Democracy in the Political Present

Democracy in the Political Present

A Queer-Feminist Theory

Isabell Lorey

Translated by Lisa Rosenblatt in cooperation with the author

VERSO

London • New York

This English-language edition first published by Verso 2022
Originally published as *Demokratie im Präsens: Eine Theorie der politischen Gegenwart*
© Suhrkamp Verlag, Berlin, Germany, 2020
Translation © Lisa Rosenblatt 2022

The translation of this work was funded by Geisteswissenschaften International –
Translation Funding for Work in the Humanities and Social Sciences from
Germany, a joint initiative of the Fritz Thyssen Foundation, the German Federal
Foreign Office, the collecting society VG WORT and the Börsenverein des
Deutschen Buchhandels (German Publishers & Booksellers Association).

1 3 5 7 9 10 8 6 4 2

Verso
UK: 6 Meard Street, London W1F 0EG
US: 388 Atlantic Avenue, Brooklyn, NY 11217
versobooks.com

Verso is the imprint of New Left Books

ISBN-13: 978-1-83976-733-3
ISBN-13: 978-1-83976-734-0 (UK EBK)
ISBN-13: 978-1-83976-735-7 (US EBK)

British Library Cataloguing in Publication Data
A catalogue record for this book is available from the British Library

Library of Congress Cataloging-in-Publication Data

Names: Lorey, Isabell, author. | Rosenblatt, Lisa (Translator), translator.

Title: Democracy in the political present : a queer-feminist theory /
  Isabell Lorey ; translated by Lisa Rosenblatt in cooperation with the
  author.
Other titles: Demokratie im Präsens. English
Description: London ; New York : Verso, 2022. | "Originally published as
  Demokratie im Präsens: Eine Theorie der politischen Gegenwart." |
  Includes bibliographical references and index.
Identifiers: LCCN 2022025475 (print) | LCCN 2022025476 (ebook) | ISBN
  9781839767333 (trade paperback) | ISBN 9781839767357 (US EBK) | ISBN
  9781839767340 (UK EBK)
Subjects: LCSH: Democracy—Philosophy. | Queer theory—Political aspects. |
  Feminist theory—Political aspects.
Classification: LCC JC423 .L64 2022 (print) | LCC JC423 (ebook) | DDC
  321.8--dc23/eng/20220729
LC record available at https://lccn.loc.gov/2022025475
LC ebook record available at https://lccn.loc.gov/2022025476

Typeset in Minion by Biblichor Ltd, Scotland
Printed and bound by CPI Group (UK) Ltd, Croydon CR0 4YY

Contents

Democracy in the Present Tense

An Introduction

Liberal democracy is falling apart – it is eroding, imploding even. Such opinions have circulated for some time. They didn't first arise with the proclamation of an 'illiberal' democracy or with the financial crisis of 2008 and the austerity policies that followed in its wake. Contrary to the assumption of a continually progressing project punctuated by temporary crises, liberal representative democracy has never been intact, nor has it ever been the best of all possible forms of government, guaranteeing freedom and equality for all. Since the formation of its modern, European form, it has been permeated by conditions of domination that have been met with continual resistance. The escalating crisis of the present is one of a perpetually contested form of governing.

At the same time, over the past decades, liberal democracy has proven astoundingly stable and adaptable. In the course of democratic renewal processes, social movements that have organized along party lines, as with the Green or left parties in many sites in Europe, have been able to gain parliamentary representation and at times even enter into government. This process can be interpreted either as a potentially infinite movement of democratization and expansion of rights, or, alternatively, as a persistent taming and integration of social movements' protest potential.

The ranks of authoritarian populist forces have grown steadily since the 2000s. Representative democracy's dynamics are now being used for immobilizing, denouncing, and turning back the democrat-ization that has already been achieved, rather than for further democratization. Liberal representative democracy's modes of oper-ation have provided an opportunity for anti-liberal forces to enter parliaments and governments through elections. A feature of repre-sentative democracy's form of government is the ambivalence of, on the one hand, a step-by-step expansion of rights and of social recogni-tion for those who face discrimination, and, on the other hand, the conservative and even reactionary dismantling of rights enshrined in immigration, asylum, abortion, and labour laws. The dismantling of liberal democracy currently being pursued by right-wing populism actually originates at democracy's centre and is deeply inherent to it.

Authoritarian-populist and illiberal forces build upon the consti-tutive inequalities and patterns of domination of modern liberal democracies. These inequalities include not only those arising from racialization, but also those between genders and sexual orientations, between owners and non-owners, between supposedly underdevel-oped colonies and civilized centres, and between citizens and those who have no (civil) rights where they reside. In its fundamental insti-tutions, liberal representative democracy is, paradoxically, profoundly undemocratic. Representing the heterogeneous many of the *demos* is not even possible.

In the administration of this basic flaw, parties and parliaments are not neutral instruments representing different interests, but rather instruments of domination for the maintenance of inequalities based on gender, law, property, education, and racialization. Moreover, as the most important organs of representation and decision making, political parties are losing more and more members, while those members who remain participate in only a few select internal party decisions and represent only a fraction of the population. 'Minorities' that are poorly or not at all represented are more or less integrated and protected. Women, workers, and migrants remain poorly repre-sented. One of the central aporias of liberal democracy is that democratization processes occur without changing the form of this democracy in its masculinist, bourgeois, and exclusionary core constitution.

In response to the effects of Thatcherism in the late 1970s, Stuart Hall developed the concept of 'authoritarian populism' to describe how, in a crisis of representation, the bourgeoisie rearranges itself as the ruling class in order to offer representation to the dissatisfied, while simultaneously blaming moderate liberal democratic forces for the crisis itself.[1] Rather than arising out of nowhere, authoritarian populism has a long history and renews itself from the bourgeois centre. In recent decades, such renewals have, in turn, taken place through the ideological shifts and renaming of political parties, and the founding of new ones. 'Moral panics'[2] fuelled by themes such as security, migration, and sexual liberalization are a recurring means of authoritarian populist mobilization.

Authoritarian populism specifically opposes a freer arrangement of gender relations and sexuality regimes. What this clearly illustrates is that a strengthening of authoritarian populist discourse and illiberal politics is not a negation of liberal democracy, or somehow other to it, but a fresh escalation of the gender inequality and sexism constitutive of this form of democracy in capitalist societies.[3] Gender and sexuality are not simply themes or issues for mobilizing the right wing. The propagation of a 'natural' gender difference by authoritarian-populist discourse includes a (re-)traditionalizing of patriarchal-heteronormative gender relations, which, incidentally, falls in line with a right-wing 'feminism' that differentiates itself with slanderous intent from the construct of 'genderism'.[4] Equality is seen as having already been achieved – as evidenced, not least, by the election of female and homosexual leaders – which for nationalist and anti-European positions simultaneously serves as a reason to delegitimize all equality policies.[5] A combination of nationalism, neoliberal politics, and biologistic 'feminism' establishes a 'femonationalism'[6] that uses naturalizing and colonialistic gender discourses to justify racist and anti-migration politics, and, through a politics of fear, shifts gender inequality onto the 'other'.[7] At the same time, the biologistic-naturalized version of gender entrenches majority society's social inequalities, which are required for stabilizing a reformulated hegemonic masculinity.[8] In right-wing discourse, violence against women is externalized in terms of patriarchal relations of violence between (im)migrant 'others', others from whom one's 'own' women must be protected and immigrated Muslim women, in their alleged sexual patriarchal subordination, must be saved.[9] Right-wing femo-nationalist discourses reduce heterosexual women to victims who must be protected – for the preservation of the nation – by men belonging to the majority society or by an authoritarian state. In this patriarchal-heteronormative proposition, masculinity, by way of a right-wing 'feminism', is able to imagine itself as not only super-ior but also enlightened and modern.[10] This type of superior masculinity is inseparable from a nationalist refiguration of white-ness which, in a reformulation of nineteenth-century biopolitical racism, enables the invocation of a 'healthy', 'pure', 'white' people (*Volk*) mediated via issues of 'gender', 'family', and 'identity'.[11] This identitarian, ethnicized *Volk* is naturalized as pre-political. Based on the discursive antagonism between 'them' and 'us' or 'the elites' and 'the people',[12] authoritarian populism claims to form an identity with the 'true people'. The authoritarian turn sustains itself mainly through discourses of the identitarian and the authentic, while rep-resentation ideally culminates in a *Führer* or leader figure. These types of discursive strategies, premised on the identity of a people, uphold the representative form of democracy and suggest solutions for its crisis.

Constructed on such an identitarian basis, this notion of 'the people' is currently posed in opposition to more than simply 'political elites' and migrants. Marked as the prime 'enemies of the people'[13] are 'genderists' and feminists, as well as LGBTQIA+ and human rights activists, because they reject reproduction in the sense of a patriarchal-racialized reinforcement of the nation. The inherently self-contradictory worldwide political movement of authoritarian populism – in oppo-sition to same-sex marriage, abortion rights, and 'political correctness' – has been ideologically fuelled by the Vatican, which invented the term 'gender ideology' and successfully ensured its viral spread.[14] Anti-gender discourse, which has made deep inroads into the bourgeoisie, continues to enable a consideration of violence against women in the public sphere in terms of lapses by individuals, and in the private sphere as 'relationship-related crime', and to structurally externalize this violence as the effect of an unenlightened patriarchy of the 'other'.[15]

Outside of feminist research, social and economic precarization in neoliberalism is often cited to explain the rise of right-wing populism, rather than analysing the focus on gender and sexuality within authoritarian-populist forces and discourses.[16] Not only is precarization often reduced to insecure hegemonic masculinities, the implication is also that it is a purely class-specific phenomenon. Structurally gendered precarization and migrants' racialized precarity are not taken into consideration. Yet precarization as a phenomenon is neither exclusively neoliberal nor homogeneous. Social, economic, and legal insecurities are so diversely shaped that they cannot be summarized in the collective subject of interest of a 'precariat'. Rather than a shared work experience, precarization is a form of political domination that began to be established across classes in the 1990s, affecting the whole of society in different ways.[17] The restructuring and dismantling of welfare states and labour markets, along with financial deregulation, were the conditions that allowed precarization to continue its spread during the financial and debt crises – reinforced by austerity policies in the EU – and to become a normalized instrument of governing.[18] This goes hand in hand with an authoritarian neoliberal reorganization of bourgeois-capitalist domination, which sounds out the extent to which a segment of the population will accept the re-formation of naturalized, patriarchal-heteronormative gender relations, including an appropriate concept of family, as compensation for politico-economic transformations. Counter to the assumption of bourgeois-liberal-capitalist societies until well into the 1970s, the initial decades of neoliberal politics have clearly shown that patriarchal-heteronormative gender relations, based on the precarization of primarily (married) women, are not at all necessary for the maintenance of a bourgeois-capitalist society. In connection with the normalization of precarization, it has been possible to largely liberalize gender relations, capitalize on plural life concepts and diversity, and utilize them for neoliberal concepts of the state.[19]

Liberal democracy's fundamental state of crisis has once again become obvious with the authoritarian-neoliberal turn.[20] In the 1990s and 2000s, it was still inconceivable for social movements to refer positively to the concept and practice of democracy. However, in the early 2010s, amid strengthening authoritarian politics and EU austerity measures, massive and sustained emancipatory democracy movements emerged, for the most part in Europe's south. These movements refused to make classic demands for more democratization or to elect representatives. They wanted to invent, practise, and live a different, new form of democracy. '¡Democracia real ya!' (Real democracy now!) was the slogan that brought together several thousand people on Puerta del Sol, Madrid's main square, for the first time on 15 May 2011. Those who had assembled earlier, on Tahrir Square in Cairo, had already begun to try out new forms of radical inclusion and organizing, as did those who gathered afterwards, on the Syntagma Square in Athens, at the sites of the Occupy movement in the United States and the Gezi movement in Turkey, and in many other places. They emphatically referred to democracy as a way of living together. They fought for new forms of democracy, for a deeply democratic life, for a new society that they wanted to invent, experience, and make happen in the present. This manifold, enduring, discontinuous trying out of new democratic practices provided the occasion for contemplating alternatives to the liberal representative form of democracy also at the level of political theory. From the aporia of liberal representative democracy there thus unfolds a democracy in the present (tense): presentist democracy.

Authoritarian populism, conversely, builds upon the contradictions of liberal democracy, in part exacerbates them, and at the same time undermines the central, liberal promise of a progressive, future-oriented democratization. This promise is based on the necessity of struggles for recognition, and repeatedly makes it seem as though the fundamental conditions of domination of representative democracy are necessary, and that this form of democracy is without any alternative. Authoritarian populism does not want to change the aporias of liberal democracy in democratization processes, but, instead, to establish them as unchangeable.

The following six contradictions are among the constituting aporias in which liberal representative democracy is trapped: first, representation is always exclusionary; it is never possible to represent *all*. The aspiration of equality is unachievable with this instrument. The concerns of those who are not represented reach the hierarchical institutions of representation, if at all, in a heavily mutated form. Usually, horizontal decision-making structures and the open formation of political objectives are blocked.

Second, liberal democracy is based on a constitutive separation between the political and the social, between the state and (civil) society. From the autonomy of the political arises the necessity for political representation, which forms the basis of the irredeemable promise of the liberal norms of equality and justice.

Third, the idea of popular sovereignty assumes the unity of popular will, which carries the constitution. The concept of a juridical constituent power of the sovereign people demands the formation of a general, uniform will. The *demos* as *Volk* cannot be indeterminate, multiple, and heterogeneous. In the juridico-political realm, it shows itself as a masculinist-general formation and demarcates itself from a dispersed, particular, and female-connoted multitude in the social.

Fourth, liberal democracy is always a limited and enclosed democracy. Popular sovereignty always acts in the context of a nation state. Those who arrive in these societies can be integrated only into the existing, ethnicized conditions. When liberal democracy feels threatened, border and migration regimes are deployed to close it down. Freedom is restricted in the name of freedom.

Fifth, bourgeois liberal democracy is constituted through the gendered separation of a public and a private sphere. The patriarchal order of a naturalized heteronormative gender dualism and nuclear family underpins the capitalistically profitable, unpaid care and reproductive work carried out by women. Social interrelatedness, precariousness, reproduction, and care are feminized, devalued, and depoliticized.

Sixth, with the normalization of precarization and social uncertainty, the neoliberal authoritarian turn becomes apparent in an intensified security apparatus. Control and surveillance increase, social security decreases. Precarization and austerity and debt policies lead to increasing individual and state indebtedness, which works to the advantage of restabilizing bourgeois-capitalist domination since debts conduce to a calculable, future-oriented conformist behaviour.

Moreover, liberal democracy's logic is reflected, in a specific way, in two fundamental problems having to do with its conception of time and history. One problem is that a bourgeois construction of history invariably believes in progress and adheres to a linear conception of time. History is told as a continuous story of the victors, of becoming civilized, of development, and of (liberal) democracy. In the context of this form of democracy, the belief and hope in a better future remains steadfast. This promise for the future does more than propel struggles for recognition, inherent to which is the desire to be inscribed in the history of the victors. The promise of linear time also influences the form of political organization. The liberal political understanding of permanent duration and resilience is inextricably tied up with an adherence to institutions of representation. The struggles of social movements are considered spontaneous, unpolitical, naive, ineffective, and fixated on presence and immediacy unless they take a second step and become institutionalized in a party or some other organized form of interest representation. Not making demands and not electing representatives confuses the chrono-political discourse regime focused on representation.

The second problem comprises a limited understanding of the present and its blindness to history. In liberal concepts of time and history, the present remains beyond the political and is reserved for contingency and emotion, a feeling understood as authentic in the here and now. Subjectivist and useless for reflection and generality, the present concerns only the particular and the moment. It is contrary to the continuance of representation, which it can only warp in its momentary intensity. The affirmation of this construction of the present as an authentic-identitarian one can be found not only in authoritarian-populist ideologies, but also in the longing for the authentic and ecstatic in the 'now' of a certain form of masculinist left-wing militance. Here, 'truth' is considered a 'complete presence to oneself and to the world', as 'a vital contact with the real', which constitutes political action.[21] Friendships form as 'irreversible bonds' through the experience of violence.[22]

Presentist democracy has nothing to do with such authenticist immediacies. It unfolds in an entirely different understanding of the present. The time of presentist democracy is the now-time as conceived by Walter Benjamin, which can be understood as an infinitive and expanded present. Now-time is a historical materialist time, in which present-day struggles are related to those of the past. These struggles actualize minor fragments of history, tear them from oblivion and create connections with those silenced by conditions of violence – fabrics of relations that might again generate, together, the force to shatter conditions of domination such as sexism, classicism, racism, and colonialism. These struggles know that 'reality' is not immediate, but rather an assemblage of conditions of domination, and they use the present – with leaps into minor pasts – to recompose the constellations of the present. They support liberal democracy's democratization processes, the struggles for recognition and expansion of rights, but go beyond them. They leave the liberal logics of linear time behind and instead practise a presentist democratic politics.

The presentist does not have a dichotomous relationship to representation; it emerges, instead, in an exodus from the dual problematic of linear, continuous narratives and authentic-identitarian fetishisms of the present. The presentist present is the political present, in which an untimely and undeferred becoming of democracy is practised. This becoming of new forms of democracy unfolds in a constituent process, which is not simply aimed at constitutional reordering, at a constitution in the sense of a basic law. More fundamentally, the constituent process of presentist democracy is instead entangled in the emergence of new subjectivations. Rather than seeing the aporias of liberal democracy as unchangeable, presentist democracy breaks them open. No identitarian confrontations of 'us' and 'them', no dichotomies of consensus and conflict or movement and party. Presentist democracy is without a people and without nation. Rather than regimes of borders and migration, the borders it confronts are sexism and racism, homophobia and transphobia, colonialism and extractivism.[23]

Currently, presentist democracy's most important struggles include the transnational queer-feminist strike movements that have formed since 2015 in opposition to violence against women and authoritarian populist politics.[24] In many places these movements were sparked by femicide, by one woman too much many falling victim to male violence because she refused to satisfy patriarchal-heteronormative gender roles.

The 'black protests' that formed in Poland in 2016 constituted a broad, emancipatory women's movement that successfully resisted an attempt by the authoritarian populist regime to tighten the country's already extremely strict abortion laws. A short time later, inspired by this success, women in Argentina called for a feminist mass strike, mobilized by the hashtag '#NiUnaMenos' (#Not one [woman] fewer). The wave of protests has since become increasingly larger worldwide. Queer-feminist strikes are not aimed solely at violence against women, authoritarianism and antifeminism, homophobia and transphobia, but also against the alliance, hostile to life, of patriarchal order and neoliberal capitalist exploitation and pillage. And the feminist wave is breaking records, such as on 8 March 2018, when in Spain alone, 6 million people across 300 cities and municipalities took part in what was hitherto the largest strike in Europe. Throughout the world, feminist mass strikes have taken place in over fifty countries.[25]

The queer-feminist strike is a political and social strike. It is directed at more than simply wage labour, and does not require a unified subject that strikes cohesively. Instead, it begins from non-identitarian mutual dependencies and affections. In Argentina they say, 'Tocan a una, tocan a todas' (Touch one, and you touch all). The strike movements refer not only to queer-feminist genealogies, but also to the occupation and democracy movements of the 2010s, which were critical of representation and adopted transversal practices of organizing. These movements consider themselves 'anti-racist, anti-imperialist, anti-heterosexist, and anti-neoliberal'[26] because, with the formation of neoliberalism, financialization, and business-oriented globalization, the attack against women and all workers increased dramatically, above all for women of colour, the unemployed, and migrant women.

Not only are the current queer-feminist struggles multitudinarian and manifold in their geopolitical spread and transversal orientation, they also draw lines through time – as in the song sung at many demonstrations in Latin America and increasingly also in Europe: 'Somos las nietas de todas las brujas que no pudieron quemar, pero es el momento de alzar nuestra voz y gritarle al mundo ¡NI UNA MAS!' (We are the granddaughters of all the witches they could not burn, but our time has come to raise our voices and shout to the world NOT ONE MORE!)[27]

Past struggles are remembered in time leaps, and the current wave of strikes is indebted to their practices and modes of organization.[28] Where a democracy movement has existed for several years, such as in Spain, this new wave joins it, to once again counter the liberal form of democracy with presentist democracy practices above and beyond borders and limitations. Starting as they do from violence against women as an expression of structural violence, from the structural devaluation of care and reproduction, from the economic and socio-political conditions of domination, discrimination, exclusion, and deportation, the current queer-feminist struggles, which involve the alliance of so many movements and initiatives, must be understood as intersectional and transversal struggles. This is the advantage of the strike as a transnational queer-feminist instrument open to a multiplicity of actors – not only women, but also, for example, precarious and migrant workers.

The wave of queer-feminist strikes takes on the challenge political theory has ascribed to the multitude for centuries, namely to be the counterfigure to that form of democracy based on the sovereignty of a people. It is more than simply a further emancipation movement that has liberated itself from the claws of patriarchy to finally become a political subject.[29] The many queer-feminist confluences conceive of themselves as worldwide multitudes: they are different and manifold and cannot be reduced to a state, a party, or a people.[30] In this sense, the strike wave actualizes and multiplies the old figure of the multitude which has haunted modern political theory as a counterpart to the people, too dispersed and too interdependent to become a masculine political subject capable of political action solely through the parameters of representation and sovereignty.

The multitude that appears in the present as an alternative to the people and populism is deeply anchored in social relations, in mutual dependencies and affections; it thwarts the liberal logics of representation, because this logic cannot guarantee its multiplicity. It is based on 'situated assemblies . . . for the production of collective intelligence, tactical discussion, and expanded networks'.[31]

The feminist multitude is striking against the *Volk*, against internationally active reactionary alliances, and against the amalgam of liberal democracy and neoliberalism. It fights again and again for the value of interrelatedness with people, things, and environments.

The reflections in this book are a beginning that takes up these struggles, actualizes the past, and conjoins them into a constellation of *democracy in the present tense*. The first chapter shows how a masculinist conceptualization of the sovereign people is based on a de-politicization of the multitude. Jean-Jacques Rousseau was the first to draft a democratic art of governing, which Foucault later grasped with the term 'governmentality'. In Rousseau's reformulation of modern political economy, the family, including the patriarchal gender order, loses its function as the model for conducting a state and becomes a hinge for governing a multitudinous population. When the multiplicity assembles and celebrates a festival, it is not about the immediate presence of those who are celebrating, but rather about exchange and shared abundance.

The second chapter shows how vehemently the dichotomy between representation and presence also influenced Jacques Derrida's early conception of deconstruction, and thereby poststructuralist thinking, since it was developed in demarcation from Rousseau. For Derrida, Rousseau advocated no more than a metaphysics of presence, of ahistorical immediacy and self-referentiality. However, this critique also applies, to a greater degree, to Georg Wilhelm Friedrich Hegel's understanding of the present. When in *Rogues* Derrida again turns to Rousseau, his judgment is milder. With the help of Rousseau's understanding of democracy, he now unfolds the democracy to come, and the present which remains in coming. It is a democracy in becoming, in movement, which is not postponed to the future: undefined, unclosed, and open to the incalculable arrival of who and what is coming.

With Walter Benjamin, discussed in the third chapter, the messianic coming proves to be a historical materialist figure with which present and past become a constellation in now-time. Benjamin breaks open the history of the victors and bases his materialistic understanding of time on affect and care. Resounding in care for the past are the voices of the silenced, who play a role in fabrics of relations in the now, situated in the resistances and struggles. With Benjamin and Marx, the social revolution of the Paris Commune is actualized, with its micropolitical practices, non-representationist experimenting, countless assemblies and alternative forms of organization, and the caring relations of neighbourhoods.

The fourth chapter unfolds a political reconceptualization of the present with the help of Michel Foucault's marginal concept of the 'present infinitive'. From this emerge the six components of presentist democracy's present: becoming, duration, indeterminacy, repetition, leap, and organization.

The fifth chapter develops Antonio Negri's concept of the constituent power of the multitude, from which a democratic social revolution emerges that re-poses the question of reproduction and care. The multiple discontinuous cycles of the Spanish democracy movement are actualized in their queer-feminist hues – from the occupations of the squares by the 15M movement through to the municipalist movement of governing the city halls.

Concluding this conceptualization of presentist democracy, the sixth chapter traces the modern genesis of the figure of the autonomous individual, its entanglement in debt and its delimitation from relations of care. Still today, this masculinist figure shapes the regimes of precarization and gender relations, and impedes the positive connotation of precariousness and social indebtedness. It is deeply entangled in the alliance of capitalism and racism, an alliance that was evident in the causes of the financial crisis in 2008. On the contrary, when practices of care and a black and queer understanding of debt are placed at the centre, democracy in the present tense appears.

1

Rousseau

Assembly, Not Representation

The form of democracy that we currently consider self-evident resulted from disputes and struggles that came to a head in Europe in the eighteenth century. These were struggles for the freedom and self-determination of the individual, which had also become manifest in legal codes since the seventeenth century. In the European history of rights and liberties, the English Habeas Corpus Act of 1679, which established the rights of a person who had been arrested to be examined by a judge without delay, was considered a crucial step toward a law-based constitution: a juridically constituted power.[1] Ten years later, the rights of the English parliament were established in the Bill of Rights; in 1787, the US constitution was created, with its opening words, 'We the people'; and in 1789, in the course of the French Revolution, the rights of all individuals were guaranteed in the Declaration of the Rights of Man and of the Citizen.

The first bourgeois constitutions, however, belong to the history of the victors, the property-owning men, and not to the women, the peasants, the slaves, and all those whose struggles were not successful enough to result in a constitution. Among the victors' struggles were those recorded in the *Federalist Papers* from 1787/88, where, in the course of ratifying the US constitution, the necessity of representation of the people, of the *demos*, was argued. The supporters of representative democracy, who favoured a federal, presidential executive, successfully opposed the advocates of a confederation. Democracy was discredited as the 'tyranny of the majority', and the Republic put forth as the fairer representative form.[2] In 1791, Olympe de Gouges published her *Declaration of the Rights of Woman and the Female Citizen*, in which she protested against the male privileges that were to be elevated to constitutional status through the French Revolution. She identified the new bourgeois regime as the 'tyranny' of men, and in her feminist constitutional writing demanded a new, egalitarian, revolutionary constitution.[3] Without having achieved even a single change to the constitution, she was executed by guillotine two years later. De Gouges's revolutionary feminist declaration was published the same year that the Haitian Revolution of the slaves, inspired by the human and civil rights promised by the revolution in France, began in the French colony Saint-Domingue. Not until thirteen years later, in 1804, was the Napoleonic army defeated and the Republic of Haiti proclaimed by its now free black citizens. It was the first independent state in Latin America.[4] In Haiti too, however, civil rights were reserved exclusively for men.[5] It was not only white French citizens of the past who considered the empowerment of black men an 'unthinkable history' – the Haitian Revolution continues to be trivialized in Europe's history of the victors up to the present.[6]

In political theory, only the US and French constitutions of white male citizens emerging from the 'Western' revolutions are considered pivotal events in the democratic implementation of general norms such as freedom and equality. Although these constitutions did not apply to everyone, according to the standard narrative they mark the constitutional beginnings of a bourgeois society that could be associated with a promise of progress – the promise that democracy can transform itself and be extended to those who were initially not included, not counted, not represented; those who were not entrusted with democracy in terms of rights and participation, freedom and equality. According to a widespread understanding of democratic development, history shows that although the eighteenth-century constitutions were full of exclusions and legitimations of domestication and hierarchization, over the course of the following centuries, those who were originally excluded were able to fight for their ongoing inclusion.[7] Understood in this way, representative democracy is dynamic and not determined once and for all; it changes on the basis of society's transformations and disputes. This is an understanding of representative democracy in which not only Europe and the 'West', but also white and masculinist predominance are inscribed as measures of progress and development. The paradigm of this understanding of progress remains hegemonic to such an extent that, to the present day, the foundational parameters of liberal democracy – such as representation, *Volk*, and the figure of the autonomous individual – have not been sufficiently deconstructed to sustainably break open the bourgeois framework of dominance.

For that reason, we will once again pose several fundamental questions: If democracy means the power of, or domination by, the *demos*, what is meant by 'the *demos* (itself) should rule'? Is the *demos* the *Volk*? Who belongs to it, and who doesn't? How should this form of (self-)government proceed? Who should participate, and how? Should all who are considered citizens participate directly, or should they be mediated via representation? What was the *demos* in the eighteenth century, and who were all the others considered not to belong to the *demos* and yet who nonetheless had to be governed? How does their exclusion from politics determine the parameters of the legal constitution of a bourgeois society? Can the constitution, once established, be broken open by the continuous inclusion of those who have been excluded? Or, instead, should the masculinist constitution be fundamentally questioned and criticized at its core?

In modern European political philosophy, manifold considerations have been employed to legitimize democracy as the rule and self-government of the *demos*. Already during the Enlightenment, the main question of democracy was not only that of the self-government of the *demos*, but also that of the form in which the countless many could be discouraged from insurrection and made controllable and governable. In the history of political theory, those who are dispersed and difficult to govern, those whom rulers have always seen as a threat and as tendentially ungovernable, are frequently designated by the Latin word *multitudo*; in French and English: 'multitude'.

The relationship of number and assembly has been a recurring theme of the disputes ever since the struggles for bourgeois constitutions. Who counts when the *demos* assembles? Who counts as part of the *demos* and who doesn't? Is the *demos* even countable? In political philosophy, the practice of ancient Greece is seen as the ideal practice of self-government of the *demos*: all the free citizens of a city or an empire assemble at the marketplace, debate, and decide on common matters. Nonetheless, when disputes arose over how to update to this form of (self-)rule in the eighteenth century, doubts about the feasibility of 'direct' or 'absolute' democracy for larger states prevailed. Due solely to its size in terms of numbers, the *demos* was considered incapable of assembling, and thereby incapable of governing itself without mediation. But if the citizen could not govern himself, he was in danger of becoming lost in the multitude, among those who were not even counted when dealing with a public assembly: women, children, the poor, slaves, and foreigners, who were incapable of acting as a sovereign subject.[8]

These questions regarding the numerical size of the *demos*, which problematize the possibility of its assembly or the necessity of its representation, conceal a further charged relationship that runs throughout the debate on democracy's forms, but is seldom moved to the forefront: the relationship between the united people of male citizens and the heterogeneous many of the multitude. By focusing here on the relationship of the *Volk* to the multitude, my concern is not to contribute to debates on mass and power, but rather to analyse gendered constructions of popular sovereignty, the basic political formations of bourgeois society, and the concomitant forms of democracy as the rule of the *demos*.

In absolutism, Thomas Hobbes already drafted essential aspects of his fear-driven state theory in terms of a threatening *multitudo* in the 'state of nature' from which the political order of representation must offer protection, but which perpetually threatens it. The *multitudo* corresponds to a 'natural freedom' before representation and before the state.[9] As a negative foil to the principle of the Own and the One, the *multitudo* exists with no defined number or clear political goal. Hobbes understands it as dispersed and ungovernable. It refuses to be united through obedience and representation in the Leviathan, and instead leads to insurgency in the political body, sickening it, and potentially even destroying it. '*Concord*, [is] *Health*; *Sedition, Sicknesse*; and *Civill war, Death*.'[10] For the first modern theorists of security and the state, it was not only the non-unified dispersed, per se, that presented a threat to sovereignty, but also its exchange in uncontrolled gatherings, which was always suspected of conspiracy against representation. Hobbes warned against the irregular political movements of the *multitudo*: 'Irregular Systems, in their nature, but Leagues, or sometimes meer concourse of people, without union to any particular designe, not by obligation of one to another, but proceeding only from a similitude of wills.'[11] The *multitudo* assembles without purpose, is associated with bias and affect, and is poised for revolt against the sovereignty. When not politically and juridically tamed, it is constructed as potentially leading to civil war, a war of all against all, linking the individual's fear of a defenceless vulnerability with the fear of a threatening, property-destroying other. The menacing exchange of the *multitudo* in its ungovernable gathering corresponds to the dependence on others in the 'natural state', fantasized as a deadly threat. Here, the individual is forced to lead an insecure, precarious life, without civil rights and entirely at the mercy of the Other.

Conceiving the *multitudo* as a horror scene of ungovernable exchange in order to legitimate political domination runs throughout Western political theory and still influences the dominant perception of democracy today. The scenario is deeply gendered and likewise excludes all that is seen as foreign. Hobbes's security-centred state theory makes the first modern promise that law and the sovereign will guarantee protection against these concerns. The construction of an original state of nature serves as the prerequisite for a juridical security state, which ends the dangerous equality and freedom of the *multitudo* and legitimizes inequality through bourgeois law and the Leviathan.[12] The individual, thus protected from (violent) redistribution (in the state of nature) should ultimately become independent from others, in that he is no longer equal to them. At the same time, through inequality and self-subordination under the social contract, property is protected.[13] Hobbes dissolves the alarming mutual relatedness in the state of nature in favour of individualized protection in the bourgeois social contract, which guarantees individual freedom and property as patriarchal rights.[14]

The conception of a modern political democracy is based on this division between, on the one hand, the consolidated, unified people, which can be represented, and, on the other hand, the menacingly gathering multitude, the heterogeneous many, those not tamed in the union. At issue is the differentiation between those who are capable of bourgeois self-governing (by means of representation) in the context of a juridical order, and those who gather uncontrolledly in exchange, tend towards revolt, and must be governed. In the logic of traditional political theory, the incalculable multitude, although excluded from the citizenry, does not exist outside of state borders. Within the state order, it harbours the danger of unlawful revolutionary gathering, of wild debate and celebration, of insurgency and civil war. Against this imagined threat, political theory has since ancient times constituted the juridical, masculinist *populus*, which still shapes debates on modern popular sovereignty.[15]

In the eighteenth century, in order to justify political representation as indispensable, the multitude was constantly presented as being too dispersed for modern democracy in two ways: for one, the male citizens belonging to it are too numerous, and too dispersed across a territory, to make an assembly seem possible. Due to their dispersal, they are denied direct participation in determining the allocation of space and the shaping of politics, rights, and the economy. The ancient idea of the assembly of free citizens thus confronts the problem of governing a population of the many who are dispersed across a territory.

But there is another reason why the multitude is understood as too dispersed: it is judged as being too emotional. The heterogeneous many – so the assumption goes – lack composure, control, and reason; they can engage in democratic practices only on the basis of sentiment, passion, affective distraction. For the proponents of representative democracy, the comprehensive participation of the multitude harbours the danger of mutual affect, exchange, and insurrection; hence its distraction and dispersion must be tamed through representation.

In the eighteenth century, there were fierce debates over whether the national, culturalist, and patriarchal *demos* of the bourgeois paterfamilias in large states such as France, or even larger ones such as the US, could or should assemble for political decisions, without representation. The advocates of representation – such as John Locke, Montesquieu, James Madison, and Alexander Hamilton – used different arguments to maintain that the citizens had to be represented by members of parliaments.[16] To oppose the danger of a 'tyranny of the majority' (Madison) and insurrections of the untamed *demos* as multitude, and nonetheless champion a pluralism of interests, the American Federalists considered representative democracy the only tenable form of rule of the people. De facto, this meant the government of the minority over the majority, of owners over those who owned less, of bourgeois men over women, of whites over blacks. The federalist founders of the United States considered the participation and affections of the multitude a threat to the polity; the passions of the multitude should not determine the daily business of politics without mediation and control.[17]

Several decades before the *Federalist Papers* and the French Revolution, but already in the midst of disputes about how a bourgeois self-government could be conceived, Jean-Jacques Rousseau firmly rejected the necessity of political representation for unifying the *demos* and taming the multitude. In his *Social Contract*, Rousseau gave an unequivocal response. However, in his idiosyncratic critique of representation, he did not simply take the side of the non-representable multitude. In his view, (male) citizens are, indeed, initially part of the multitude, which he also conceived as countless, undefined, and politically 'blind',[18] in keeping with his political theory precursors. But when the citizens assemble – and thus, in a certain sense, step out of the multitude – the number of those assembled plays no role. As soon as the citizens are assembled, they are able to form the sovereign without representatives. In Rousseau's opinion, the dispersal of citizens across a territory does not prevent their coming together. In response to his contemporary critics, he points to the Roman republic, where, despite its magnitude in terms of numbers, 'the Roman people' were able to assemble frequently and regularly.[19]

Rousseau knows that only those men who had citizenship rights belonged to the *populus* in Rome: they alone are relevant for the question of the size of the people, which dictates the debates over feasible or unfeasible assemblies of citizens. He is entirely aware that many more people were living in Rome, not only those who (still) had not attained rights to citizenship – who could, however, potentially gain them (such as freed slaves and citizens of conquered communities)[20] – but also 'subjects, foreigners, women, children, and slaves'.[21] With this precise listing of those who were not counted, he names those whom he knows lived alongside the Roman *populus*. These many Others without citizenship status surface continually in *The Social Contract*, and belong to either the multitude or society depending on whether they are indefinite or definite. But they never belong to the sovereign, are never among those who act politically or are able to enact laws.

Rousseau's failure to present a consistent theoretical framework is often highlighted; the contradictory interpretations of his work are implicit in the texts themselves, primarily because he did not adequately clarify the relationship between individualism and collectivism, or between the particular and the general.[22] Feminist readings of Rousseau have stressed, in different ways, the fundamental heteronormative gender difference that runs through all of his works.[23] The dichotomies inherent in his work reveal inconsistencies in part due precisely to his gendered political theory. Rousseau's writings illuminate the theoretical contradictions that were accepted in nascent bourgeois society in order to keep women and non-citizens out of the political. The politically active, sovereign *peuple* capable of forming its own laws embodies something quite different to the *volonté générale*, the general will, and is, instead, reduced to the masculinist and particular in itself.

Rousseau is a striking figure in this regard. On the one hand, in the nascent phase of bourgeois society and the nation state, he contributed significantly to the establishment of a particularistic and misogynist image of women,[24] alongside which a form of masculinity could stylize itself as the general human. On the other hand, with his critique of representation and advocacy of the republican

festival – which he considered no less strictly heterosexual and hierarchical in terms of gender – he also paradoxically supplied the first
aspects for a queer-feminist understanding of democracy that makes
do without a people and is conceived from the heterogeneity and
interrelatedness of the multitude.

  In contrast to the liberal understanding of democracy that was
taking shape in parallel, Rousseau grasped that this form of governing was not primarily about numbers or counting, and that political
and societal assemblies are indispensable. Unlike the terms used for
the other possible constitutions discussed in ancient Greece, most
influentially by Plato and Aristotle, the word 'democracy' does not
contain any reference to number-justifying the necessity of representation: monarchy contains the word *monos*, which refers to the
rule of the One; while oligarchy comes from *hoi oligoi* and signifies
the rule of the few. 'Democracy', however, does not reveal how
many the *demos* contains. It refers neither to any defined number,
nor to the minority or majority of a population, but rather to the
power of the many as an inclusive gathering that makes no reference
to the limits of a nation.[25]

  However, it would be too imprecise to define democracy, independent of its representative variant, simply as the power of the many.
Josiah Ober has shown that the suffix *krátos* in *demokratia* means
'power' in terms of strength and empowerment, 'the capacity to do
things',[26] rather than rule of the many over the few. In ancient Greece,
the *demos* was composed of many socially differentiated individuals
who were free to pursue their interests and did not have to be united
to act in conjunction with others. Admittedly, not everyone had full
citizenship rights, and the many acted in a 'public' space that was
differentiated from a 'private', feminized one. However, in this argument, what is of primary importance is that democracy as the power
of the varied many did not have to be bonded to representation in any
way. With this etymology, the negative understanding of democracy
as the dominance of the masses over the few seems merely a repetition
of those ancient, anti-democratic polemics that did not take early
democratic practices seriously. For not everyone had the same capacity to do things or could act in the same way. These capacities were,

apparently, not viewed as being inherent to individuals. Only when citizens (male and female) were perceived in their social differences, and not as uniform, did it become clear that many of them had to be supported in order to participate on equal footing in the shaping of common affairs. A lottery for public offices, and speeches in assemblies, can be seen as such supportive equalizers.[27] In accordance with this etymological-historical interpretation of the Greek term *demokratia*, this form of governing does not require either the amalgamation of a people or representation. The capacity to do things is not a capacity that everyone has to the same degree, but instead refers to the many different individuals who, in their social heterogeneity, shape common cohabitation. *Demokratia* guarantees that the capacities of the individual can be lived out for the benefit of the common.

When, in the eighteenth century, Rousseau drafts his form of democracy as critical of representation, he cannot engage with social heterogeneity at a political level. The political is reserved for male citizens. In developing his conception of the political, he concentrates on the constitutional significance of the citizens' assembly and the general legislation resulting from it. Rousseau is clearly aware that representation by the few is not needed for the citizens' self-government, and he does not question the capacity of individual citizens to do things in principle. His reservation is that nothing general occurs when individuals do different things. In his understanding, unity is required for the general, and only male citizens are capable of forming that unity. However, in no way do they automatically act in the interests of all: 'Nothing is more dangerous than the influence of private [particular] interests in public affairs.'[28] When citizens are not assembled, they pursue their own separate interests. For that reason, he concludes: 'To use the term in a rigorous acceptation, a true democracy has never existed, and will never exist . . . We cannot imagine a whole people continually assembled to take care of public affairs.'[29] The *peuple* that decides on the general laws is not a permanent institution, but instead always arises when the citizens assemble. Beyond these meetings, the male citizens pursue their particular interests and, like all the others, are part of the *multitude*. By focusing on the division between *peuple* and *multitude* in this reading of Rousseau's concept of democracy without representation, my aim is not to offer any further variants of the topos of the divided people.[30] Rather, I am compiling the elements for a conception of democracy on the basis of the heterogeneous multitude. This requires an investigation of the constructions of the *demos* or of the *peuple* in which the multitude is depicted as the non-political Other.

For Rousseau, the assembled citizenry is the foundation of the legislative power. It is the *peuple* as legislative sovereign that possesses the *pouvoir législatif.* 'The sovereign cannot act except when the people is assembled';[31] and 'sovereignty cannot be represented', since only the *volonté générale*, the general will, is sovereign. 'The deputies of the people then are not, and cannot be, its representatives, they are only its commissioners; they can conclude nothing definitively.' The legislative *peuple* is, in principle, not representable, since, when there are representatives, 'as soon as they are elected, the people is enslaved and has no power'.[32] No elected government, no parliamentarians, and no officials can act in place of the assembled people; representation in its full sense is impossible.[33]

In this way, Rousseau drafts a legislative constituent power without representation. His *Social Contract* rests on this non-representative juridical constituting. When the citizens assemble and form the legislative sovereign, in their performative act of association they constitute a 'collective person':[34]

> This act of association [momentarily] produces a moral and collective body[35] composed of as many members as the assembly has votes, which receives from this same act its unity – its common being [*moi commun*], its life and its will.[36]

This forming of a unity of the *peuple* does not refer to any prior identity or natural state; it is performative. Rousseau leaves no doubt as to the tradition of collective political life within which he understands this *moi commun*, this collective 'public personage'.[37] He defines it as a union of citizens corresponding to the Greek *polis*, rather than to the territory of the sovereign. The public personage, he emphasizes, formerly took the name of the city, the *polis*, 'and now takes that of republic, or body politic. This is called the *state* by its members when it is passive; the *sovereign* when it is active.'[38] The way he links the sovereignty of the *peuple* with this understanding of the *polis*, however, does not allow him, in his conception of the juridical-political, to move to the forefront the citizens who are interrelated in their heterogeneity, doing things for the general welfare; but rather, the political unity is at the forefront.

The citizens, allied by contract, must unanimously form the *volonté générale*,[39] so that the emerging sovereign becomes indivisible, and only thus can it determine the 'general best'. The particular voices of the individual members must be disregarded.

> There is often a great difference between the will of all [*volonté de tous*] and the general will [*volonté générale*]: one regards the common interest only; the other regards private interests, and is only the sum of individual wills [*volontés particulières*].[40]

In the formation of the sovereign, it is preferable for 'the citizens to have no permanent associations among themselves' and no communication with one another. 'But when they divide into factions and partial associations at the expense of the whole, the will of each of these associations becomes general with regard to its members, and individual [*particulière*] with regard to the state.'[41] Different interest groups and individual associations or parties damage the unity of the sovereignty. In the sphere of the juridical-political, communication, and thereby social relations, are considered simply a negative gathering of individual vested interests. Everything particular must remain in the sphere that is separated from the *peuple*, in the *multitude*, where it can only gather and amass. Like the multitude, the particular is 'blind'[42] to the general political will that characterizes the sovereign. The particular is manifold and connected through exchange and communication; it is not suitable for homogeneous melding. Only when it is isolated and solitary can it dissolve within a higher-order general. Contracts cannot be made on the basis of mutual relatedness; what is needed are citizen-individuals who are separated from one another and can be considered, first and foremost, legal persons capable of entering into a contract. In the ideal contractual sovereign, all particular relations are erased so that only individuals, detached from one another, assemble, and can transform their mere gathering, dissolving as the sovereign. The state as the general arises from the suspended particulars of the male citizens, who are also always the property-owning citizens.

> Whoever dares undertake to establish a people's institutions must feel himself capable of *changing*, as it were, *human nature* itself, of *transforming* each individual who, in isolation, is a complete but solitary whole, into a *part* of something greater than himself, from which in a sense, he derives his life and his being; [of changing man's nature (*constitution*) in order to strengthen it;] of substituting a limited and moral existence for the physical and independent life [with which all of us are endowed by nature]. His task, in short, is to take from a man his own powers, and to give him in exchange alien powers which he can only employ with the help of other men. The more surely these natural forces are dead and annihilated, the greater and more desirable are the acquired ones, and the more solid and durable the establishment [*constitution*]; so that when the citizen is nothing and can do nothing save by help of all the others, and the force acquired by the whole is equal or superior to the sum of the natural forces of all the individuals, it may be said that legislation has reached the highest point of perfection to which it can attain.[43]

What Rousseau sketches here is the citizen and man as human. By nature, this human is a 'complete' and 'solitary whole' and equipped with his 'own powers'; he is autonomous as an individual in his physical existence. Care, reproduction, and social interdependence are not relevant to this conception of a politically competent bourgeois masculinity. However, Rousseau is entirely aware that in its 'natural', independent constitution, this male body is incapable of survival. Independence thus has to be replaced by a 'partial and moral existence': the male individual must quasi-denaturalize, revoke his non-viable autonomy, to bond contractually and as a solitary whole, to become part of a larger new, constitutional whole – precisely so, as though social interrelatedness, which has been forced into the sphere of the unpolitical, the particular, and the private through the political construction of transcendent, masculinist sovereignty, must somehow be compensated for, not as a relation of heterogeneous individuals, but as a connection within a uniform dissolution. The republic replaces the erased social and sexual bonds.[44] To this end, the male citizen must quasi-relinquish his physical body; his 'own powers' have to be destroyed and replaced by a legal and political existence resulting from that destruction. The performative act of concluding a contract is not a process, not a transformation, but an instantaneous substitution through the masculinist collective body, the legislative power, that emerges only at that very same moment.[45] It is literally a substitution of constitutions – Rousseau uses *constitution* in a double sense: moving from the physical constitution of the individual man to the general (state-)constitution. This bourgeois masculinity constitutes itself violently, as the political-juridical collective can be achieved only through a voluntary, subjugating self-abandonment. That is the price to be paid for this juridical constituent power without representation, in which the bourgeois man becomes the masculinist *peuple*, representing an allegedly ungendered general.

The social contract gives rise to a special form of bourgeois-masculine subject formation. Every male citizen concludes 'a contract, so to speak, with himself'.[46] This is a bourgeois (self-)contract 'between an obligation to one's self, and to a whole, of which the individual forms a part'.[47] The contract with one's self correlates with a male subject constitution, which Rousseau stipulates as necessary in the context of the self-rule of the *demos*. He connects political freedom with subjugation in a historically novel way. With the performative act of concluding a political contract, with the emergence of the association, the bourgeois lawmaker renounces his own legislative, and thus becomes a subject.[48] The citizen is equally sovereign and the one who is subjected: both are 'identical correlations'[49] and characterize bourgeois masculinity. In this political theory, being free and being obedient constitute male autonomy as a sovereign subjugation under the constitution: as the bourgeois subject who is capable of acting politically.[50]

Rousseau not only describes this ambivalent form of bourgeois subjectivation, which remains influential today,[51] he also drafts a historically new form of the executive, which he bases in the non-representable legislative. It is interesting how Rousseau solves the problem that because the non-representable *peuple* is not permanently assembled, the sovereign thereby does not embody the government, and also cannot be represented by it: the *pouvoir législatif* is assigned a *pouvoir exécutif*, a non-representing government as an administrative power. The executive is an exclusively administrative power and not a representative of the legislating sovereign. Since in Rousseau's conception of a republic the legislating sovereign cannot be represented, there is no permanent political institution of assembly, such as that of a parliament.[52] The political *peuple* assembles only when dealing with changes to existing laws, or to create new laws with which general affairs are to be regulated. And only then is the *pouvoir législatif*, as the power of the citizens, efficacious in determining 'state laws – or also constitutional laws'.[53]

However, an executive in the sense of an administratively executive power becomes necessary not only because the sovereign is not permanently assembled, but also – as Rousseau clearly states – because the citizens' political engagement is not self-evident. He laments that 'under a bad government . . . they foresee that the general will, will not prevail, and finally domestic cares absorb their attention'.[54] The political collective of the *peuple* must be asserted continuously over quotidian cares. Against the backdrop of the citizen who tends toward privatization, the institutionalization of a government appears to be a false or double base for the security of the state.

But how can the indivisible sovereign entrust the executive with the business of government, even temporarily? Rousseau's argumentative manoeuvre for this is as follows: indeed, the general *will*, which forms only when the citizens assemble, cannot be represented, but the *power* can transmit itself; it can be shared.[55] 'For the will is general, or it is not.'[56] The principle of the self-legislation of the *peuple* is brought to bear only for fundamental laws.[57] In contrast, a particular will does not have any force of law; it is either private or – and this is pivotal for Rousseau's concept of government – it is an act of the magistracy, that is, an administrative act: as such, it can present only a decree or a regulation.[58] The government correlates with a particular expression of will, below the legislative. Even the level at which the separation of powers occurs is based on the crucial division into particular and general: the executive, responsible for the 'politically particular', simply passes and manages regulations, not laws. It is an executing and administering power, thus a constituted power, but without being representative.[59] The government as administrative magistrate can, with 'vigor and celerity in enforcing the laws . . . prevent vexations, correct abuses, foresee seditious enterprises'.[60] Any lack of a division between the legislative juridically constituent power and the executive constituted power would be highly problematic. The *peuple* as sovereign would then, at the same time, be the *pouvoir exécutif*. 'The right and the fact would be so confused, that it would be impossible to tell what is law and what is not law.'[61] 'The legislative power once established . . . becomes a question of establishing also the executive power.'[62] When the *peuple* is not assembled, the executive governs. When it is assembled, there is no government; the executive is suspended.[63] 'It is not wise for him who makes the laws to execute them; nor for the body of the people to turn its attention from general views to particular objects.'[64]

However, Rousseau values the government primarily to the extent that it serves the sovereign.[65] The moment the government usurps the legislative of popular sovereignty, 'the social compact is broken'.[66] The state dissolves, and no one is bound by the laws anymore. For Rousseau, 'the abuse of government' bears 'the common name of *anarchy*'.[67] The legitimation of resistance against a government that aims to usurp the legislative arises from the impossibility of representation, which cedes to the male citizens as *pouvoir législatif* the right to political revolution. Rousseau conceives a 'codification in law of the right to insurrection'.[68] Even when the state or constitutional laws are no longer sufficient, 'the people is always master, and can change its laws, – even the best'.[69] In the most extreme case, it can suspend the constitution/the contract, as the collective sovereign cannot impose any law that it cannot collectively change. 'The sovereign, having no other force than legislative power, acts only through the laws.'[70] The social contract is thus revisable and laws can be considered bad or obsolete. This is an idiosyncratic variant of juridical, non-representationist constituent power and, at the level of representation critique, is more radical than what Emmanuel Sieyès would propose several decades later in the context of the French Revolution and the legitimation of the constituent assembly of representatives.

The male citizens, who form the non-representable and only intermittently acting *peuple*, qualified to suspend the constitution, exist not only when they act politically in unity; they also have a life beyond their political existence, before their formation as sovereign. They are part of the figure that is opposed to the political *peuple*, set in the sphere of the social: the figure of the *multitude*. Rousseau frequently uses this term for an indefinite number of people: he identifies the multitude as 'scattered', 'many', 'indeterminate', 'unknown or despised', 'blinded', or simply as 'blind'.[71] For Rousseau, the indeterminate, vulnerable many are not capable of collectively evolving a general political will; due to its isolation and dispersal, a multitude can be easily subjugated. In order to be able to act politically, and protect themselves, the dispersed citizens must therefore unite into a *peuple* as the body politic. 'As soon as this multitude is thus united [*réunie* also means 'assembled'] into a body, one of the members cannot be injured without attacking the body, and still less can the body be injured without the members feeling its effects.'[72]

Of course, it is not the entire multitude that unites and forms the collective political body. Rousseau separates from the rest of the multitude the men capable of equality among themselves, and thereby of becoming the *peuple*, and only these few are capable of sublating their differences in the general of the collective body. He knows that by substituting the physical constitution of the citizens for the constitution of a collective body, the differences, asymmetries, and hierarchizations in the politically indeterminate existence of the multitude,[73] all who live in the state territory, cannot be nullified. But these inequalities remain excluded from the sphere of the state: for

Rousseau, the political forms beyond the 'natural' inequalities of the social.[74]

This social includes not only the figure of the multitude and the not-politically-viable particular. The administrative form of governing apparently also requires the idea of 'society'. In contrast to the juridical-political *peuple*, in Rousseau's conception society is not formed, it does not arise performatively, but instead corresponds with 'nature'. As Marx noted critically, Rousseau naturalizes the *société* and thereby the social.[75] This is apparent not least in his understanding of the family as 'the most ancient of all societies, and the only natural one'.[76]

In my interpretation of Rousseau's conceptual mélange, society is a category that includes not only the particular and the affective (a category that promotes connectedness, as I will show later based on the example of the festival); the indefinite, diffuse multitude, which is blind and incapable of political action, is also inherent to society, or at times even corresponds to it. The aspects Rousseau wants to highlight here are significant. The designation 'multitude' is no longer suitable, it seems, when his aim is to emphasize a capacity for freedom and sovereignty in private, which means that this also applies to women. In such cases, he speaks of society, where, in contrast to the multitude, active behaviour is possible. In a republic, the sovereign-associated *peuple* cannot simply be subdued and controlled; as a society they have to be governed.

> There will always be a great difference between subduing a multitude and governing a society. If scattered individuals are successively enslaved by a single man, in whatever number it may be . . . I do not see a people and its chief; it is, if you will, an aggregation, but not an association; there is neither public property nor political body.[77]

Rousseau is the political theorist who, in the eighteenth century, began drafting that art of governing which Michel Foucault identified as 'governmentality'. Starting from the freedom of the individual, he designs a historically new form of governing which brings the

political and social action of citizens into focus and thereby perceives
not only that there is a political *peuple*, but that across the territory
there are 'scattered' people who do not form the *peuple*. Rousseau
understands that with the formation of a bourgeois society, politico-
economic transformations, and the growing number of those living
within the state borders, the issue is that of governing a population
that goes beyond the *peuple*.[78]

At the same time, as mentioned earlier, Rousseau is also the one
who perceives that in the governed society, a special form of bourgeois subjectivation becomes possible in the ambivalence between
freedom and subjugation, through which women, too, subjectivate
themselves in a special way.

For Rousseau, every person is born free, also the woman. But she
does not attain the political freedom bestowed upon the bourgeois
man. She is not capable of the general, as she is fully and entirely
defined by her sex and steadfastly remains in the societal particular.
Even when men and women have the same organs, needs, and faculties, and are equal as human in this regard ('the machine is the same
in its construction'[79]), 'where they are unlike, [it has] to do with the
characteristics of sex'.[80] Solely on the basis of her sex, the woman
cannot transform her 'natural' freedom into political freedom. The
woman's place is the family, the household, the private.[81] She remains
in the sphere of the societal and the politically indeterminate multitude. Bound to her passions and affects, she cannot become an active,
contract-forming part of the *peuple*. The man as *citoyen*, on the
contrary, is capable of politics and embodies the general.[82] He can
disengage from his 'natural' body and thereby from his sex and his
desires. The separation of the political and the social, which emerges
clearly with Rousseau, and which fundamentally characterizes the
bourgeois political order, is based on this heteronormative gender
order.

For Rousseau, the ambivalence between freedom and subjugation
constitutes not only the subject of the male citizen. The woman, too,
must subjugate herself in her gender-specific freedom. In this ambivalence she must, however, establish a gendered subjectivation in the
private sphere complementary to the man. In his pedagogical

writings, Rousseau clearly states that he does not consider gender a
naturally given quality; despite the naturalized social, gender is something that must be exercised, that first arises through practices.
Therefore, in the bourgeois private sphere also, self-conduct and
self-control are necessary. In that sphere, however, the game of freedom and subjugation does not unfold as the constituent power of the
citizen, but, rather, as heteronormative gender relations. By withhold-
ing her desire, and thereby first awakening his, the woman controls
both herself and the man. Through her sense of shame and her
self-control, she subdues the man, but at the same time also herself.
He is 'dependent on her goodwill', as she 'compel[s] him in his turn
to endeavor to please her, so that she may be willing to yield to his
superior strength'.[83] These heterosexual structures of desire establish
mutual conditions of dependence and domination, with which
Rousseau legitimizes the exclusion of women from active political
citizenship.[84]

Man is subjugated not only as a citizen by laws of his own making,
but also in his sexual desires by the woman. But – similar to his 'natural' physical constitution – he has to shed this double subjugation if he
wants to form a contractual association and thereby the (male) general
with other citizens: as subject of the law, will, and reason, he must free
himself from the woman in a sexual regard.[85] As part of the political
sovereignty of the *peuple*, he cannot remain dependent on her. He
must become an independent human who supposedly has no gender.
Only in private is he 'a male now and again', while 'the female is
always a female'.[86] It is not only the general will but also the norm of
the general human that is fundamentally rather than incidentally
based on liberation from the affective domination of the woman,
imagined as a threat. The ideas of law and reason are also therewith
inherent to a specific form of bourgeois autonomous masculinity
which believes itself to be freed of its gender.

In this scenario of bourgeois masculinity, the woman cannot
become a free human in political terms, and thereby an adult. She
cannot conduct herself in a political sense; she must be controlled by
the man and is ultimately condemned to an existence that is dependent on him.[87] Defined in such a manner by Rousseau, women remain

rooted in the multitude as politically passive, immature citizens needing protection. The masculine popular rule requires the construction of a complementary, dependent, politically unfree female citizen at its side, not least to legitimate the largely male, heterosexual (state) duties: protection of the weak who are passive and dependent; and protection from the other man, a rival for the children. This is one of Rousseau's most fundamental fears, on the basis of which he composes his bourgeois (gender) order. A man must beget many children, and he must be sure that they are his own. For if it occurs that he raises someone else's children, then everything falls apart. The 'faithless wife . . . destroys the family and breaks the bonds of nature; when she gives her husband children who are not his own . . . To my mind, it is the source of dissension and of crime of every kind.'[88]

While the social contract protects the male citizen from 'all personal dependence',[89] the institution of the family as the sphere of the (married) woman protects from the moral dangers of abnormal societal developments. Rousseau argues time and again against women who will not allow themselves to be bound to their maternal duties and to the household. Leaving one's own children to a wet nurse, or refusing to bear children at all, not only leads to the collapse of domestic life but disturbs the entire moral order.[90]

During Rousseau's lifetime, gender relations were not understood exclusively in the way he favoured, which is why his arguments for a heteronormative gender order are so vehement. He even allows the protesting women in *Émile* to have a say, indirectly. He knows that the women who were his contemporaries had long not accepted their exclusion from full civil rights and from the entire realm of the political. The struggles that Olympe de Gouges formulated in her *Declaration of the Rights of Woman and the Female Citizen* in 1791 were clearly audible even thirty years earlier with Rousseau. The assertion of a bourgeois-patriarchal gender order was, already in the eighteenth century, the outcome of struggles to the detriment of the protesting women.

This female part of the multitude, which could not be so easily tamed, is included in *Émile*: 'Women do wrong to complain of the inequality of man-made laws; this inequality is not of man's making, or at any rate it is not the result of mere prejudice, but of reason.'[91] 'Vague assertions as to the equality of the sexes and the similarity of their duties are only empty words.'[92] But Rousseau's concern was not simply to reject the equality of the sexes. When he denounced women's unconventional urban life, holding rural fertility up against it, his concern, corresponding with contemporary discourses, was also with patriarchal population policies:

> Women, you say, are not always bearing children. Granted; yet that is their proper business. Because there are a hundred or so of large towns in the world where women live licentiously and have few children, will you maintain that it is their business to have few children? And what would become of your towns if the remote country districts, with their simpler and purer women, did not make up for the barrenness of your fine ladies?[93]

Rather than a mere continuation of a patriarchal gender order extending back to antiquity, this nexus of population growth and political and moral order is due to an incisive transformation of the modern European political economy. In the eighteenth century, it is not only the bourgeois desire for freedom and self-determination that expands; the European population also grows immensely, agricultural production increases, and financial wealth accrues. All of these changes necessitate new forms of governing as well as a new political economy. Rousseau made crucial proposals for a new understanding of political economy in a pioneering article in the *Encyclopédie* by Diderot and d'Alembert, seven years before *The Social Contract* and *Émile*.[94] One of his main points is to assign the institution of the family with a function fundamentally different to that it had fulfilled from antiquity through to his own era.

In his thoughts on a republic, this restructuring of the family was necessary in order to distinguish the general from the particular, the political from the social: not only as a bourgeois nuclear family with the woman as moral nourisher and educator, but as an institution that would no longer be a model for the self-legislation of the *peuple* or the government of a society. The leading of the *oikos* lost its function as the role model for conducting a state: the rule of the one, such as that of the paterfamilias or the king, was to be replaced by that of the *demos* consisting of equal male citizens. The family could no longer be a model for the state, as otherwise the transformation could not be accomplished from particular to general, from man to mankind, from *multitude* to *peuple*.[95] Rousseau therefore argues vehemently for the separation of the private economy from the economy related to general affairs.[96] In an economy thus split, the family becomes the educational, disciplinary hinge between the naturalized gender order and the social contract, oriented on law and reason. A fundamental feature of the new, modern political economy is its guarantee of patrilinear blood relations. Since, above all, the family is assigned the function of raising the (male) citizen, it should be based on the certainty of paternity.

With the conception of the contract and the *volonté générale* in *The Social Contract*, Rousseau invents a specific form of bourgeois-juridical sovereignty, which builds upon the administrating and directing executive's art of governing. As Foucault notes in his lectures on *Security, Territory, Population*, in this new political economy that no longer emanates from the *oikos*, the 'problem of sovereignty' is posed with exceptional poignancy in relation to the challenge of governing a population.[97] Rousseau rises to this challenge, but his bourgeois 'theory of power' remains grounded 'in law and the system of law'.[98] The juridical-political perspective, which relies on the formation of an indivisible sovereignty of the *peuple*, would already reach its limits during Rousseau's era, which he seems to anticipate, and this is perhaps why his political theory appears, in part, inconsistent. For the principle of governing a population, and with that, the principle of biopolitics, is *omnes et singulatim*: it governs all, not only the *peuple*, and each individually. 'And what does population mean? It does not simply mean to say a numerous group of humans, but living beings, traversed, commanded, ruled by processes and biological laws.'[99]

The historically new challenge of governing a population is especially evident in Rousseau's concept of a masculinist sovereignty, which is accompanied by the shadow of a naturalized and feminized multitude, by those who do not belong to the *peuple*, but are very clearly part of the population. He thereby moves in the context of the emerging bourgeois-capitalist paradigm of domination, which is shaped by the construction of a naturalized, binary, and heteronormative gender difference along the separation between private-particular and state-general affairs. In *The History of Sexuality, Vol. I*, Foucault recognized this binary 'idea of sex' (*idée de sexe*) as a central hinge for a biopolitics that first became dominant in the eighteenth century, and then mainly in the nineteenth.[100]

Rousseau's writings are dealt with in detail here not only because he conceptualizes a non-representationist form of the republic in its tense relationship to a new, gendered political economy oriented on the governing of a population, but also because he imagines a form of legislative power that comes about through the abilities and empowerments of individual citizens. This constituent power operates without representation, yet nonetheless remains trapped in a legal paradigm; it is therefore merely a juridical constituent power, in contrast to Antonio Negri's re-conception of a constituent power that is decidedly not limited to a juridical framework. Rousseau's juridical constituent power is based on the merging of the assembled citizens into a unity. Precisely this imperative of a unity contradicts the conception of a constituent power that goes beyond the juridical, a power which in a radical way emanates from the heterogeneity and interrelatedness of singularities not melded into a whole.[101] Individuals mutually related and dependent upon one another, and the socialities resulting from this, are unwelcome in Rousseau's understanding of the juridical-political sphere, and for that reason they are made particular and often feminized, situated in a societal multitude construed as pre-political. Nonetheless, he perceives the necessity of social bonds, and the way he imagines this societally in terms of exchange and assembly is extremely interesting.

Rousseau's sexism has been repeatedly mentioned, and his vehement advocacy of a heteronormative and hierarchical gender order, which excludes women from the political, comprehensively discussed. Here, however, at the end of this chapter, in unfolding how Rousseau, from his representation-critical perspective, imagined the convening

of the multitude as a republican festival, we can abandon his bourgeois masculinism and seek inspiration for a new, queer-feminist
conception of democracy.

Rousseau produces a comprehensive critique of representation
which applies not only to the political but also to the societal. He deals
in detail with how societal existence is shaped when the sovereign is
not assembled. He rejects not only the representation of the sovereign,
but also the theatrical stage. He does not want to imagine an acting,
non-subordinated society on the model of spectators at a theatre.
With his critique of representation, however, Rousseau does not
escape into a metaphysics of presence,[102] nor does he defend the
immediacy of the physical body or praise the authentic as opposed to
mediation or acting.

His essay 'Letter to d'Alembert' was published in 1758, four years
before *The Social Contract* and *Émile*. In it, he explicitly formulates a
critique of the theatre. For him, the theatre is an obscure site of
aesthetic representation, offering 'exclusive entertainments that close
up a small number of people in melancholy fashion in a gloomy
cavern, which keep them fearful and immobile in silence and inac-
tion'.[103] The performance on the stage can be frightful; in the darkness,
unable to move or raise its voice, the audience is damned to sit and
idly endure. The closed space of the theatre thus is a metaphor for
passivity and obedience.

Rousseau contrasts this theatrical domestication and immobility
with the assembly of the many outdoors as they share in celebrating a
festival: 'It is in the open air, under the sky, that you ought to
gather . . . let the sun illuminate your innocent entertainments; you
will constitute one yourselves, the worthiest it can illuminate.'[104] He
has no problem with acting when it is not delegated. Without the
stage of an institution such as that of the theatre, those who come
together become, themselves, actors in the movement. 'What will be
shown in them [these theatres]? Nothing, if you please.'[105]

I would like to highlight several aspects that Rousseau invokes in
favour of the festival to show how they rupture the dichotomy of
presence and representation. When he emphasizes the bustle of everyday life rather than the actor or spokesperson on the stage, he does

not favour an authentic conception of the present; he does not set mediation in opposition to being present, but rather opposes construction to representation. His concern, in various ways, is with movement and exchange, with the construction and awareness of bonds in the present. In this regard, Rousseau offers an understanding of acting that goes beyond staged performances. Enthusiastic about Geneva, he writes, 'Everyone is busy, everyone is moving.'[106] That is the drama that the city offers. 'The city appears, as it were, multiplied by the labors which take place in it';[107] it becomes dynamic, manifold, and even seems larger. Rousseau emphasizes the theatre of everyday life in motion, the movements in the now. In *The Social Contract*, the *polis* is still a positive role model for the republic, though he doesn't dare foreground the movements of the city, this interrelated heterogeneity, in his conception of the political. However, what he does adopt from urban society for the conception of the juridical-political are assemblies for which no representation is necessary.

In Geneva, Rousseau observes that the city dwellers assemble and exchange views in various contexts on a regular basis. Meetings in taverns are no longer adequate to resolve disputes, react to events, and 'deliberate coldly and calmly'.[108] These debates are republican activities, which take place in so-called circles, a practice of assembly that is not exclusive to men. Women, too, have their recurrent gatherings.[109] 'The citizens of the same state, the inhabitants of the same city, are not anchorites; they could not always live alone and separated';[110] they must discuss matters on a regular basis. A republic accounts for that; it is what comprises it. Rousseau understood such bonding assemblies, integrated into everyday life, as 'imitations', or repeated dramas 'befitting free men'.[111] The play on a theatre stage, on the contrary, comprises a mental dispersing of sorts, which undermines republican activities, permits little concentration, competes with the assemblies in terms of time, and shows imitations as mere spectacles.[112] 'The theatre of repetition is opposed to the theatre of representation, just as movement is opposed to the concept and to representation, which refers it back to the concept', writes Gilles Deleuze in *Difference and Repetition*, making no reference to Rousseau.[113] In movement, the affective forces of an encounter can have an effect on the mind, without mediation, but nevertheless not immediate.

In his critique of the theatre of representation's 'exclusive entertainments',[114] Rousseau is even able to say something positive about the movement-spectacle of travelling artists.[115] The republic doesn't require a single 'public theatre': 'one needs even many', which arise when the many 'assemble often and form among themselves sweet bonds of pleasure and joy',[116] when they celebrate a plethora of public, open-air festivals. This is a theatre of movement, in which 'vibrations, rotations, whirlings, gravitations, dances or leaps' are invented, 'which directly touch the mind'.[117]

The republican festival appears in 1758, in the 'Letter to d'Alembert', as a type of climax to the open play in movement, in exchange, communication, and dance: 'Let the spectators become an entertainment to themselves; make them actors themselves; do it so that each sees and loves himself in the others so that all will be better united.'[118] Those celebrating are 'gay, and tender', they 'seek to communicate their joy and their pleasures. They invite, importune . . . All the societies constitute but one, all become common to all.'[119] It is a play that produces the common; an open, bonding, hospitable sociality to which anyone can be invited, one that takes up and admits difference and heterogeneity in the unfolding of the common. The common is not the general, as it does not suspend the particular. The common, however, does not simply put together the particulars and connect them with one another. The common exponentiates the particular, the special, the singular, to a 'sight of the abundance',[120] created through freedom.

At the republican festival, it is the multitude in the abundance of the common that assembles, acts, and moves in a republican sense. Spokespeople and mediators are not necessary. Should the festival and assemblies be forbidden and disappear from the public realm, appearing in their stead would be 'private meetings', where people are compelled to 'hid[e] themselves as if they were guilty'.[121] In this regard, too, Rousseau opposes clandestine gatherings. He wants the squares to be occupied, the exchange and bonds celebrated in an entirely public sphere: 'Plant a stake crowned with flowers in the middle of a square; gather the people together there, and you will have a festival.'[122] Here, unlike in *The Social Contract*, all who celebrate at the festival belong to the *peuple*. When Rousseau writes *The Social Contract* just a few years later, only those who form the sovereign belong to the *peuple*. Had he written about festivals in his political writing, and seen the formation of the common as a political act, he would have had to speak of the multitude as assembling in the squares, exchanging views, and celebrating their mutual relatedness – in the movements of dances and leaps. He would have had to speak of a multitude surrounding bourgeois democracy and a people, however construed.

2

Derrida

Democracy to Come

It was Rousseau's critique of representation that the young Jacques Derrida was grappling with when he began to develop the notion and practice of deconstruction in his 1967 text *Of Grammatology*. Representation is fundamental to the deconstructive salvage of writing against the unmediatedness of the voice. Derrida problematizes this unmediatedness in Rousseau, not because his assembly of citizens manages without representation, but more fundamentally in terms of the self-referentiality because of 'hearing-oneself-speak' – the primacy of speech over writing. He accuses Rousseau *in toto* of a masculinist metaphysics of presence, and rather than simply criticizing the political constitution of the Republic in *The Social Contract*, he focuses primarily on Rousseau's conception of the festival in 'Letter to d'Alembert':

> The origin of this society is not a contract, it does not happen through treaties . . . and *representatives*. It is a *festival* [*fête*]. It consumes itself in *presence*. There is certainly an experience of time, but a time of pure presence, giving rise neither to calculation, nor reflection, nor . . . comparison: . . . Time also without differance.[1]

Therefore, Rousseau's thinking belongs 'to the metaphysics of presence, from Plato to Hegel, rhythmed by the articulation of presence upon self-presence'.[2] Rousseau is, however, not simply caught 'within that implication of the epochs of metaphysics or of the West'.[3] Much more important is the concept of history that accompanies the metaphysics: that 'this history of metaphysics, to which the concept of history itself returns, belongs to an ensemble for which the name history is no longer suitable'.[4] This ensemble is the 'presence present to itself', which, taken out of time, describes a moment without history.

It seems as though Derrida's critique of this presence without history applies more to Hegel than Rousseau. Hegel is the one who dialectically grasps the presence in the present tense as not *in* time and yet as an immediate moment. He places the logos at the centre of his thinking, the unmediated return of the spirit to itself, of the absolute spirit, which speaks without mediation, without interlocutor, and hears itself speak.[5] Derrida turns away from dialectics for precisely this reason, because it 'is governed, as it always has been, by a horizon of presence'.[6] Yet the question is whether Rousseau, who is critical of representation (and thoroughly worthy of critique for his masculinism), is deserving of the accusation of harbouring a metaphysics of presence. In the following, my concern is not to confront Derrida's deconstruction of metaphysics with yet another reading of Rousseau. Instead, Derrida's arguments in *Of Grammatology* lead me to a consideration of the problematic that his plea for representation and writing is based on a critique of self-referentiality, and thereby on a type of essentialism, which has created, beyond Derrida, a deconstructive knowledge that perceives beyond representation only the immediate, self-identical, and authentically 'natural'. Abandoned by this is the possibility of conceiving of the present in a way other than through the paradigm of immediate presence, essence, and identity. The understanding of history thus remains captive in a Eurocentric linearity of a philosophy of history, and makes it difficult to comprehend democracy as anything other than liberal and representative.

The self-referential presence of the spirit is part of Hegel's understanding of the present, which still has a great influence today. Conserved from his complex conception of a dialectical present are mainly the aspects of presence and immediacy. Hegel's present arises from the dialectic of the eternal as the absolute, true, and universal present, and the now as the concrete, individual present.

The first dimension corresponds to 'the eternal, which is present [*gegenwärtig*]';[7] the present of the spirit, the reason, the self-thinking thinking, the logos. For Hegel, reason, being eternally present, is present everywhere in history, a history that, as a dynamic of sublation, is striving for maximum rationality. Reason is eternal because, as endless truth, it steadfastly pursues history and remains unchanged through all temporal and spatial transformations. In its presence this eternity is not the beyond, and not the future, as it does not belong to the flow of time. 'Eternity is not before or after time, not before the creation of the world, nor when it perishes; rather is eternity the absolute present, the Now, without before or after.'[8] Eternity is not in time, but rather, time itself; it is the idea, the spirit, at once present, future, and past: eternity is 'true present'.[9] This absolute present is, because past and future are not: 'the non-being of the being, which is replaced by the Now, is the Past; the being of the non-being which is contained in the Present, is the Future. In the positive meaning of time, it can be said that only the Present *is*, that Before and After are not.'[10] 'Eternity will not come to be, nor was it, but it *is*.'[11] The past, on the contrary, 'has been actual as history of the world'.[12] Thus, in its not-being as the past it is not eternal, yet reason as eternal is present in it everywhere. On this basis, there is a philosophy of history for Hegel, although, as we will see, the task of philosophy is to comprehend the here and now.[13]

The second dimension of the present is the concrete present, the discrete, individual present of the now. This now 'is the result of the past, and is pregnant with the future'.[14] The being of the now is not eternal, but, rather, limited; it constantly becomes the non-being of the past, and the non-being of the future becomes the being of the now. The concrete present is in a steady movement of dissolving the temporary differences of past and future being 'as passing over into nothing, and of nothing as passing over into being'.[15] 'The immediate vanishing of these differences into *singularity* is the present as *Now*.'[16] The now is merely a fleeting, discrete temporal moment, a subjective, sensuous feeling.[17] The impression of the senses passes quickly; 'it *is* nothing as the individual Now',[18] a short, '*finite* present'.[19] In this permanent passing of the present being, Hegel understands the now as being without mediation. It is immediate, without representation. In order to have existence as something that has been, it must first be reflected on and mediated. 'The Now' is not time itself; it is the immediate determination of time,[20] the 'pure immediacy'[21] of the here and now, without an absent origin. The immediate present *is*, and at the same time has disappeared, in that another has replaced it. In its immediacy and fleetingness, the concrete present, the here and now, is ultimately without history, an ahistorical moment, with whose passing and reflective comprehension teleological world history realizes itself further.

Hegel understands the state as eternally present, as absolute spirit whose perfect historical form can never be realized. It is located in the dimension of the absolute present. In contrast, he sees the social relations of the family, the kinship relations in the private realm, stuck in the concrete now and thereby in immediacy.[22] In Hegel's theory, the family enters into a dialectical relationship with society; as gender-specific connoted spheres of private and public, they find unity in the state as the realm of the political.[23] Hegel allows democratic participation only by means of representation;[24] a radical inclusion of the heterogeneous many does not occur, since an unmediated participation of the particular would be no more than the immediate sensuous presence of an individual, no more than an aesthetic awareness in the now, but not political action.[25] In this idealist perspective, the other side of political representation is a metaphysical presence as particular immediacy, which as such cannot be political, but instead remains self-identical in the social and aesthetic.

For Hegel, the task of philosophy is to comprehend the here and now. He situates it in the dialectic of the absolute present oriented on reason, and the concrete, moment-like now. To illustrate the philosophical task, he uses an ancient Greek saying that also plays a role in Marx and Benjamin (and in the next chapter).

When the philosophy of history explores reason, then, it is concerned with the absolute present, which is present everywhere in the past; yet at the same time philosophy must remain in the now. It must comprehend what is, 'because *what is* is reason'.[26] Hegel explains this necessary concentration on the being of reason using the ancient

Greek saying from one of Aesop's fables, which is translated into Latin as '*Hic* Rhodus, *hic* saltus': '*Here* is Rhodes, jump *here*.' (The historical context is long-jump competitions on the Greek island of Rhodes.) As Hegel remarks, he changes the old saying only slightly, substituting 'rose' for Rhodes, while the leap becomes an invitation to dance: '*Here* is the rose, dance *here*.' With this slight change, Hegel illustrates the temporality of philosophy, whose task is to comprehend reason as what *is here*. 'To recognize reason as the rose in the cross of the present'[27] means precisely not to jump, not to jump beyond Rhodes, the rose. It would be 'foolish to fancy any philosophy can transcend its present world',[28] as that would mean carrying out a normative philosophy occupied with the future, building a world '*as it ought to be*',[29] not as it is now. For Hegel, such a normative future world exists only as opinion and imagination. Philosophy is not about drafting utopias.

Hegel writes that recognizing reason as a rose in the present means 'to find delight in it, [it] is a rational insight which implies *reconciliation* with reality'.[30] The invitation to dance is directed towards philosophy, which in the here and now should take pleasure in reason, should celebrate it.

Let's return to Derrida's critique of Rousseau, whom he accuses of a yearning for metaphysical presence. Rousseau prefers the presence of assemblies, voices, and speech: small communities, in which the unmediated coexistence of the citizens and the 'unanimity of "assembled peoples"'[31] are possible. This presence signifies a 'completely self-present'[32] being, the perfect self-identity, selfhood, and feeling. In his deconstruction, Derrida not only trims representation-critical and anarchistic references from Rousseau, but also imputes to him a conception of a present pregnant with immediacy and presence in the sense of Hegel.[33] And precisely when Derrida deconstructs Rousseau and his gendered considerations, he reproduces, at the same time, gender-specific dichotomous attributions, which conceive of feeling, emotion, immediacy, and presence as female, and rationality, reflection, deferral, and representation as male.

When, with Rousseau, representation is suspended, and at the republican festival the public no longer watches but rather appears in common and passively/actively determines what happens, this is not about extinguishing 'the difference between the actor and the spectator, the represented and the representer, the object seen and the seeing subject',[34] as Derrida accuses him of. Such an extinguishing would be no more than authenticism, or – as Derrida formulates it – 'intimacy of a self-presence', 'the consciousness or the sentiment of self-proximity, of self-sameness'.[35] In the public festival, Derrida sees no more than the presence of the identical, the community of the own ones, in correspondence with those political forms without 'representative difference'[36] which Rousseau prefers in *The Social Contract*: the political committees, as well as the assembled, free, legislative *peuple*.[37]

Derrida does not want to acknowledge here that Rousseau invokes the festival as an assembly, allowing the 'audience' to abandon the stage, in that it leaves its role in the scenario of representation and becomes the many who move and dance, mutually affecting one another. Notwithstanding the critiques of a 'united people', which only when assembled becomes sovereign, Rousseau's considerations transgress the metaphysics of presence. The public of the theatre becomes communal; at the festival it foils the dichotomy between *publicum/privatum*, public and private. In doing so, it doesn't simply leave the private, the dark space of viewing, and enter into the light of the public realm.

In order to break through both the dialectical as well as the deconstructive juxtaposition of immediate presence and mediating representation, political action must be newly defined with reference to practices based on mutual affections and dependencies that allow new forms of democracy to arise, which, being without traditional forms of representation, cannot simply be categorized and discredited in terms of being present and as physical presence. But how can the dichotomous perception of presence and representation be broken open even more? How can aspects of Rousseau's republican festival, such as movement, exchange, and affection, be expanded in the conceptualization of an unclosed democracy, a democracy that suspends borders, opens borders, and is not limited to a people?

For that, a reconceptualizing of the present is necessary, a reconceptualization which, with the deconstructivist critique of the metaphysics of presence, has been all too hastily banished from some poststructuralist thought. Interestingly, these thoughts on the present can be expanded with a focus on both the temporal as well as the unclosing aspects of democracy by way of Derrida's later writings; in particular his book *Rogues*, in which he gathered all of his contemplations on a 'democracy to come' and produced a revised reading of Rousseau.[38]

Does the to-come in 'democracy to come' mean that this democracy has a future? Is it in its ideal form, or at least its better form, in the future, is it still yet to come? Or does the to-come refer more to the present, to the now, to a special form of present tense? What does the to-come have to do with hospitality, with open borders? And how do we have to understand the present so that what is to come, that which comes, which arrives, has a place? What understanding of democracy is tied to that?

I would like to scrutinize Derrida's 'democracy to come' – positioned against the background of the critique of liberal representative democracy – in terms of its contribution toward rejecting all the promises of a democratization postponed to a future, fighting for alternative forms of democracy in the present, and trying them out in a present that is more than a fleeting moment, more than physical presence, and instead an expanded process of constituting.[39] Remaining – or rather, becoming – in this expanded present without a rationality of self-referentiality, however, repeatedly causes discontent: everything that we are accustomed to identifying as utopia, as futurity, seems thereby lost. As though everything could only be better in the future and the present won't be changeable; as if beginning in the now were not possible. For that reason, too, Derrida's unclosed democracy to come provides an interesting opportunity to think about how, in an untimely grasp of the present, what is to come can be understood effectively without reference to the future.

In *Rogues*, which is heavily influenced by the terror attacks of 11 September 2001 and the subsequent reactions of 'Western' democracies, Derrida gathers his earlier considerations on democracy to come and expands upon them. He makes clear that the reason why we speak at all in different ways about democracy, why we can fight at all over different concepts of democracy, lies precisely in the concept of democracy itself, as this concept cannot be unambiguously defined. Democracy is indeterminate and never itself. It lacks a self, an own, an essence. Consequently, *there is* no true and genuine democracy. As Derrida says, it cannot present itself as already existing and complete.[40] Democracy remains open of necessity, and there are consequences to that. It harbours the danger of being occupied by the extreme right in a way that attempts to make this constitutive indetermination controllable with the determination of identity. Fascist and authoritarian governments repeatedly come into power in formal, democratic ways.[41] Within 'Western' democracies, the ranks of right-wing and racist parties grow steadily, parties that strive for an ethnically homogeneous – and at the same time heteronormative and patriarchally hierarchized – equality only for citizens ethnicized in certain ways. Everything that is imagined as different is, at best, excluded. Derrida shows that this identitarian 'autoimmunization' of democracy is based on a 'double *renvoi*':[42] the *reference* to everything different and foreign within the community that is imagined as homogeneous, and the *sending off or expelling* of the other from the community.[43] With this double *renvoi*, democracy is moved to a later point in time. However, such a self-limitation, which attempts to base itself on the construction of a true identity, is not at all a strategy employed solely by extremist right-wing parties. As self-limiting strategies, autoimmunitarian attempts at identitarian foundation are widespread reactions to the fundamental indetermination of democracy.

The reference to an identity, an own, a self (*ipse*), marks a circular movement, a return – the idea of selfhood, self-referentiality – which in the reference itself draws a border, a circle that limits, that borders, a community.[44] This selfhood, which circularly refers back to itself, does not necessarily require a reference to something original, for example an ethnically or nationally [*völkisch*] determined identity. This self-referentiality grows out of the bourgeois categories of sovereign self-determination, autonomy, self-legislation, sovereignty, from the *krátos* as the power of the *demos*. It is a selfhood that makes its own laws, that makes itself, auto-nomously. With this etymological

interpretation, Derrida initially follows Émile Benveniste, who emphasized the gendered connotation of the noun *krátos*: it identifies, in a
political sense, 'the "power" as personal advantage'[45] which is possessed by he who is 'master of himself' and thereby has (the) authority.
Derrida refers to the correspondence of this circling self-positing with
the masculinist power and potency of 'I can', of 'one's self' as lord and
master. The etymological traces that, with many detours, have been
inscribed into this selfhood refer steadily to ownership, property, the
authority of the lord, usually that of the master of the house who, as
host, sets the conditions of his hospitality himself.[46] This masculinist
self-referentiality becomes 'a principle of legitimate sovereignty, the
accredited or recognized supremacy of a power or a force, a *krátos* or a
cracy'.[47] Derrida identifies it as 'phallo-paterno-filio-fraterno-ipsocentric',
from which, in European modernism, the 'political theology . . . of the
sovereignty of the people, that is, of democratic sovereignty', unfolds.[48]
The self-referentiality is thus not due solely to a national or ethnic
understanding of democracy, but is constitutive for liberal democracy
which starts from the sovereignty of a people. Popular sovereignty is,
in a masculinist sense, self-referential. These notions of sovereignty
and of a superiority circulating around oneself cannot be separated
from the idea of wholeness. The whole is that which is circumnavi-
gated, in a revolving, returning self-reference. The circle, the turn,
'makes up the whole and makes a whole with itself; it consists in totalizing, in totalizing itself, and thus in gathering itself by tending toward
simultaneity'.[49]

The concept of a totalizing, homogenizing equality, of course,
opposes the freedom of the individual, understood as having the
autonomy to decide for oneself.[50] One of the main aporias of liberal
(representative) democracy is revealed here: the ultimately self-
destructive autoimmunization through circular wholeness, through
the assembly of all who are the same, which, however, not only is
impossible but also limits the freedom of the individual in the assim-
ilating propensity of a community of the equalized. Mainly in times
of crisis, and under real or imagined threats, a democracy that
revolves around itself tends again and again to dangerously immunize itself by means of a masculinist security politics.

Under the pretence of protecting democracy from its enemies, in its warlike self-defence it comes to resemble its enemies. Threat, protection, and security become indistinguishable, especially in the interior of a democracy, ever more authoritarian and subject to policing. Democracy protects and maintains itself in a Carl Schmitt–like logic of antagonism between friend and enemy, by threatening itself, by destructively autoimmunizing itself.[51] With reference to minorities labelled as 'different', there is either an intensified proclamation of their integration and assimilation, or a dismissal, a return, a deportation of the 'Others' labelled as a threat. Parallel to these practices of autoimmunization, the coming of democracy is postponed to the next election or some other later point in time.[52] The possibility of repealing democracy through free, democratic elections on the basis of the free decision to limit freedom is part of the aporia between equality and freedom – and, as Derrida writes, 'one of the many perverse and autoimmune effects of the axiomatic developed already in Plato and Aristotle'.[53]

'Another truth of the democratic' is incompatible with this ipsocracy and phallocracy; it clashes with 'the truth of the other, heterogeneity, the heteronomic and the dissymmetric, disseminal multiplicity, the anonymous "anyone," the "no matter who," the in-determinate "each one"'.[54]

In *Rogues*, Derrida clarifies that, for him, the concept of democracy to come is not about a form of democracy to be completed in the future. He formulates the talk from which he delineates himself as follows:

You know, the perfect democracy, a full and living democracy, does not exist; not only has it never existed, not only does it not presently exist, but, indefinitely deferred, it will always remain to come, it will never be present in the present, will never present itself, will never come, will remain always to come, like the impossible itself.[55]

Thirty-five years after his reading of Rousseau in the 1960s, when he was just developing deconstruction, Derrida associates him with precisely this understanding of democracy oriented towards the never-coming future. In *Rogues*, there is no longer any mention of a metaphysics of presence when Rousseau despairs over 'any democracy ever being presently possible, existent and presentable'.[56] Rousseau sees 'what makes democracy unpresentable in existence',[57] but understands it as an impossibility remaining in the future. In his new interpretation, Derrida shifts the temporality of Rousseau's Republic from the presence of the present into the absence-preserving future. With this gambit, Derrida has freed the present of the suspicion of metaphysics and opened it up for his deconstructive thinking. Now he can preserve his own understanding of democracy to come from the future and leave it in the present.

Ultimately, Derrida sees that Rousseau is not focused on an unchangeable essence of democracy, but, conversely, points to democracy's permanent malleability. In *The Social Contract*, Rousseau writes that, more so than any other government, the 'democratic or popular government' tends 'so strongly and so continuously to change its form', and, more than any other, demands 'vigilance and courage' to maintain it in its changeable form.[58]

The reason for the indetermination of democracy, as already mentioned, can be found also, for Rousseau, in the word itself: 'To use the term in a rigorous acceptation, a true democracy has never existed, and will never exist.'[59]

The impossible permanent presence of the entire citizenry, which cannot incessantly assemble, the impossibility of the being present of the sovereign, of the unrepresentable *demos*,[60] likewise prevent democracy from *being* in the sense of an essence of democracy. Democracy does not *exist*; it is constantly transforming, indefinite. In this sense, all that exists is a becoming of democracy. For Rousseau, the reason there is no true, perfect democracy consists also in the fact that the people don't have the virtues of the gods; not vigilance, nor courage, nor endurance, nor force. But they have to strive for it, fight for it, and 'better perilous liberty than peaceful slavery'.[61]

Derrida offers an interesting interpretation of this passage from Rousseau: for one thing, in the chapter on 'Democracy', Rousseau does not write about God, and thereby not about one indivisible sovereignty, as he does otherwise in *The Social Contract*, when writing about the formation of a sovereign general will.[62] Rousseau writes in the plural, of gods, without saying how many. The number plays no role. It is this *more than one* that heralds democracy, according to Derrida.[63] On the other hand, Rousseau employs a concept of freedom that makes it possible to understand freedom as no longer the antipode of equality. The freedom fraught with danger, which is to be preferred over servitude, arises in the dynamic of the changeability of democracy itself, through its indetermination, and is no longer directly connected to individuals.

Jean-Luc Nancy, whose book *The Experience of Freedom* Derrida refers to,[64] clarified in his work on the concept that *krátos* does not necessarily have to designate a masculinist ability for self-reference and autonomy. Instead, according to Nancy, *krátos* refers to freedom as the 'force of the thing', and demo*cracy* revolves around precisely this force of freedom. Such a shaping, transforming force of freedom reverses the interpretation of a self-referential power or force of a *demos*. In addition, as 'force of the thing', freedom disengages from the agency of the subject, which Josiah Ober emphasizes in the etymology of *krátos*.[65] Equality then no longer means the equality of persons, who as similar form the *demos*, the *Volk*. On the contrary, Nancy's understanding of freedom entails a radical heterogeneity. As force of the thing this freedom breaks open the border between the animate and the inanimate. It disengages from identity and delimitability, and thereby from countability, from number and size, from discipline, and from the biopolitical, statistic-oriented relationship of democracy and poll.

But when the meaning of democracy is opened up to such an extent, the question is raised: How far should democracy go? To whom should it extend? Up to what number can a republic assert a claim to democracy?[66] What number signifies the majority? How many can come (additionally)? How many are allowed to arrive? Who and how many will be welcomed and how? Who is granted hospitality?

Derrida closely links his understanding of democracy to come with this question of hospitality. The enclosed democracy, which

limits itself in an autoimmunizing move to the construction of a self
(in the form of a national-normalized citizenry, of a people, a community), offers hospitality only in a second step: first, it constitutes
itself as the 'master/lady of the house'. Only *after* taking in those who
are equal on the basis of origin and birth, and expelling all unequals –
both the unequal citizens as well as the unequal, foreign others (in
different ways, by marking, hierarchizing, or excluding) – can it
imagine, under certain circumstances, hospitality. The exclusion is
primary, hospitality as (re-)absorption secondary. It is a limited and
conditional hospitality, one that does not take into account the fact
that those who are positioned as other, foreign, and rogue, also (can)
belong to the *demos*.[67] The enclosed democracy is an auto*immuniz*ed
community (*communitas*), which refuses the exchanging of *munus*,
which also involves hospitality, in a way that can be deadly for those
who come/arrive as 'foreign'. In ancient Roman understanding,
im-munis is a person without *munus*, to whom no obligation or duty
(*Abgabe*) is assigned, a person who does not return a received gift or
good deed, who does not fulfil the obligation to return, who cannot
or need not reciprocate.[68] For another practice of hospitality, the
exchange of the *munera* must be broken open in a way other than this
immunizing one.

Unclosed democracy has no use for conditional hospitality, which
is based on exclusion. Unbounded democracy breaks with the
construction of a natural homogeneity as well as with sites of origin
and provenance. At the start is the rupture with hegemonic ideas
of democracy, and this different start means for Derrida a divide, or
rather a crack, a joint, a deferral – also of the beginning – in order to
start, to mark, an '"originary" heterogeneity that has already
come',[69] and that can befall only with what comes, in order to open
up the democracy. Derrida's position is thus not that democracy is
impossible in the present, and in this sense always only coming in
the future. Instead, he reverses the autoimmunizing *renvoi* as refer-
ral and deferral to the others, to a deferral, a *différance* in the
present, which makes identitarian presence impossible and becomes
an expanding movement of the present time, 'a dis-located time of
the present'.[70]

Rather than postponing the promise of democracy indefinitely into the future, Derrida proposes a different way of dealing with the present. When he speaks in French of *démocratie à venir*, with the orthographic separation of the *à* from *venir*, at the same time he turns away from the word *avenir*, which in French means future. Quite explicitly, he instead puts *à venir* (to come) close to *devenir* (becoming).[71] *À venir* means a coming, not as something 'in the future' separated from the present, but as something that *remains in coming* – a movement or dynamic that recurs in the present. The durability of what is to come, the becoming, is neither teleological nor continuous, neither linear nor anticipatory. It is without horizon and far from the economy of redemption.[72] Derrida's figure of to-come does not mean the future, but rather an expanded, unforeseeable present, which is not, but remains in the process of becoming. This present has no connection to the identitarian presence, to 'there is', to essence, or to immediate presence.[73] The present that remains coming to be is a becoming, a present that endures in the unforeseeability of movement.

The to-come of *à venir* puts great value on the arrival, but without this being the end of the movement, an arrival that is unforeseeable, incalculable, contingent. This to-come is discontinuous in its course, in its duration, and points to what and who comes, to the unforeseeable event, to the coming of any others whom one did not see coming, to that which is coming without being visible.[74] It is about the event that cannot be awaited, anticipated, calculated.

A hospitality that faces the unforeseeable, the indetermination, the always precarious to-come in the present, is without conditions; for Derrida, it is 'absolute hospitality'.

Absolute hospitality requires that I open up my home (*chez-moi*) and that I give not only to the foreigner (provided with a family name, with the social status of a being foreigner, etc.), but to the absolute, unknown, anonymous other, and that I *give place* (*donne lieu*) to them, that I let them come, that I let them arrive, and take place in the place (*lieu*) I offer them (*avoir lieu*), without asking of them either reciprocity . . . or even their names.[75]

My 'at home' is not an inward-oriented relationship to self, not an immunized 'in principle, inviolable' 'home',[76] but, rather, becomes an 'unconditional refuge'[77] for what is to come, and opens itself to the surroundings. When Derrida speaks of absolute hospitality, he does not necessarily have a fixed, immovable home in mind, a built place where what or who is to come can be awaited, as though only they were in motion. The site of giving place is also incessantly changing, is in the strict sense home-less, is becoming, on the way – not least due to the unforeseeable and ongoing return of the to-come.

This mobile hospitality breaks with the duty of giving, with the exchange of *munera*. The to-come is not obliged to the return of a *munus*.[78] Beyond Derrida, who in this context focuses mainly on the juridical break of the gift without reciprocity, I would like to emphasize that this radical hospitality is social precisely because it suspends the exchange and debt economy of *munus*, the duty to be given (*Ab-Gabe*), and demands no advance, gives no loan that has to be paid back.[79] Whoever comes is invited, is welcome to come, to take place. This practice of radical inclusion suspends the logic of *munera* as a condition of belonging to a community (*communitas*), in that it gives excessively, in an unconditional social giving of hospitality: this openness of gathering with any others, in mutual pleasure, enjoying the radical heterogeneity, can also be understood as a festival.[80] In contrast to Rousseau, this pleasure is one that, without the obligation of *munus*, does not conclude or limit interrelatedness and cooperation through the idea of a people, but instead is precariously in motion in the incalculable present and remains in coming. The hospitality which breaks with the exchange logics of *munus de-munizes*, emphasizes mutual openness, which deconstructs the asymmetry between the master of the house and the guest/foreigner.[81] It begins from a sociality that does not give primacy to autonomy and self-referentiality, but instead risks embracing the fundamental relatedness with those to come that cannot be suspended.[82] The hospitality of democracy to come, with all of the eventfulness of the unforeseeable to-come, is also a sort of stance, which as a social practice goes beyond the event of the arrival or the festival. The self-referential subjectivation of metaphysics is broken open, the social practice remains radically turned toward the other. Joining, to expand the _With_, is always possible.[83] The always possible festive pleasure is found in talking with one another, eating and living together; in short, in the *'undeniable . . .* experience of the alterity of the other, of heterogeneity, of the singular, the not-same, the different, the dissymmetric, the heteronomous'.[84] In contrast to Rousseau's festival, radical hospitality as attitude and social practice is not a recurring event, but a form of life.

The to-come of democracy to come is not an attribute for Derrida, not a mere variant of democracy. *Démocratie à venir* corresponds rather with the concept of democracy itself, which is the only form of government that inherently involves the non-measurable, the incomparable, the imponderable – that which is to come. Derrida does not have utopia in mind when he talks of what is to come. 'I mistrust utopia, I want the im-possible.'[85] The event is possible only as impossible, as incalculable, unexpected, as the arrival, which inscribes in what is to come (*à venir*) as a becoming (*devenir*).

The democracy to come is situated in a present that is understood as new, different, and untimely, also because, with what is to come, Derrida wants to emphasize the necessity of acting. Democracy to come does not allow any deferral in time. The *à venir* 'of democracy is also, although without presence, the *hic et nunc* of urgency, of the injunction as absolute urgency. Even when democracy makes one wait or makes one wait for it.'[86]

It is an acting without deferral, without following a norm or a rule, without knowing 'which path to take'.[87] For this reason, democracy to come also does not announce a classical, political revolution. It remains coming, and in that way lets itself be understood in the context of permanent, molecular, social revolution. The impossible possible is a 'weak', 'vulnerable' force 'without power', which 'opens up unconditionally to what or who *comes* and comes to affect it',[88] the mutual, de-munized relatedness. This precarious force in the now corresponds with Walter Benjamin's 'weak' messianic force,[89] which permanently considers the Messiah's coming in daily life, in the now, as a possibility. It is messianic, and thereby 'always revolutionary'.[90] The messianic force of the expanded present evades the masculinist *krátos* of identitarian presence and affirms the radical heterogeneity which stems from the *krátos* as the freedom in the force of the thing. With it, democracy can be separated from auto-nomy, the *nomos* from *autos*, and in this way, a law, a *nomos*, is conceivable that does not emanate from the self, but rather comes from the other. Even more than around an ethical *nomos*, which starts from the unforeseeable arrival of the other, a perspective emerges in which democracy can be thought, in general, more in the modes of sharing, affecting, and infecting. Democracy has the possibility and the duty 'to de-limit itself', to suspend its borders, to practise 'self-delimitation'.[91]

3

Benjamin

Leaps of Now-Time

In his final text, 'On the Concept of History', written while fleeing from the Nazis in 1940, Walter Benjamin emphasized the necessity of a weak messianism.[1] The Messiah, who can appear at any moment of daily life in the present, is a secular figure rather than a theological one. The messianic coming in the present is characterized by a particular relationship to the past, with which an unusual conception of time is expressed. Benjamin assigns historical materialism – a historiography schooled in Marxism – the task of understanding this conception. The only historical materialism that can be moored with a weak messianism is one that concentrates on the present and dissociates from all future-oriented progressive and developmental narratives. Benjamin wants to 'attain to a conception of history' (VIII) in which the 'historically understood' (XVII) does not follow any idea of progress or linearity. On the contrary, every idea of progress and every politics with regard to the salvation of '*future* generations' (XII, emphasis in original) must be broken up, interrupted, burst open. In 1940, in the midst of fascism, Benjamin clearly sees that it is not the exception, but rather the rule (VIII); rather than marking a break in civilization, it is part of the ideology of progress, which blossomed in the European nineteenth and twentieth centuries, mainly in the teleology of history.

Only a historical materialism that recognizes and preserves the messianic spark is capable of effecting this break, this blasting of dominant thinking along the lines of linear progress. An entirely different understanding of the present is required, an understanding that not only is interwoven in a special way with the past, but also focuses on affect and care in an untimely way – nothing that would ever occur to a materialism interested in merely 'crude and material things' (IV).

To the linear, bourgeois historicism that secures domination Benjamin opposes a conception of time understood from the perspective of the ruled and of class struggles. This other time of struggles is interwoven with secular-messianic materialism through a linkage of present and past that is doubly relational: firstly, in this present, the sparks of the past are perceptible, sparks that come into or arrive in the present but that were, of course, not foreseeable by previous generations. Nonetheless – and this is the second, contrary relation – those living in the present are awaited by those from the past. For Benjamin, 'there is a secret agreement between past generations and the present one', a connection with the past as 'a breath of air that pervaded earlier days' (II). Their silenced voices resound like an echo when we listen to them, when we actualize them in the present. It is this sensed breath of the past, these voices that are once again audible, that correspond with the '*weak* messianic power' (II, emphasis in original). This power is a force that is given, one that breaks with/from/out of the past into the present, as something to which the past has a claim (II). It doesn't simply exist, it *is* not; instead, it signifies potentiality in every moment of everyday life.

But the messianic force also reveals itself as a capability of the materialist historian of the present, with which she is able to fan 'the spark of hope in the past' (VI), doing justice to the claim of having been awaited, allowing herself to be claimed by the suppressed voices of history, actualizing the struggles and redeeming the past in revolutionary practices that break open the continuities that secure domination.

Nothing that has happened is lost; it can be tracked down again and actualized. Benjamin turns against traditional messianism, which believes that 'only a redeemed mankind is granted the fullness of its past' (III), and only then would it be able to refer to *all* of its single moments, as citable/to be summoned only on Judgment Day

(*Jüngster Tag*). In contrast to this judgment on redemption that has been postponed into the future, Benjamin understands *every single moment* of the past as being citable in the present. 'Each moment it [redeemed mankind] has lived becomes a *citation à l'ordre du jour*' (III) – which day is the youngest day (*der jüngste Tag*). The past does not allow itself to be judged only on Judgment Day, before the court of God, at the end of history. What has been, in its slightest moments, can already be put on the order of the day, the *ordre du jour*, invoked in the order of the current day, which is always the *jüngste Tag* in history. The notion of citing that Benjamin uses several times in his theses on the philosophy of history (see XIV) is also a letting come, an active summoning of the past into the present, which in the order of the day comes into contact with that which is occurring. In the order of the day, the present already becomes one that is compiled, and history a 'construction' (XIV).

Citing past moments, voices, and events does not mean a literal rendering, an eternal, authentic adherence to that which has been. 'The true image of the past flits by' (V). It moves quickly and quietly and, contrary to the suggestion of the linear progressive history of the victors within which the suppressed fall silent, it cannot be captured. The image of the past flashes as a moment in a moment in the present. It breaks open the linearity and, appearing inconspicuously, is over again in no time. 'The past can be seized only as an image that flashes up at the moment of its recognizability, and is never seen again' (V). The truth of the past can be recognized only in movement. It runs from the present and escapes it when the present fails to apprehend the inconspicuousness, fails to make a concept of history in accordance with it.

A historical materialist who not only is schooled in Marx, but, with Benjamin, also pierces every history of progress, sees in class struggle not only a 'fight for the crude and material things', but also the 'refined and spiritual things', the affects and the affections, which 'are alive in this struggle as confidence, courage, humor, cunning, and fortitude, and have effects that reach far back into the past' (IV). The persistent liveliness of the refined and spiritual things in the actuality of the struggle provides the force to 'constantly call into question every victory, past and present, of the rulers' (IV). The inconspicuous of the weak messianic force recurringly makes all past moments on the order of the day citable and open to criticism: the past is mobile, it can be changed, the voices of the silenced can be heard again and can play a role in the now. Rather than great changes of the past, these are mere inconspicuous ones, but they are precisely those that must be understood (IV). Only in this way is the present comprehensible as a historical 'constellation' (XVII).

The historical materialist has the capability, in the now, of 'articulating the past' (VI), summoning and actualizing it. These are moments that flash up in the struggles, in the re-assessment of the past, in critically tearing from the history of the victors what has been forgotten and annulled. 'It means appropriating a memory as it flashes up in a moment of danger' (VI), in a moment of remembering that cannot be planned, but 'unexpectedly appears' (VI), suddenly and immediately, and which must be recognized and interpreted in a way that does not again fall prey to the conformism of temporal linearity, but instead serves to actualize the histories of the non-conforming and disobedient. They are memories that have to be broken off and regained from the history of the rulers, memories that set alight 'the spark of hope' (VI).

The refined and spiritual things, the affects and affections, do not correspond with the historicist 'process of empathy' (VII), which requires forgetting the later course of history, as supposedly knowing nothing about it, trying to understand and empathize with a historical subject. According to Benjamin, this empathy of bourgeois historiography corresponds with *acedia*, 'indolence of the heart' (VII). The tremendous accusation he therewith hurls almost incidentally at Fustel de Coulanges – a renowned French historian first of antiquity and later of the Middle Ages, whom he cites by name – can hardly be underestimated. Fustel strove to empathize with the religious ideas of the ancients in order to understand their political institutions.[2] The experience of death served for him as the starting point: ancient societies had to be understood through their ancestor worship and veneration of the dead. When Benjamin accuses Fustel's historicist method of empathizing with religious thought of *acedia*, he discredits it in the context of medieval theology as a deadly sin. He uses a word that was most likely translated by 'medieval theologians' (VII) – as Benjamin explicitly mentions – from the ancient Greek *akēdia*, 'carelessness' (from *akēdeo*, 'not caring', 'forgetting', and *kēdos*, 'care'), into the late Latin.[3] *Acedia* as carelessness, or – as translated in the seventh thesis – 'indolence of the heart', was considered one of the seven deadly sins, distinctly distancing itself from God and, in general, from all spirituality – and implicitly also from every messianism. Included in *acedia* are states of mind, such as sorrow and melancholy, that are based on nothing other than the lack of care, which at the same time goes back to what Fustel understands as a methodical virtue: forgetting, which in the end means nothing other than disinterest. *Acedia* describes the lack of warmth, the spiritual listlessness, the lack of access to the 'refined and spiritual things', which the historical materialist must understand. The flash of the true historical image in the present cannot be perceived through empathy with the past, precisely when – forgetting all subsequent events – it imagines itself to be deep in (ancient) history. The empathy with the ancients' experiences of death that Fustel demonstrates can only be an empathy with, and a caring for, the victors, for the central actors of a linear bourgeois historiography, which projects its beginning back into antiquity and musealizes the trophies of this triumphal procession through to the present. 'Whoever has emerged victorious participates to this day in the triumphal procession in which current rulers step over those who are lying prostrate' (VII), to whom no care is given. The spoils drawn along with this procession are the 'cultural treasures' (VII).

Rather than with an empathetic historicist who cares only for the victors, this historiography of victory must reckon with 'a historical materialist [who] views them with cautious detachment' (VII). In this distancing, this refusal to play the watching *claqueur*, a care becomes possible that enables a diachronic caring for the true historical image flitting by; just as the 'horror', the 'anonymous toil', the slavery on which the colonialist exhibiting of civilization is based first becomes perceptible at a distance from the triumphal procession of the colonialized cultural goods. 'There is no document of culture which is not at the same time a document of barbarism', reads Benjamin's famous conclusion to the seventh thesis.

Rather than starting from *acedia*, the lack of care and spirituality, for which all messianic force is inaccessible, a historical perspective of the ruled begins from the present. Such a perspective – as it can be formulated beyond Benjamin – stems, on the one hand, from a synchronous temporal sense of mutual care as sociality and thereby of relatedness with others; on the other hand, however, as care, it also refers to a concept of history that attends to the diachronic relationship of becoming and decaying: through an awareness of the atrocities carried with the history of victory, and through a commitment to their actualization in the present. This diachronic care is a care in the now and about the now; situated in the history of struggles and conflicts, its 'task [is] to brush history against the grain' (VII).

Unlike bourgeois historiography, with its myth of progress saturated with ideas of domination, a materialist understanding of history that brushes against the grain requires the construction of history in the present, a construction in which 'that which has been, is constantly redefined by the present day [*das Jetzt*]'.[4] This redetermination does not correspond to an addition of a mass of facts, 'to fill the homogeneous, empty time', but is rather a 'constellation saturated with tensions' (XVII).

The present is anything but a homogeneous temporality that is over in no time, that immediately passes by and in the future will have been. It is not a moment and 'not a transition' (XVI). The present of the materialist understanding of history that is open to secular messianism is a construction and 'constellation' (XVII, Addendum A) of several interwoven temporalities, simultaneities in productive difference and confrontationality, because the suppressed and forgotten are actualized. The constellation is like a tissue, a meshwork of relationships in which one's 'own era has entered, along with a very specific earlier one. Thus [the materialist historian] establishes a conception of the present as now-time shot through with splinters of messianic time' (Addendum A). This interweaving with a certain epoch, as Benjamin formulates it in Addendum A of his theses on the philosophy of history, does not mean that only *one* moment that has been, *one* past event, can be woven together with the present. There are many, manifold splinters. Understanding the present as a constellation therefore means assuming several actualized pasts in their relationships of tension with one another in an extended now-time, which as a constellation is to be understood rather in the plural as several nows. The manifold now-time is a constructive temporality, in which history incessantly forms, the creative hub in which historical constructedness, the composition of various moments of time, is practised and becomes obvious. In its entanglement with the past, now-time is not a temporality that remains self-identical with itself, as immediate and identitarian presence, as an authenticity of body and affect, or as a pure mental state. It is a composite movement.

For Benjamin, the multiple messianic splinters in/of manifold now-time are monads in which 'the entire course of history' is 'preserved and sublated' (XVII). However, the individual dialectical monad enriches now-time only when it is blasted out of the homogeneous course of the history of the eternal victors, when the historicist linearity is broken open, when the sparks of hope from the past (VI) become perceptible in the revolutionary practices of class struggle, when now-time vouches for them, halts the progress that secures domination, and brings to a lasting standstill the 'homogeneous, empty time' (XIII) that is filled by the victors. In the woven now-time, the 'oppressed past' (XVII) of the revolutionary struggles will then be understood historically, when in 'every second', in every moment of everyday life, 'the small gateway . . . through which the Messiah might enter' (Addendum B) remains open, when the Messiah's coming remains possible, entirely unpredictably, in the now. In now-time, the suppressed who do not appear with their practices and subjectivations in the history of the victors, who do not count for precisely that reason, are able to turn their gaze to that which has been.

Benjamin's materialist understanding of history turns the historical gaze to the political. The task is to shape the now-time constellation of present and past as emancipatory. But it is precisely such practices that change society which are opposed by the homogeneous progressing of the rulers' time, by the claim of a development that has no alternative, which ultimately serves to discipline and prevent insurrections, and even more so, different social orders. Practices that (fundamentally) change existing conditions are rendered impossible. This is evident even in the critical belief that capitalism's history of exploitation and accumulation constantly renews itself and will therefore remain forever unstoppable. Emancipatory changes that are postponed and deferred to the future also prevent acting in the present.

At the same time, however, in now-time, revolutionary perspectives emerge that oppose the narratives of counterinsurgency and securing domination with common political acting. Starting from the struggles in now-time means learning to understand how, with the strategies of the denial of these struggles, for one, history is construed as a historicist continuum of the victors, and for another, emancipation is deferred to the future. 'What characterizes revolutionary classes at their moment of action is the awareness that they are about to make the continuum of history explode' (XV). The struggles for the material as well as the refined and spiritual things begin with the affects and affections, in the midst of mutual care. This does not at all mean that now-time is conciliatory; on the contrary, it is full of tension and, ultimately, 'a condition of violence': 'the fate of the past continues as the present', and at the same time it is a temporality that 'makes accessible, what at one time was possibly different historically, to prevent the continuation of violence, suppression, and exploitation'.[5] In this way, the present reveals itself as 'a fundamentally political moment'.[6] Revolutionary practices in now-time are what generate lasting discontinuity and change societal conditions.

In his theses on the concept of history, Benjamin goes through various diachronic constellations: from the angel of history driven into the future, to the revolutionary tiger's leap. All of these perspectives emerge in the present, all interrupt the course of time, and all are, in their own way, resistant. They are always interrupting movements in now-time.

Benjamin had already purchased Paul Klee's *Angelus Novus*, a watercolour drawing in shades of yellow and light brown, in 1921, one year after the work was completed, and he had friends bring it to him several times, including during his flight from the Nazis. When he had to leave Paris in 1940, before the invasion by the Wehrmacht, the drawing was left behind once again. The *Angelus Novus* is only one of several drawings in a group of works with angel motifs by Klee. In the ninth thesis, Benjamin brings this angel – with his oversized head, his raised arms that suggest wings, and his short legs and bird's feet – into his text and calls him the 'angel of history'. The angel looks to the right, past the observer, his eyes large and mouth open, his tousled hair standing on end. Benjamin clarifies: 'This is how the angel of history must look' (IX).

Here he creates a figure that recognizes the continuity of domination but is unable to fundamentally break through it. The angel appears – as explained at the beginning of the ninth thesis – 'about to move away from something he stares at'. He seems to adopt the attitude of the historical materialist, who, as observer of the carnage of the victors, must distance herself in order to perceive the cruelties. The posture and facial expression of the angel reflect this: 'His eyes are wide, his mouth is open, his wings are spread.' He gazes at the atrocities of the victors, at the countless dead, the defeated of history. His back is turned toward the future; 'his face is turned toward the past. Where a chain of events appears before *us*, *he* sees one single catastrophe, which keeps piling wreckage upon wreckage and hurls it at his feet' (IX, emphasis in original). But the angel cannot burst open the past; he sees it, but he cannot change it. What remains is his horror, which makes him freeze and incapable of acting. The angel stands in the midst of the storm of historicist continuity and the mono-linear movement of progress, which blows against his wings with such force that he cannot withstand it. With his horrified gaze at the suffering of the past, he cannot fundamentally break open the dynamics of a continuous narrative of history.

This looking backward while being driven forward is one of the aspects of the angel of history. Nevertheless, he is not an instrument of historicism. He sees wreckage, not an orderly layering; he sees the dead, not victors. Within the continuous forward movement, and despite it, he changes the gaze. He sees what the history of the victors means, and perhaps – this is the second aspect that comes into its own in the figure of the angel – this recognizing/visionary/seeing gaze is what, at precisely the same moment, first calls forth the progress as a storm. If the angel were always standing in the storm, and at one moment capable of turning his gaze to the horrors of the past, then the storm of progress, the history of the victors, would be primary. If, instead, progress and the *awareness* of the atrocities occur simultaneously, then the angel would always turn his gaze with or within the movement of progress, and the storm would always try to nonetheless push the backward-staring angel into the future.

But a third dynamic of action and reaction is also possible: the gaze that is turned and perceives the past differently could be the moment triggering the storm. The resistance of the angel to the future-oriented history of the victors would then be primary. The storm would be an instrument used by the victors to fight against insurrection, and not first the directional movement or the speed of their historicism. The task of the storm would then be to drive the angel to give up his resistance against the force of continuity that secures domination. In this reading, the stormy energy of progress would be a reaction to a resistant attitude in the present that disturbs continuous time, that does not accept the history of the victors. Yet, in this interpretation also, the angel staring into the past is no match for the storm; he is not a figure of now-time breaking open the historicist continuum of time. Seeing the history of the victors as the history of the dead and wreckage, and being horrified, is thus only a first step of resistance, on the basis of which the movement of the tiger's leap in now-time must be found.

The angel of history is not a figure of the struggles; he cannot fundamentally disrupt the continuity of history. He does not have much at this level with which to oppose the windy ideology of progress that wants to eternally postpone now-time. In contrast, with the 'tiger's leap into the past' (XIV), Benjamin introduces a figure that emerges in the struggles of now-time, which is devised in a form strikingly parallel to Marx's analysis of the bourgeois and social revolutions in 'The Eighteenth Brumaire of Louis Bonaparte'.[7] The tiger's leap can be performed in a bourgeois costume. The tiger then leaps (around) in the arena of the existing conditions of domination and reinforces them with costumes and images from the past. But the tiger can also be materialist-revolutionary, leaping without a command from the ruling class, 'in the open air of history' (XIV) and without the ideological roof of the arena of domination, composing the time fragments in now-time. The tiger senses the spark of hope, the actual in the past, and tears it away for the present – but not always for that of the (true) revolutionary struggles.

In Benjamin's eyes, Robespierre and others achieved a tiger's leap in the French Revolution. They made the break with the *Ancien Régime* legible through references to the Roman republic, among other ways by citing the ancient clothing. For Benjamin, this was a tiger's leap in a bourgeois costume, akin to the strategies of fashion when it actualizes a past style. 'Fashion has a nose for the actual, no matter where it stirs in the thickets of long ago' (XIV, translation altered). Benjamin's critique of the French Revolution is very similar to Marx's in 'The Eighteenth Brumaire'. In 'the classically austere traditions of the Roman republic', the bourgeois gladiators, according to Marx, 'found the ideals and the art forms, the self-deceptions, that they needed in order to conceal from themselves the bourgeois limitations of the content of their struggles and to keep their passion at the height of the great historical tragedy'.[8] Yet according to Benjamin, in the French Revolution, in contrast to the angel, the break with the continuity of history was achieved, namely through a present leap into the past, which tracked down the actual therein. Nonetheless, both the French Revolution and fashion remain 'in an arena where the ruling class gives the commands' (XIV). The 'leap in the open air of history' (XIV), by contrast, happens only in the suspension of the ruling command, only in the bursting open of conditions of domination. It is a leap that takes place under the conditions of the ruling class, that breaks from its command while leaping, and goes beyond it. Only this type of leap into the open, into freedom, 'is the dialectical leap Marx understood as revolution' (XIV): the social revolution.

Marx emphasizes the practices of 'the social revolution of the [first half of the] nineteenth century' as opposed to the mere bourgeois struggles.[9] Such a revolution

> cannot begin with itself, before it has stripped off all superstition in regard to the past. Earlier revolutions required world-historical

recollections in order to drug themselves concerning their own content. In order to arrive at its content, the revolution of the nineteenth century must let the dead bury their dead.[10]

The revolution that leads to fundamental societal changes has to turn to the present and its own problems. That means revolutionary struggles in now-time, possibly in costume, but without the spectacle principle. Such social revolutions

> criticize themselves constantly, interrupt themselves continually in their own course, come back to the apparently accomplished in order to begin it afresh . . . until the situation has been created which makes all turning back impossible, and the conditions themselves cry out:
> Hic Rhodus, hic salta!
> Hier ist die Rose, hier tanze![11]

At the conclusion to this impressive passage, Marx quotes Hegel's adapted version of the ancient Greek saying from one of Aesop's fables. Hegel turns leaping into dancing, to make it clear to the philosophers that they should not be concerned with ideals oriented on the future, but should rather turn to the rational, as can be found in the present-day state.[12] Marx's interest is obviously a different one. For him, too, 'Hic Rhodus, hic salta!' is a saying that refers to the present.[13] He does not emphasize, like Benjamin, the leap into the past, but mainly the change of the societal conditions in the present, the renewed critical beginning, the attention to and patience for persistent but discontinuous struggles, for the recurring experimenting conducted for as long as it takes until the conditions begin to dance and a reversal into the rulers' continuous (supposed) lack of alternatives is no longer possible. However, Marx breaks sharply with that which has been. In his description of these processual, recurring struggles, Marx's concern is precisely not with a leap into the actual of the past, but with a final break from the past. For him, this break is the condition for the irreversibility of societal changes.

Benjamin goes further. The tiger's leap not only breaks the continuity of domination in the present, but also changes the past. Rather than breaking with that which has been, the leap builds a discontinuous relationship of becoming and decaying: it is concerned with tracing resistant and revolutionary moments and practices in the past, in order to tear them away from it as discontinuous splinters, which could historically have been possible in a different manner, but were broken off through violence, suppression, and exploitation. With this blasting out of past practices for actualizing (rather than conserving), now-time becomes for Benjamin a political and extended temporality, manifold composite presents. This plural now-time of the struggles is not a time that can be isolated, not a time of the absolute event. It constructs untimely constellations into potentialities in the past, to go beyond the angel's shocked presence and rediscover the political present in the 'thickets of long ago' (XIV).

If we were to follow Marx's 'Eighteenth Brumaire' from 1852, and let the dead bury the dead, we should no longer refer today to the Paris Commune of 1871. Past revolutionary practices would be finished, with no relevance for now-time. Twenty years after his Brumaire text, Marx, a contemporary witness, granted that the Commune had achieved a decisive revolutionary break. In 'The Civil War in France', written during the time of the Commune, he emphasized its new, creative self-government, 'which breaks the modern State power'.[14] Clearly recognizable in actuality, this 'revolution against the *State*'[15] was, however, not sustainable. The political conditions were not permanently changed, not enduringly inspired to dance, but were brutally smashed by the French army in the 'Bloody Week' of May 1871, with an estimated death toll of 20,000 to 30,000.[16] Nevertheless, if we affirm Benjamin's revolutionary tiger's leap under the free sky, then the suppression of the Commune becomes not just another failed revolution. In the Commune, several constellations can be tracked down and their energy released once again. The way in which such an actualization can take place, however, depends greatly on the interpretation of the events that are designated as the Paris Commune.

When the Commune is understood simply as an insurrection, as a single major break, many resistant practices get lost.[17] Marx himself fostered such a one-dimensional interpretation with the title of his influential text 'The Civil War in France', even though he offered a much more manifold reading. Along with attempting to identify a single break, it also makes little sense to want to establish a triggering event, an origin, or a founding moment.[18] Beyond the martial narratives, such as the storming of the Bastille, the Parisian women represent a non-violent resistance at the beginning of the Commune. According to contemporary chroniclers, it was the women who started it all on 18 March 1871. Already underway in the early hours organizing food, it was they who sounded the alarm and enabled the defence of the cannons of the National Guard.[19] But such founding narratives that inscribe the actions of women in (revolutionary) history also tear the events of 18 March away from a manifold process, which had long persisted by this time, such that this day becomes merely a contingent concentration of practices and events. The discontinuous concatenations of the years before, which cannot be synchronized in linear time, are not taken into consideration when the Commune is assigned a single, spontaneous start.

In the midst of bourgeois rule, which had increasingly turned against the working class over the course of the nineteenth century, unfolding in the late 1860s recurring practices of resistance were continually being recomposed and, in part, building on one another.[20] Crucial for this was the establishment of freedom of the press and assembly in 1868: attacks on the state and the bourgeoisie increasingly became a key component of ever more radical speeches. A significant movement including countless assemblies and clubs arose.[21] At many meetings, women's exclusion from politics and discrimination against them in everyday life were also discussed repeatedly as the 'women's issue'. Patriarchal gender relations were questioned, while possibilities of divorce and of 'free relationships' were just as much a part of the discussion as education, prostitution, and the reorganization of women's work.[22]

In 1869, ever more assemblies were disbanded, which repeatedly provided occasions for protest. In May 1870, the right to assemble was even repealed for four months, but afterwards the assembly halls quickly filled again. Demands for local autonomy and self-government could be heard increasingly frequently at a municipal level: a decentralist structure should succeed France's centralist one. The call for a Commune also grew louder. After the removal of Napoleon III in early September 1870, insurgencies spread throughout France: during the proclamation of the bourgeois Republic in Paris, communes were already declared in Toulouse, Marseilles, and Lyon.[23] Several of these insurrectionary practices were followed by violent confrontations with government troops, leading to suppression of the protests.

At the same time, class-specific coalitions of labour movements increased in these years. The removal of the ban on assembly facilitated the organizing of strikes, the frequency of which surged, as did the number of those involved.[24] In many sites, club meetings transformed into gatherings committed to changing society, and produced a 'collective understanding . . . of an urban public'[25] expressed in new social contexts mainly as mutual care. Discussed at the assemblies were problems of social reproduction and everyday life, such as prices for rent and food. In urban vicinity, relations of care were newly shaped, as with the organizing of the people's kitchens during the Commune, 'Whereas the class composition seems to have been relatively heterogeneous, the constant was mutual acquaintance from the neighbourhood.'[26] New pedagogical practices that had begun to spread in the 1860s – whereby primarily women's groups attempted to wrest the educational system from the clergy and improve the situation of women's education – also brought a great number of young women teachers from the provinces to Paris. Several of them, such as Louise Michel, became key actors in the Commune.[27]

When censorship of the press also ceased in September 1870, a phase of excessive experimenting with all possible media ensued: countless newspapers arose, myriad political posters and placards hung in the cities, and caricatures and political murals were frequently seen. All moves and all positions were distributed quickly and widely, also among the many who could not read or write.[28]

The Paris Commune was not the telos of a proletarian struggle, and neither did civil war or insurrection break out on 18 March 1871.

Rather, we should speak of heterogeneous practices, struggles, and movements in an extended, discontinuous, and manifold now-time.

> The movement developed so rapidly and so widely, specifically because there was *no* unified party apparatus, *no* unified ideological line. Instead, revolutionary micropolitics developed spontaneously, local committees and council-like systems were founded, and expanding grassroots movements arose everywhere.[29]

This was an experimenting, and a recurring beginning of social and political organizational forms in a non-uniform present. There was no definitive programme for overtaking the state apparatus, and the concern was not simply with replacing political personnel. Instead, in the long movement of the Commune, non-representationist practices were developed in manifold experiments. The bourgeois order of the state that Marx had emphasized was broken open precisely in this minimization of parliamentary or party-like representation. No deputies as representatives and no advocates for interest groups were employed, and hence there was no segregation of the political realm from the social. Assemblies and committees sent delegates to the Commune's boards who had an 'imperative mandate' – were directly accountable, could be replaced at any time – and received an average wage. Exchange between those represented and those representing was to be guaranteed. In Marx's words: 'The *Commune* – [that is,] the reabsorption of the State power by society as its own living forces.'[30] It 'was to be a working, not a parliamentary, body, executive and legislative at the same time'.[31] Without a separation of powers, it should be a 'Social Republic',[32] in which the bourgeois division of the political and the social was abolished and the bourgeois logic of representation transformed into a new societal form of self-government.

Due to the exclusively male-occupied central committee, this self-government was, however, limited in its abolishment of the bourgeois logic of representation. Women would be excluded as active citizens in this respect for decades to come.[33] But the new form of municipal self-government did not simply manifest itself in the new practices of councils and dependent mandates, and it was not merely about a new manner of leading.[34] In his essay 'Paris, Capital of the Nineteenth Century', Benjamin described the Commune as the climax of the 'spontaneous energy and the enthusiasm with which they set about establishing a new society'.[35] New networks, communication systems, and new relations of care, designed primarily by women, were invented in the socialities of the everyday life of the Commune. During the siege of Paris by Prussian troops, women organized the means of heating and nourishment, while men secured the fortifications. Women revolutionized social reproduction – first and foremost in the areas of education and the care of small children – and women's working conditions, which could be improved, at least, by higher wages.[36] Social services, such as child care and free, secular mandatory education, were achievements of the Commune that were later taken up in part by the Third Republic.[37] Due to their exclusion from the representative form of bourgeois politics, the women of the Commune devised specific types of resistance and new organizational forms. They were a decisive part of the countless cooperatives and neighbourhood groups that formed out of economic necessities, including the people's kitchens and clinics for the wounded. New socialities arose from mutual care in the struggles of now-time. Women also appropriated diverse economic and military contexts to which they had previously been denied access. Many were involved in spontaneous actions, bore arms, and propelled barricade battles.[38] The politically engaged women of the Commune did not act in a social realm separate from the political – the invention of its organizing evaded such a bourgeois gendered division. Also due to their exclusion from masculinist structures of representation, which extended into the labour movement, women tended to stand for the revolution's micropolitical practices: the majority did not take a dogmatic political position, and were de-centrally organized in neighbourhood and vigilance committees and informal women's groups.[39] They were often the contact point between the Council of the Commune and those not directly represented there. Lacking the right to vote, women burst apart the separation of the political from the social; their major contribution to the Paris Commune ensured that it cannot be understood as a one-time insurrection.

Benjamin's concept of the Commune as the producer of a new society is also central for the recurring interpretation of the Commune as a festival. In the mid-1960s, for example, Henri Lefebvre saw the Commune as 'a long festival'[40] that extended from 18 March 1871, a reading that had a significant influence on the reception of the Commune around 1968 and beyond.[41] The metaphor of the festival seems to suggest itself when established political institutions are abolished and those assemble and organize who are not a part of the political *Volk* but instead form the multitude, when women and men act together, and the bourgeois-masculinist order of the political is suspended. Especially in its limited transgression, carnival is indeed the other side of the political and of the hegemony of the heteronormative, and the festival for Rousseau ultimately located solely in the social. In the Commune, on the contrary, the conditions were dancing due to manifold experiments with forms of social organization, due to the constituent power of the multitude, and due to its novel ways of instituting and organizing in a different social order. Self-government was no longer that of the sovereign masculinist people (against a monarchic ruler), but rather that of the social multitude in its temporal and spatial heterogeneity, which reshaped living together as mutual care. The self-government of the Commune released the elements of the new society in the present, elements that had already developed in the crisis of bourgeois rule. In Benjamin's fourth thesis on the concept of history, this image is found again in those struggles in which 'the refined and spiritual' things are present in a way other than as 'a vision of spoils that fall to the victor' (IV). It is the social revolution that develops from the bourgeois historical teleology, that breaks with it, steps out from it.[42] The dancing of the conditions was not a temporary transgression, but rather a dis/continuous revolutionary and militant festival, of which individual splinters can be actualized, in a tiger's leap from today.[43]

4

Foucault

Present Infinitive

In an interview with *Nouvel Observateur* in 1977, Foucault described himself as a 'historian of the present'.[1] Such a historian breaks with all forms of historicism and starts critically from the present. It is an understanding of the present that has consequences; it means expecting the revolution, facing the problem of the 'return of the revolution'.[2] But this return is not a reversion to past revolutions, as in historicism, which draws on the past to solve the problems of the present.[3] The return is not retrogressive, but is an actualization. In Foucault's interpretation it corresponds with the permanent possibility of a reversal arising out of the dynamics of power relations in which resistance is not relegated to being a mere effect. Resistance is 'coextensive'[4] with power, and accrues steadily in power relations that are constantly reversible. It is from this dynamic of power and resistance that the possibility of the return of the revolution arises.[5]

Foucault's way of analysing history makes it possible to 'criticize the present'.[6] Revolutionary practices are not simply strategies or tactics coming from the past that are handed down and passed on. The resistance of struggles in the present unfolds its force in that which evades actual relations of power. These are struggles that are not oriented on law and representation as though power comes simply 'from above'. They are struggles that come – like power – 'from below'. As events rather than continuities, they emerge in bodies, in the subjectivations.

Foucault designated the present also as *actualité*.[7] Actuality is closely entangled with his question of who or what we are in the present. Foucault seeks an answer neither to the question of being nor to that of identity. He is interested in what we could *become* in the present, how we might become different, or de-subjectivate ourselves. In his text 'Subject and Power', he defines this more precisely with reference to Kant: 'When in 1784 Kant asked, Was ist Aufklärung?, he meant, What's going on just now? What's happening to us? . . . Kant's question appears as an analysis of both us and our present.'[8] This type of 'critical analysis of our world',[9] a critical analysis of the present, means understanding the relations of power and conditions of domi- nation that determine who can become a subject and who cannot, and how in both cases we are bound to a supposed own, original 'identity', which either binds us together and discriminates us in groups and/or individualizes us and separates us from one another and makes us (self-)governable. We do not escape such identity politics 'at a future date', in promises of 'liberations, revolutions, [or an] end of class struggle'.[10] Rather, we refuse in the present 'what we are', and what we are forced to be. According to Foucault, we must liberate ourselves 'from the state and from the type of individualization which is linked to the state', and instead look for new forms of subjectivation, of becoming different.[11]

Foucault frequently raises the question of what we are in the pres- ent. This arises from his understanding of history, which is heavily influenced by Nietzsche, whose critique of history links the question of ontology with ways of thinking time.

What we are in the present, Foucault argues, is not a matter of identity, but rather a matter of discontinuity, experience, and de- subjectivation.[12] What we are in the present is a question of how history is perceived and how revolutionary practice is understood. This ques- tion is one that cannot be posed with continuous, linear, teleological concepts of history, as these negate struggles against conditions of domination and exploitation, making them invisible. These struggles correspond with a different temporality, a discontinuous history which Foucault, referring to Nietzsche, calls 'genealogy'. Genealogy perceives ruptures, events, and beginnings. And, even more, the genealogical perspective – according to Foucault in his 1971 essay 'Nietzsche, Gene-alogy, History' – must emphasize the singularity of events.[13] It must seek that singularity 'in the most unpromising places, in what we tend to feel is without history – in sentiments, love, conscience, instincts; [genealogy] must be sensitive to their recurrence'.[14] Similar to Ben-jamin's philosophy of history, genealogy is also occupied with constellations of affects and affections rather than with the search for origins and linear developments. Without origin and without sub-stance, the idea of an essential identity is, indeed, abandoned; but not the countless beginnings.[15] That is the main act: to destroy the subject, the identity, the origin – these pillars of historicism – in order to con-ceive of other temporalities in which the understanding of the present determines how struggles are contemplated. It is important here to think of the beginning as both singular and multiple. Not remember-ing everything, being able to forget, is crucial; as Nietzsche writes, this requires 'the capacity to feel *unhistorically*'.[16] It must be possible for something unique to take shape in the present, without a past found-ation and without identity. One must be able to dare to begin again and affirm becoming in the present. The practices of acting, thinking, and feeling never merely continue that which has been; they are not simply routine and habit, but also involve experimenting, stumbling, reorient-ing, re-organizing. In his critique of historicism, Nietzsche identifies such practices as 'unhistorical'. The past has to be forgotten to a certain extent, 'if it is not to become the gravedigger of the present'.[17] Only in the unhistorical can a 'historical event' begin, without the 'suprahistor-ical' condition.[18] The event is, then, according to Nietzsche, historically unhistorical, when in present becoming it gains its force without conjuring up the eternal or the unalterable.

In order to live at all in the present, one must be capable of ignor-ing the linear narrative. This defence of the present, however, is not sufficient to fundamentally change societal conditions. The past cannot simply be repressed: for the critique of conditions of domin-ation, of ongoing exploitation and injustice, it is vital to analyse the past in its continuities and ruptures, and to be aware of the wreckage and the dead, in order to act against such conditions, to change, burst open, and discontinue them.

The event also does not form without a relation to the past. It relates in a new way to what is past, the abiding, and the unknown. It is unique, but not because it was possible to observe it only once, isolated from existing conditions; rather, it is singular and at the same time temporally and spatially relational because it distinguishes itself through its power of re-constituting. The event can replace what has been lost, recompiling and reshaping fragmented forms. As Nietzsche says, it has 'plastic power', a force that is effective in time, that (re-) forms.[19] The event shapes history in the present. It is a force in becoming, which is situated, conditioned by the relationship of forces, and does not contribute anything to the idea of historical truth. Plastic power is dependent on the environment, the surroundings, the 'horizon around itself'.[20] Precisely because a recomposition occurs in the event, it is not isolated but relational and conditioned in its creative force. It can concatenate with other events. In the constituting of the event from heterogeneous fragments, new ways of life, political practices, and economies are affirmed, which do not cast off their descent [Herkunft], but instead multiply them.

Against the backdrop of this Nietzschean understanding of history and the event, genealogy's task, for Foucault, 'is not to show that the past actively exists in the present, that it continues secretly to animate the present, having imposed a predetermined form to all its vicissitudes'.[21] Genealogy has no interest in finding the single origin, the one identity. The genealogical present is shaped by countless beginnings, by dispersal, the dispersed.[22] The genealogical analysis observes the event in the context of its repetition, its 'eternal recurrence', as Nietzsche says.[23] This analysis breaks with the metaphysics of an eternal truth and thereby evades the presumptuous objectivity of historians who imagine themselves outside of time and supposedly able to empathize unburdened with the respective epoch. Repetition is the basis of 'historical sense', which feeds into the becoming of everything considered immutable: the body, feelings, subjects, the continuity of time.[24] Affections are perceptible only in becoming, not as a restricted identity.

Historical sense is situated in disputes and struggles; it looks at the proximate and into the depths to unfold dispersions and differences.

It has more in common with medicine than philosophy, says Foucault, insofar as the latter constantly denies the body in order 'to secure the sovereignty of a timeless idea'.[25] Historical sense is always infected, always has a beginning that is muddled, 'impure', and ambiguous.[26] From one and the same sign, both sickness as well as the 'seed of an exquisite flower' can arise.[27] The beginning is always contaminated.

When Foucault turns away from the concepts of origin and a deterministic past, when he claims that there is no reversion and that in contingency we become what we are in the present, he is influenced not only by Nietzsche. Simultaneously with his text on Nietzsche, his essay 'Theatrum Philosophicum' discusses Gilles Deleuze's then recently published books *Difference and Repetition* and *The Logic of Sense*.[28] Foucault and Deleuze had previously worked together on the complete edition of Nietzsche's works, and at the start of the 1970s both were now occupied with conceiving of the present differently.

Both distance themselves from a linear understanding of history that has little regard for the present, and thereby for the struggles. An event cannot be understood when the actual is 'a former future where its form was prepared', or simply 'the past, which will occur in the future'.[29] Such a teleologically bordered present demands 'a metaphysics of a crowned and coherent cosmos, of a hierarchical world'.[30] Instead, Foucault speaks of a present infinitive (*un présent infinitif*) as a present that is (in the process of) becoming.[31] Reduced to neither the instant of presence nor the physical definition of a point without extension, it breaks with the linear depiction of history without becoming independent of the past. With the term 'present infinitive', Foucault supplements his understanding of genealogy and event. He forges the new term from the meanings of the grammatical present tense and the infinitive and, together with Deleuze, calls the sense that arises therein the event-sense.[32] Although Foucault speaks of the 'present infinitive' only in his discussion of Deleuze's books, and the term is not further explicated, he gives clues as to how his genealogical analysis of the present can be further unfolded. Against the background of the present infinitive, it becomes possible to speak in a new way of repetition – the Deleuzian understanding of repetition inspired by Nietzsche rather than Hegel.

I take the concept of the present infinitive as an opportunity to unfold six conceptual components for a political redefinition of the present: 1) becoming as expansion of the present, 2) duration as multiplicity, 3) indeterminacy as measureless difference, 4) repetition as transversal return, 5) leap as actualization, and 6) organization as instituting practice.

(1) The first component refers to the proximity of the infinite (as endlessness) to the infinitive (as verb form). The verb designates the action, the doing, the practice, the event, what is happening at the moment passively as well as actively. As infinitive, the verb introduces sense into language. Here the verb is 'becoming', not 'being'.[33] Becoming in the infinitive withdraws from the instant of presence, the immediate, and allows another grammar of the present tense, another comprehension of the present. Foucault cites 'to die' as the perfect example of an event-sense that is both the shifted tip of the present (tense) 'and the eternal repetition of the infinitive'.[34] It is the anonymity of death that is of interest, not as something that subjectively ends, but rather as the endlessness of any death. The sense of the verb 'to die' is not to be moored to presence, to an instant. Dying occurs in an expanded present. It is 'never localized in the density of a given moment, but from its mobile tip it infinitely divides the shortest moment'.[35] The mobile tip widens the present; in its movement it expands it, and splits and multiplies the instants so that they allow for expansion, repetition, return. In its movement, the tip shifts the limitation and finitude of the instantaneous present simple. It is the verb that pins the event-sense: 'the infinitive tip of the present'[36] that becomes a becoming. Separated from what is instantaneous presence, the present is exposed to what is coming, the becoming.

With the appeal to that verb form that does not express any person or any number, the infinitive refers to a now that cannot be appropriated. It does not refer to one or several persons or things, to the one or the many as definable identities. It is a present that is not focused on the separation of individuals. It is infinitive because it is, in a sense, impersonal. In Foucault's terminology, it can be understood as an actuality that favours 'de-subjectifying'.[37] As this type of temporality, it refers to the blending of bodies, to affections, to the mutual dependencies of singularities. Connections and relatedness are not created between two existing poles, subjects, or entities that must first be separated in order to then conceive of the relationship between them. Starting from infinitive, unlimited, infinite mutual relatedness no longer allows individuals to appear as separate and autonomous, but instead makes them perceptible as singularities who have always been affected by and with others, who change together along with other singularities, who are constantly in exchange with, communicate with, and become infected with them.[38]

This component of the present infinitive, its 'impersonal' expansion and affection, is the key reason why the present cannot be reduced to its immediacy and authenticity. It has the force of constituting only because, as Foucault says, it is an effect 'produced entirely by bodies . . . colliding, mingling, or separating'.[39] As Deleuze, whom Foucault paraphrases here, formulates it in *The Logic of Sense*: 'The event results from bodies, their mixtures, their actions and passions.'[40] The present infinitive is thus always – as in Spinoza – a *product* of the affection of bodies (and thereby also of things), because bodies are never independent of one another, autonomous and closed, but are openly in relation to other bodies, ecstatic, precarious, indebted.[41]

Foucault also refers to mutual affecting and being affected when he speaks of the relationships of forces in describing relations of power. 'An exercise of power shows up as an affect',[42] according to Deleuze in his book *Foucault*, which is anything but a book about Foucault. From a biopolitical governmentality perspective, affecting also means conducting and governing.[43] But not only that: with compliant affection, at the same time, resistances emerge.[44] It is precisely because of mutual affection that, in struggles against repression and discrimination, the one body becomes the body of all.

(2) The second component of the present infinitive refers to duration. Beyond presence and identity, a special form of duration is already shown in becoming, which emerges through extending movements and repetitions, through affecting relations of power and resistance.

While this duration of becoming does not lack orientation, it has no goal insofar as the directions do not exist beforehand but emerge in acting, in experimenting, in becoming, in the affections and relations of power of the expanded present. They are directions in which, corresponding with Nietzsche's historical sense, everything will again be led toward becoming, toward that which has become, both as what has been in the past, as well as in its actualized constellation in the present (tense), which can therefore be changed. In the present of becoming there is no subsequent temporality of the future, only the expansion, the various durations, of the present.

The expanded present is not tied to the past in a linear way, to a past that it lets pass by in the reflecting representation; it is not an immediate, authenticist, identitarian presence, which achieves meaning only through a representation that feeds it to the past. The present infinitive does not mark a moment of transition between past and future, it cannot stay in continuity with the past. The present must be understood as a discrete, expanded temporality, as the present tense in motion, but not without a relationship to that which has been. It is an enduring process, a process of change, which endures precisely because, through the different repetitions of new beginnings, institutings and destitutings, it moves (further) with interruptions.

For that reason, inherent to this present as discrete temporality, there is in addition to the duration of becoming a second dis/continuous form of duration. It corresponds with the dis/continuity that is interrupted by countless beginnings and reveals itself as the duration of multiplicity. Both forms of duration – that of becoming and that of multiplicity – are inseparably intertwined.

Crucial for understanding duration as dis/continuous and recurringly interrupted – and not as a linear course, as uniformity and invariability – is to connect it with concepts of multiplicity. Henri Bergson differentiates between two types of multiplicity, the second of which is pertinent to the understanding of dis/continuous duration. The first type of multiplicity is numerical multiplicity, or manifoldness (*Vielheit*).[45] This manifoldness is a quantitative multiplicity, which divides the many into individuals, allocating and distributing the differences in their countability. Numerical manifoldness lives from the tension between the one and the many, and the possible unity of the many. It is a multiplicity of the external, the number, the order.[46] This way of thinking lies at the base not only of the logic of representation, but also of the idea of the *Volk* and the Hegelian idea of political democracy as 'all in one'. When democracy is conceived in terms of this type of multiplicity, the many must always be led to the one, the general and democratic representation; because in their great number they cannot be assembled, their numerical manifoldness must be united in the *Volk*, the general will, and its representation.

The other Bergsonian conception of multiplicity is that of the multiplicity (*Vielfalt*) of duration. Number does not play a role here; in this sense, the multiplicity is infinitive. This duration emerges through difference (differentiation) without negation. It is the duration of the multitude, not that of the *Volk*. This concept of multiplicity underscores the many, countless folds in their immanence, their qualitative difference.[47] The folds cannot be strictly separated from one another, they overlap, fold together or unfold successively, or apart from one another. The manifold is in a state of permanent change and in this sense continuous; it unfolds in an enduring process of differentiation. This processual duration of the manifold changes incessantly, because inherent to it are multiple beginnings and breaks, and the breaches that emerge from them. In Bergson's terminology, it is a virtual duration, which identifies the present precisely because it is permanently actualizing in differentiation. It cannot be divided in the name of the number, or numerically.

Duration as multiplicity does not simply identify a perpetuation of multiplicity; it, too, exists in the plural. It includes an immeasurable plethora of durations, which are very different from one another. Duration as multiplicity means the simultaneity of several durations in the present. Bergson offers the example, which Deleuze takes up, of sitting on the bank of a river observing the flowing of the water, the gliding of a boat, the flight of a bird, in coincidence with 'the ceaseless murmur in our life's deeps'.[48] This 'coexistence, [of] a simultaneity of fluxes'[49] which surround us, shows the ability to have 'the privilege of being one and several',[50] as Bergson writes. Being one and several means perceiving the durations of other living beings and things, the durations of the surroundings, and melding with them. This manifold duration is ecological, binding, and divisible, but it does not split apart and does not come into contradiction with what is split off, with the others. The multiplicity of duration is without negation; it is an affirmation of the different in the ecology.[51]

(3) The third component of the infinitive is its indeterminate differentiation. Here, the Latin adjective *infinitum* does not mean simply something without end, something endless. It focuses instead on the missing *finis* as the missing boundary. The infinitive refers to the unbounded, unstriated, undetermined, to that which is without determination, without measure or telos. *Infinitum* means something indeterminate precisely because it is not bound to identity, and also not to negation. The indeterminate is not something *un*differentiated here, not indifferent or without difference. Rather, it is dispersed and in this sense decidedly differentiated, precisely because it is indeterminate: a measureless difference.[52]

Measureless difference is indeterminate multiplicity, not united manifoldness. Measureless difference precedes that other form of difference that is based on judgment and division, on sorting and segmenting, which serves to hierarchize distinctions. Measureless difference is not beyond power relations. It denotes that excess, that plus of multiplicity that reveals the permanent failure of the identitarian claim of hierarchizing and segmenting difference, highlighting its limitations and making them contestable.[53] Measureless difference is the environment, the surrounding, of hierarchized difference.

'The greatest effort of philosophy was perhaps directed at rendering representation infinite (orgiastic)',[54] when reason becomes 'sufficient reason . . . the ground which no longer allows anything to escape'.[55] Here, Deleuze criticizes Hegel's ineluctable linking of reason and representation, which strives to 'save' all difference through mediation. But even when the infinite, orgiastic representation claims to measure and mediate every single difference, and differs precisely in this claim from the finite 'organic representation'[56] that determines the difference in the term, fixes the difference to an identity, limits and thus entirely subordinates it to an identity – even when the orgiastic representation 'discovers the infinite within itself' and also finds 'tumult, restlessness and passion underneath apparent calm' or 'the limits of the organized'[57] – difference must, indeed, 'leave its cave and cease to be a monster'.[58] Reason constantly strives to mediate difference. However, there is always something that cannot be driven from the cave, that evades this logic of representation, regardless of how infinite it tries to become, regardless of how far nothing substantial seems to be beyond it: what evades it is measureless difference, which cannot be grasped through identity and representation, and which, when the light of mediating and striating reason does not shine on it, can only be imagined as dark and obscure. It is a difference which, in repetition, is not bound to the logic of the similar, the same, the assimilation,[59] but is rather mobile, without mediation, a manifold, measureless difference, which neither converges in a unity nor depicts the opposite or the entirely other. This difference is not one 'between' two things or identities separate from one another. It is the uncivilized surround.[60] The manifold difference, in its dispersal, is always singular; but it is indebted to, rather than separated from, what differentiates it. Rather than being bound to identity in negation, the multiple difference comes into play in *affirmation*, in reinforcing its dispersal, as indeterminate differentiation, as mutual indebtedness and infection. Measureless difference dances on the wavering tip of the present (tense).[61]

(4) As indeterminate differentiation, as measureless difference, the infinitive is entangled with a non-dialectical understanding of repetition, where difference in the mode of repetition is not led back to identity.

Nietzsche is the one who introduces this repetition as 'eternal recurrence' that makes no reference to a unity or identity. This is an infinitive repetition because it concurrently multiplies and shifts the understanding of the present, moving the eventfulness of the present (tense) to a dancing, shifted tip, in a recurring untimely present.[62] The tip moves in the rhythms of relationships of power, as well as the coexistences and constellations of time. For Deleuze, the recurring movements correspond to dancing in Nietzsche's sense, rather than to leaping and transgressing in Kierkegaard's sense.[63] Without standing still at the mediation, the recurring dancing movements drive the deed onward, the forces that, as relations of power, have unmediated effects on actions and, at the same time, fuel resistance. Eternal recurrence is a 'vertiginous movement'[64] of repetition, which dissolves the ego and is founded on the death of God. In this repetition, the scattered multiplicity and thereby also the de-subjectivation become obvious. 'The present', writes Foucault, 'endlessly recurs. But it recurs as singular difference.'[65]

What is dancing here is not Hegelian reason. The vertiginous movement on the mobile, non-identitarian tip of the present bears instead the potential of the dance as the rhythmic movement of a militant festival which, as in Marx, sets societal conditions in vibration.

In a non-identitarian understanding of repetition, there is no major, incisive event and no linear succession of events. There is only their return and coexistence. In the present infinitive an event repeats, 'devoid of any grounding in an original, outside of all forms of imitation, and freed from the constraints of similitude'.[66] It is a repetition that affirms the event in its singularity and in doing so leaves it dispersed, does not put it into a line, a concept, or a developmental history. On the tip of the manifold, expanded present, it is never only one event, one decisive moment, that takes place, but, as Stefan Nowotny writes, always a 'swarm of events'.[67] The event itself is measureless difference, 'always already manifold, a complexity'; it exists 'only in plural' and is contingent, according to Nowotny. No determined act causes the event, and no sovereign action can halt it.

> On the contrary, it is much more the concatenations of events that sometimes seem to link presumably insignificant actions with astonishing consequences and may conversely lead to the weight of endeavors undertaken by presumably significant actors to thwart the event being the measure of their impotence and even their ludicrousness.[68]

When, nonetheless, from time to time, it makes sense to speak of *one* event, this is because 'the focuses of events and concatenations of events constituting "one" event'[69] appear coherent, so that a swarm of events can be given a specific name, such as the 'Paris Commune'. But the multiplicity cannot be captured through any representation of the *one* event.

In the swarm of events, the assemblage of singularities that have occurred and are occurring, the return does not take place on the surface. It is just as little horizontal as it is vertical, and is also not oriented on limits and limitations. Instead, it is a *transversal return*, because it is a dimension of time as well as space.[70] The transversal return is the dynamic modus of an open, heterogeneous assemblage in which events emerge and come to recur. The singular events communicate with one another through time and space, as part of a present social constellation or as splinters broken out of the seeming continuum of time.[71] They compose and discompose. They are more or less compatible, strengthen or hinder one another, interlock or tear apart. Swarms of events can be tied and indebted across borders, in alliances, concatenations, and infections. When and how they proliferate or subside is difficult to anticipate, but when they spread they can be highly contagious. They flow from the surround in which they are not intended and provoke its reversal.

(5) The fifth conceptual component belonging to the assemblage of the present infinitive, and which likewise affects the relationship of present and past, can, initially, also be explicated by way of Bergson. It is the figure of the 'leap into the past',[72] which Bergson created several decades before Walter Benjamin's tiger's leap, and which shapes both Deleuze's and Foucault's assemblages of the time of the actual and that which has been.

Benjamin's 'tiger's leap into the past' takes place in the struggles of now-time, but it does not always succeed in bursting open the conditions of domination and the history of the victors associated with those conditions. Struggles can also serve to reproduce existing relations of power and domination and reduce the tiger's leaps to aesthetic circus exercises, with the rulers clapping their approval in the arena.

For Benjamin, a revolutionary tiger's leap must sustainably rupture the conditions of domination and allow the present to become political by breaking the linear time of the victors and composing now-time as a new constellation of past and present. The tiger senses the weak messianic spark in a different constellation, the actual in the past, and blasts a past loaded with now-time out of the continuum of history. The struggles are not abandoned and left to the past; they are remembered and return as altered fragments. This actualizing in the leap changes not only the present, but also the past in the present. In the composition of the historical constellation, the present expands into a manifold now-time. History is construed in the present, in which the present simple can be neither a point nor a moment or instant, but is always movement.

Bergson does not situate the leap into the past in the context of social struggles, as Benjamin does, but uses it in a more general way to make the remembering of the past in the actual more understandable. The past, according to Bergson, 'only reappears to consciousness in the measure in which it can aid us to understand the present and to foresee the future'.[73] When we remember, we jump into the being of past, in one leap, all at once. Only when this abrupt leap has been made, when the move to the past has taken place, when we retrieve a memory that occurs to us, does the fog gradually lift, and 'from the virtual state [the memory] passes into the actual',[74] gradually gains flesh, form, and colour. The leap into the past reveals the discontinuity of duration, even when the subjective feeling seems to be an experience of coherence and linearity, which subjects bound to their identity must create in order to constitute themselves in accordance with a bourgeois narrative of history, and to take hold of their past in accordance with a liberal-capitalist possessive individualism, and, therefore, be (made) responsible for it.[75] But the past cannot be possessed in a biographical linearity; it is the constructive force of memory that breaks with the linearity of time. Bergson emphasizes that what we remember are images, but not 'this image, pure and simple'[76] that leads back to the true past. The image of the past that is actualized through remembering always nestles within the present, which changes it. The image is never fixed, but always in becoming.

No true image can be captured, or, as Benjamin says: 'The true picture of the past flits by',[77] flashing, with no possibility of holding on to it. The past cannot be peeled away from the present; neither of them is a temporality that can be isolated.[78] The past exists as an image within the same time as the present; both are coexisting spheres, not successive moments. 'The past is "contemporaneous" with the present that it *has been*.'[79] In this coexistence, the duration of the expansion corresponds with various temporalities in the now. Past and present accordingly do not form 'any coexisting whole' or totality of time.[80] Instead, the actual and the actualization coexist with one another, and repeat, return, in one another. They follow one another and exist simultaneously. 'And, in the actual, an irreducible pluralism reigns',[81] through leaps, actualizations, differentiations, and inventions of the new.

This new emerges, not least, in the evoking actualization of splinters of the past, which in abrupt leaps are blasted out from a merely ostensible continuum. Never reconstruction of the same, always recurring construction: in a creative act, the past becomes present, nestles within the present.[82] The actualizing leap contradicts neither the duration nor the beginnings and the event. It is related to them and, like them, is a constitutive part of the permanent differentiation in the present, which comprises duration as multiplicity. It requires a leap in the form of a breaking out of the supposedly unchangeable succession of societal conditions, so that in the present infinitive a breach emerges again for creative acts of actualization and differentiation.[83]

(6) This conception of return, duration, and leap enables us to rethink institution and organization, and thereby arrive at the sixth and final conceptual component of the present infinitive. Duration is no longer separate from practice, instituting no longer automatically separate from movement. Bergson emphasizes that the duration of multiplicity (in contrast to numerical manifoldness) is not characteristic of order, but, rather, of *organization*.[84] Developing the thought further, and in the context of the invention of new/alternative forms of political and social organizing, Bergson's differentiation makes clear that we have interpreted organization for too long solely through the order of the

number and the One, the subordination of the many under the One. In contrast, a form of organizing as multitude does not lead to the One, is not led by one, is not centralistic or unifying; it is a form of organizing that affirms the heterogeneousness of multiplicity starting from the dynamics of affection, that enables the broad and enduring involvement of the many through radical inclusion. This involvement is not simply a countable participation in individual events or happenings, but a recurring affection and involvement in the swarm of events, without the formation of a revolutionary subject. The transversal return of radical inclusion is not practised at a single level; it is not simply horizontal, via open assemblies occurring side by side, but takes place at several temporal and spatial levels simultaneously, transversally and trans-locally.

Such practices, being not only constituent but also instituent, produce both new forms of institutions as well as a new understanding of duration, which is made up of countless beginnings, destitutings and institutings in an enduring and persistent experimenting.[85] The repetitions produce multiplicity because they do not simply repeat individual practices, compositions, strategies, or ways of communicating. Within a transversal assemblage, repetition takes place between the levels, neither simply horizontally nor vertically. In this space–time assemblage, micropolitical processes, everyday practices and subjectivations, which are disregarded in the traditional conceptions of institution and organization, come to the forefront. Instituting and organizing can be understood as forms of duration which take place in constant recomposition, in an enduring constituting: as duration of a transversal assemblage of differentiating repetitions which enable institutions of the multiple and of the common.

In a talk with students around the time he was contemplating the present infinitive, Foucault spoke about the events of May 1968. The students remarked that the movement as an occupation of a societal space could have gone much further if a left-wing discourse had provided it with a perspective, or a utopian direction. Foucault negates this, saying that he opposes utopia with experience and experiment: rather than the future vision, practices of/in the present; rather than the non-site, the actual situatedness.[86] With regard to May 1968, of far greater importance than the question of utopia was the fact 'that thousands of people exercised a power that did not assume the form of a hierarchical organization'.[87]

At the end of the talk, Foucault makes another important remark: a student says that the movement was not capable of seeing 'the whole of society . . . or society as a whole'[88] and intervening in it, not capable of formulating the general from particular experiences. Foucault responds that 'the idea of a "whole of society" derives from a utopian context' built on (historicist) dreams accruing 'within this highly individualized historical development that culminates in capitalism'.[89] Experiences, strategies, or actions that include the whole of society are doomed to fail. This idea of society in its wholeness and totality must be abandoned. Revolutionary practices not only resist such ideas, but also break with the logic coming from the past of 'until now',[90] which suggests a linear continuity up to the present.

In one of his final texts, 'What Is Enlightenment?',[91] Foucault again asks the question of what we are. Once again with reference to Kant, he continues to work on understanding the dynamics of enlightenment and critique. For that – and this becomes clear a decade and a half after he drops the concept of 'present infinitive' – the problematizing of the present is not sufficient. Missing is the appraisal of the revolution and the subsequent possibility of the return of the revolution. In his lecture 'What Is Critique?' from 1978, Foucault had tried to answer this question with the help of Kant's 1784 text 'What Is Enlightenment?', but that was not possible. Kant's text *The Conflict of the Faculties*, written after the French Revolution, first provided Foucault with the decisive impulse.[92] In this 1798 text, Kant introduces the revolution as an event, and in Foucault's interpretation, an event in which revolution does not signify a great, one-time break, a 'revolutionary upheaval', as that does 'no more than turn things upside down'.[93] 'What matters in the Revolution', according to Foucault in his reading of Kant, 'is not the Revolution itself, it is what takes place in the heads of the people who do not make it or in any case are not its principal actors, it is the relation they themselves experience with this Revolution.'[94] In reality, the revolution is what 'does indeed complete and *continue* the process of *Aufklärung*'.[95]

The revolution in question here is not a political one in the traditional sense, but a social revolution, one that takes place in minds, that concerns ways of living, forms of knowledge, the 'fine and spiritual' things. 'The question', writes Foucault, referring to Kant, is 'what is to be made of this will to revolution, this "enthusiasm" for revolution'.[96] Precisely how we view the possibility of the return of revolution is how we also answer the question of 'what we are in our actuality'.[97] When critical analysis of the present expects the revolution it actualizes recurring refusals of subordination, the singular and common will to not be governed in that way. Such a critique is inventive, opening a space and a time in which new political subjectivations, new forms of living together, can emerge.

5

Negri

Democracy and Constituent Power

Within the liberal political order of Western modernity, revolution is not expected. Struggles usually serve for the expansion of democracy; revolution is excluded from political-theoretical discourses on democracy as an unforeseen event. Revolutionary processes and emerging constituent power are positioned beyond the calculable framework, or are situated in pre-political times. Revolution does not count as politics. According to Foucault, 'the question of the revolution has dominated . . . all politics';[1] politics is always found before or after the return of another revolution. Without the French Revolution, for instance, there would be no understanding of politics in a liberal bourgeois sense, no representative democracy. For the bourgeois order, the revolutionary beginning is the constituent force that suspends the preceding absolutist order and institutes the new order by means of a constitution. The revolutionary process that breaks open the old order is integrated into the new order as its juridical constituent power, so that its disintegrating threat is tamed in the frame of the legal order. In this context, constituent power is not seen as politics, but as the (revolutionary) power of making a constitution.

The way we consider the return of the revolution is crucial, since it affects how we understand the struggles in the present, how we grasp what we are in the present, and our understanding of constituent power. Within the left, too, a discursive figure has tenaciously persisted in which constituent power is a power focused on making a constitution, which is in line with political revolution understood as a unique, major rupture of the liberal capitalist order. The possibilities of such a rupture are either longed for or neutralized to the greatest extent possible, depending on the political position. In a liberal bourgeois understanding of democracy, they are tamed in a continuous process of democratization in which inequalities can be eliminated through struggles for recognition. The condition for such struggles is a lack of inclusion. Indispensable for liberal democracy is that all are not taking part in the same way from the outset. This form of democracy needs the exclusion of those who do not (yet) count, who are not (yet) represented; it needs the multitude excluded from the political realm, otherwise the progressing democratization would come to a standstill: representative democracy would be deprived of its future-oriented promise of democratic progress.[2] The compelling argument of the twentieth century was: if the particular individuals of the multitude are not considered through representation, a pluralist formation of general interests, and step by step, then there will be the danger of totalitarianism. In this narrative, the democratizing process can never be completed; it must inevitably always be progressing, otherwise fascism threatens.

The democratic-capitalist division of labour between a realm of the political and a realm of the social,[3] and the maintenance of this form of democracy as a continuous process of democratization from a historical/historicist perspective, are based not only on the deferral of a comprehensive participation of *all* members of society to the future. What must be prevented above all is the self-governing of the *demos* as 'all'; at the same time, it cannot become present as a heterogeneous multiplicity.

Vigilance in the face of totalitarian structures is instrumentalized in order to legitimize the autonomy of the political, with its dynamics in the social, in the struggles for recognition, as well as the necessity of mediation. At the same time, a dichotomy is established between representation and immediacy, between enduring political institutions and momentary social struggles. This dichotomy repeats a Hegelian understanding of time that associates the immediate, authentic, and momentary with a disregarded present. In contrast to this vanishing present of unmediated identitarian presence, representation and enduring institutions are an expression of reason and of a linear understanding of time, capable of creating a continuous arc from past to future. In this way, a more fundamental reconceptualization of democracy is blocked.

My considerations regarding a new democratic perspective of the present as a political temporality in motion are to be understood as critiquing not only the liberal form of democracy and temporality, but also left positions which, while they award social movements great importance and certify their situational intensity, disregard those movements that are not aligned with established political institutions. Social movements are understood as being merely a temporary phase or as an aid to political revolution: they mobilize the many for a possibly more successful takeover of the state apparatus, but then quickly vanish again when not institutionalized as a party, union, or other form of representation of interests. These typical chrono-political assessments are often justified by arguments for the efficiency and necessity of prompt, concerted action. The unforeseeable event of collective revolutionary practice is welcomed; it can most definitely be understood as a revolutionary moment, but is not conceded any duration – it immediately disappears again in its pure presence. Established in such disappearing presence, the practice, discredited as 'spontaneistic', is considered by many to be ineffective when it does not institutionalize, as only in this way is its continuance guaranteed.[4] Institutionalization is thus conceived as a necessary *next* step in the chronology of a mapped-out development. The striation of complementary poles – such as spontaneity and organization, movement and party, horizontality and verticality, critique of representation and necessity of representation in the existing political system – fails to acknowledge that in the practices of the social and political movements, new forms of instituting and organizing can arise *concurrently*, as practices that break through the familiar chrono-political logics, including the accompanying obligation of representation.

To counter such liberal and left chrono-politics, I would like not only to propose a different understanding of democracy in the present infinitive, but also to link it with a new understanding of constituent power and constituent process. Such a process, unlike in liberal democracy's theoretical discourse on the state and international law, does not have to end in and with a constitution; it goes beyond that.[5] It also does not simply stand in opposition to constituted, institutionalized political power as part of an existing political system. Instead, it is about an understanding of space and time that stops interrupting the discontinuous constituent rhythm of revolutionary becoming and considers 'revolutionary becoming with respect to political constructions and constituted being'[6] as possible. It is a social revolutionary becoming that places mutual care at its centre and no longer excludes it from the realms of the political and organization.

The predominant understanding of constituent power in modern political theory is constitutional: constituent power is seen as the legislative force that creates the fundamental legal framework of a societal order. In the governmental form of democracy, it is closely connected with the conception of popular sovereignty, the self-legislation of the *demos*. In order to understand constituent power in a radically different way – decoupling democracy from the *Volk* and nation, and removing its Eurocentric conception of time – the *demos* must be understood no longer as *Volk* but as multitude, a multitude capable of unfolding a new constituent power and, along with this, other forms of democracy.

For this, democracy must no longer be analysed solely within the limited framework of a sovereign juridical power oriented exclusively on law and the norm. Foucault already insisted on this in the 1970s, yet political theory continues to focus on the dynamics of sovereign power in its analysis of power and domination.[7] Only against the backdrop of the liberal conception of the political as autonomous is power understood as something that comes from above, that is concentrated in the state, the government, and the legal apparatus. This form of power asserts itself through bourgeois subjects that are considered independent and autonomous. They are, however, themselves effects of power relations that go beyond the limited sovereign power, and which cannot be analysed with this focus on power. Understanding constituent power as a variant of juridical sovereign power correlates with an oversimplified understanding of democratic-capitalist power relations. This type of restriction not only 'covers up' coercions through disciplinary techniques, but also fails to address the biopolitical governmental dynamics of power relations and the modes of subjectivation associated with them.[8]

Understanding power relations as biopolitical governmental relations of forces means steering the perspective toward affections and grasping both the techniques and strategies of conducting and governing and the simultaneously occurring resistances.[9] Starting from the struggles in now-time does not mean driving forward a continuous liberal democratization, but rather inventing new forms of democracy in discontinuous returning movements that break open the limitations of liberal democracy.

All forms of representative democracy are framed by the discursive figure according to which, because it is not possible for all to assemble due to the great numbers involved, the numerically many individuals that count have to be represented.[10] Through institutionalized representation, duration is sought as chronological linearity and continuity, which tames the heterogeneous many in their multiplicity. The multitude, dispersed in its distribution and affection and spontaneistic in its organization, is kept outside of the politically relevant *Volk*.

In contrast to the represented manifoldness, numerical and preserved in the One, the other duration of the multitude emerges without negation, without exclusion from the affirmation of multiplicity. It is a multiplicity that is permanently changing because it forms in returning processes of differentiation in which the present is permanently actualized. Beginnings, breaks, and the breaches that emerge from them are immanent to such processes. It is not the continuance that corresponds with the duration of multiplicity, but the simultaneity of multiple *dureés* or durations in the present. The duration itself is a multiplicity, not a uniformizing, hierarchizing temporality. In the multiple duration of multiplicities, the heterogeneous many can remain dispersed, without having to be separated from one another as singles, as countable individuals. In this understanding of duration, it is possible to perceive the multitude as manifold singularities that are nevertheless not separate from one another. They are bound in environments and by their surroundings, affected by other bodies and things.

A constituent power that does not domesticate the multiplicity is radically different to a constituent power that is limited to legislation, that counts the many and makes a constitution in the name of a people. The constituent power of the multitude, however, with all of its differences, by no means emerges outside of forms of institution. It goes hand in hand with different practices of instituting.

Before developing this understanding of a multiple constituent power that is not disciplined and neutralized, a few brief explanatory notes are necessary on state and constitutional theories of a constituent power that is limited to constitution making. Up to today, these debates have been about how to understand the relationships between multitude, *Volk*, and representation. Here, constituent power is always conceived starting from law and the state; it is a force that makes law, and is connected to the question of what it means – in terms of constitutional law and on the premise of a separation of powers – that in a democracy 'all power is in the people'. Sounding out the relationship between constituent and constituted power, between the force that makes a constitution and executive force, means striking a balance in the relationship of the many to unity, since the dilemma of liberal democracy consists in its starting from the premise of the heterogeneity of the many, for the act of creating a constitution, but subsequently having to tame or neutralize its (potentially) revolutionary power so that representation appears as an indispensable paradigm of a people, however understood. Should the many function as constituent, as creating a constitution, then they are those who exist 'before the law' and consequently can also suspend it. The state-theoretical ideas of Hermann Heller, for example, who advocated for the democratic principle in the Weimar Republic, placed the will of the non-united many at the very start of a legal order. When constituent power is understood as a force that creates law, then according to Heller it demands a beginning *before* the law. After the constituent act, this force that sets up the legal order but is simultaneously dangerous must then be united and represented as a people, so that 'the people as unity reigns over the people as multitude'.[11]

In liberal political theory, however, the multitude is not only united and neutralized in the interior of the order as a revolutionary force, it is also domesticized in the private realm – a variant that Paolo Virno points out in *A Grammar of the Multitude*. This private dimension of the multitude refers not only to the personal; in the sense of the Latin *privus*, it also means to be robbed of something, to be '*deprived of*: deprived of a voice, deprived of a public presence. In liberal thought, the multitude survives as a private dimension. The many are aphasic and far removed from the sphere of common affairs.'[12] Imprisoned in the private, the realm of not-general, particular interests, the many are considered individuals incapable of acting together politically. 'The people are the collective, the multitude is concealed by the presumed impotence, as well as by the immoderate uneasiness, of single individuals.'[13]

When the multiple is not formed and organized as a collective subject that speaks with one voice, it falls outside of the realm of the political. However, it is not only denied political agency, a gesture of domination that could be countered with an extension of democratic rights as per a politics of recognition; the autonomy of the political, which is constitutive for the form of liberal representative democracy, is also based on the gender-specific differentiation between a public sphere and a private sphere assigned to women who are responsible for family, household, care, and reproduction. When the multitude is situated in the feminized sphere of the private, those who do not count are positioned not only in the allegedly pre-political realm of the personal, subjective, and particular, but also in a sphere that allows primarily physical and emotional immediacy and authenticity and that makes political organization unthinkable, as either a people or class.[14]

The dispersed multitude, with this unpolitical and private positioning, reveals the gendered and racialized aspects of the distinction between *Volk*, representation, the public realm, and political action on the one hand, and multitude, immediacy/non-representation, the private realm, and (political) incapacity on the other. The (national)

Volk, connoted as masculinist and often as white, corresponds to the union of rational citizens who are capable of political action that is chrono-politically progressive and growth-oriented; their complementary other is depicted by the feminized and naturalized multitude of the dispersed, emotionalized, and isolated individuals, the multiple others, the hierarchized difference of the backward colonies.

In *Insurgencies: Constituent Power and the Modern State*, Antonio Negri presents a theory of constituent power that breaks not only with the constitutional understanding of this power, but also with its basic juridical connotation. Departing from the three thinkers who inspired him in the conception of a non-juridically-oriented constituent power – Machiavelli, Spinoza, and Marx – as well as the genealogical lines they draw through modern political theory, Negri shows in the final chapter of his book that they, too, remain rooted in three central components of European thought: the ideology of creation, natural law as the basis for the social, and transcendental philosophy.

Negri defines the first component as the 'ideological dimensions of Western thought: the Judeo-Christian tradition of creativity'.[15] It is the burden of the One. Although Machiavelli, Spinoza, and Marx maintain a type of creative atheism rather than represent any theological positions, they are unable 'to avoid in a definitive manner that point of the Judeo-Christian tradition in which all experience is brought back to unity. To expropriate God of its creativity is not decisive, if we allow creativity to be defined still by the unity of the creative project.'[16] The ideology that creation emerges only from the One, that power and force must be connected to unity and unification, also means adhering to the idea that there is a 'creative project', a finality, a historical linearity, or continuous progress. Along this type of continual axis of time, the potentiality and 'the strength of the multitude is always conceived . . . in the figure of the unity of the multitude'.[17] Yet the strength of the multitude is based by no means simply on number alone; it does not exist in the numerical manifoldness, but in the multiplicity 'of the "many", that is, the strength of singularities and differences'.[18]

Similarly, according to the idea that the many are a collective or plural subject, or that they have to become one, the multitude can ultimately only be thought of as a unity. The logic of unity is not simply broken with by emphasizing collectivity and plurality; limiting the multiplicity of the singularities is accepted, as is the tendency to conceive of them as a homogenized and limited organism. In contrast to this, understanding constituent power *without* a unifying political figure means allowing the potentiality of the multitude to occur in political action as multiplicity.

When Negri understands the multitude not as isolated, dispersed individuals, but, following Deleuze and Guattari, as singularities that are simultaneously unique and related to others and their environments, it becomes clear that attributing a constituent power of the multitude does not simply mean that the dispersed many who do not form a people, who pursue their particular interests in the private realm, should now finally be politically strengthened. The multitude of countless constituent singularities is a composite figure that does not allow for the logic of the autonomy of the political; it corresponds to the indeterminate *demos* that is not determined to be a people.[19] Such an understanding of the multitude breaks open the separation of the political and the social, as singularities in their mutual dependencies and affections can never be situated beyond the social.

In the second component problematized by Negri, constituent power is understood in natural law terms as a force before the law, before the constitution. This is one of the traditional ideas of constitutional theory: the dispersed many come together with their individual faculties and combine their forces to give themselves a constitution. In contrast to this, there is a constituent power – which is my concern here, following Negri – that does not exist exclusively pre-constitutively; it is not a force necessary *before* the constitution and for its constituting, which can or even must then disappear again in the order of the constituted power.[20] This other constituent power is not before the law in the sense of being an origin: it is not a start, its history is not linear, and it is not composed additively. It is excessive and measureless and does not orient itself *primarily* on the law. It is not genuinely juridical and does not inevitably result in a constitution. It is constituent to the extent that it is detached from the tradition of constitutionalism.

The third component which constantly surfaces in the debates about constituent power – according to Negri, its transcendental philosophical component – is its dissipation. In order to tame the constituent power of the multiple singularities as a multitude, this power is individualized and distributed among separate individuals, privatized and particularized. Disassembled and separated in this way, it is no longer capable of collective political action; stripped of its social relatedness, it becomes an unassociated quantity of private interests that cannot be politically organized. This individualization then forms the basis for the idea that in order to act with political efficacy, the dispersed individuals would need to join together, in a secondary step, to form a collective, united subject – as though at the beginning there was the dispersed autonomous individual, as though the heterogeneous singularities were dispersed as individuals separate from others, without affections, contexts, or dependencies.

Feminist political theory has repeatedly problematized the masculinist idea of autonomy and freedom. That individuals can always potentially find collectivity, that it is ultimately possible for separate individuals, under certain circumstances, to join the revolution and form a constituent force that suspends the law, is a liberal imaginary. But in this imaginary, as Negri pointedly formulates it, the moral has priority over the political, whereby constituent power is separated 'in the empty individual intentionality'.[21]

Liberal democracy lives from the struggles to extend the applicability of laws and norms such as equality and freedom. This future-oriented promise of a potentially endless progress of democratization is based on the individualization of constituent power and on the logic that only united *subjects* can act with political efficacy. In the inevitably concomitant mode of representation, the constituent power of multiple constituent singularities disappears in the corresponding chrono-political form of organization. In order to last, in this representationist logic, every emerging social movement must, in a next crucial step, lead to a representative form of organization. Here, the constituent power has never managed 'to free itself fully from the progressive concept of European modernity and its plot of rationality'.[22] The paradigm of unity and individualization remains committed to the linear narrative of time as progress. Discontinuity, eventfulness, and contingency are discredited by superficial continuity coupled with visibility.

Conceiving of the potentiality of the multitude as constituent power beyond constitutionalism and linearity implies an understanding of democracy different to that of its liberal form. When democracy is conceived in Negri's sense, without the constitutional representation of the people as 'omnilateral expression of the multitude',[23] the heterogeneous *demos* can no longer be contained in the constitution (the constituted power) and ignored as constituent power.

In order to understand constituent power in its radical form, it is necessary to break with the liberal, bourgeois form of democracy based on a separation between a political realm and a social realm, a sphere of the public and one of the private. It is also a break with the strategic phobia in relation to the multitude, with the fear from which Western political philosophy arises. The multitude can no longer be treated under the dictum of the 'social question', which is always problematized when the conditions of domination threaten to become unstable and the revolt of the poor, the precarious, those without a voice appears to draw near; when, in the ruling order, the multitude can no longer be reduced to the social and the private separated from the political, defamed as driven by irrational passions, reckless, irresponsible, and unpredictable, as a wild crowd that can only be penetrated, dominated, and categorized by (masculinist) political rationality.

In a non-constitutionalist understanding of constituent power, the process of constitution is never complete;[24] it is a matter of a becoming of democracy in the present. The focus is not on an external constitution, but on the process of self-constituting; not on a subject of representation, but on democratic modes of subjectivation.

Constituent power in this most advanced form means establishing possibilities and procedures within and beyond traditionally understood constituted power, and outside of but also within instituted state apparatuses, experimenting with organization models, collective forms, and modes of subjectivation that resist – at least for a while – subservience. While not breaking with every form of constituted power, this new constituent power unfolds new relations and other modes of instituting – not in a separate realm of the juridically political, but rather as inextricably bound up with questions of social reproduction and care. Constituent power does not signify a one-time act, neither an act of making a constitution nor an act of revolution as an irrupting event linked to the takeover of control. It is not a limited process with the legal text of a sovereign nation as its product, but an unfinished process of constituting by heterogeneous singularities: a process of invention that is not driven by an interest in containing the radical heterogeneity of the multitude in the identity of a national people. It is a power without a people, a power that is not suited for populism, or for being limited to a national framework. The constituent process of the multitude corresponds instead with an enduring discontinuous social revolution that re-poses the questions of social reproduction and care. The discontinuous cycles of democracy movements since the start of the 2010s in Spain provide an example of such an enduring constituent process in multiplicity. At the same time, they show the extent to which the democratic constituent power of the multitude is queer-feminist.

The subprime crisis of 2007 and the financial crisis that spread in 2008 had massive consequences throughout the world. In Europe, the multiple crises had dire effects for the structurally weaker economies of the southern European countries.[25] In the name of masculinist austerity policies imposed by the EU,[26] authoritarian neoliberal governing intensified in Spain, as in other European countries: private indebtedness rose, as did the indebtedness of municipalities as well as the national government; at the same time, related governmental discourses tracing economic debt back to moral debt were actualized. Precarization increased greatly, the labour market was restructured, social rights were dismantled, and unemployment, mainly of youth, rose precipitously, wages and social services collapsed drastically and health care became more precarious; the housing shortage worsened, while ever more people lost their homes following increasingly aggressive forms of evictions by banks and the state administration. This form of governing, with its concentrated brutality, was new to the European Union, and was implemented with particular harshness in Greece, even more so than in Spain.[27] This period of fundamental restructuring of political economies in Europe was, however, not only an era of authoritarian austerity policies and reinforced authoritarian populism; in southern Europe, it was also formative for left, socially transformative modes of subjectivation and social practices. Crisis debates after 2007 focused not only on economic issues, but also on the more fundamental crisis of representative democracy. In Spain, where the 'transition' to democracy had occurred only slightly more than a decade before the transitions in eastern Europe, ever more cases of corruption accumulated in the 2000s, primarily in the conservative Partido Popular (PP), but also in the governing social democratic party PSOE.[28] For that reason, it seems obvious to interpret the name of the group appearing in early 2011, '¡Democracia real ya!', and its main slogan, 'They call it democracy, but it isn't', in terms of a fundamental critique of representative democracy. However, corresponding with the name of the group, the social struggles of the new occupy movements, not only in Spain, also found their common denominator in the search for real democracy in the here and now.

These movements experimented with multiple forms of horizontal assembly, without establishing horizontality as either origin or dogma. Rather than rigorously rejecting political representation, they attempted, in their dispersal, to break open the political system with representation-critical platforms 'from below', and to shape a new social politics for all. They began recurringly at the municipal level, in the neighbourhoods, in urban space.

Already the occupation of central squares – such as the Puerta del Sol in Madrid on 15 May 2011, and subsequently in more than sixty other cities in Spain – made clear that it was not about making demands on the rulers. In the midst of the long-observed crises of representative democracy, the occupiers began to practise alternative forms of democracy while organizing and instituting in the squares. The heterogeneous many who assembled did not elect leaders; they arranged themselves in camps and tent cities, and in no time at all, with the support of friends and neighbours, organized a functioning infrastructure on the public square, including temporary housing, provisional gardens, information booths, people's kitchens, libraries, and improvised computer networks.

> For weeks and months, the occupiers developed inclusive practices of assembly in plenaries and commissions. While the Twitter feeds helped facilitate rapid changes in course in actions and demonstrations, direct communication in the assemblies was characterized by long, patient, horizontal discussions. Collective moderation, sustained care work, the development of a specific code of sign language and the methodology of radical inclusion afforded the intensive experience of self-organization in multiplicity for hundreds of thousands of people.[29]

The decentralized 15M movement stretched across all of Spain; rather than one uniform manifesto, multiple local manifestos were agreed upon in the *asambleas* of the respective cities. This movement for occupation and assembly formed an exodus out of the liberal-democratic consensus of the transition, in which the two-party system of PSOE and PP was depicted as the best possible form of government. Until then, any questioning of this dualist representative democracy had been countered with visions of confusion and chaos and, ultimately, the discursive spectre of once again falling into the dark days of the dictatorship. The movements of 2011 broke not only with this consensus of representative democracy, but also with representative democracy in general.[30]

These movements did not come out of the blue. In the desire for an entirely different democracy, new forms of common political action get ready for a tiger's leap, which does not have to be based on a conscious decision as to where, in which past practices, the actual will be tracked down. Often this is collectively known, remembered and actualized in common practices. These are practices that create a breach for the concatenation of failed, broken-off, and successful revolutionary practices from the past to enter: the councils and social revolution of the Paris Commune; the identity critiques and problematizations of social reproduction and care by feminist and queer movements since the 1970s; the strategies of the Zapatistas from the 1990s; the instrument of horizontality employed in the Argentinian revolution of 2001; the practices of the alter-globalization movements and the EuroMayDay movement of the precarious.[31] In the 2000s, this transnational movement of the precarious was very strong in Spain, as was the movement for adequate and dignified housing, which demanded this right anchored in the Spanish constitution.[32] Emerging from this in 2009 was the platform of those affected by mortgages, PAH (Plataforma de Afectados por la Hipoteca),[33] within which the Madres Unidas por el Derecho a la Vivienda Digna organized, as mothers fought for affordable living space to live together with (their) children. From 2011, charged by the energy of the 15M movement spreading throughout the country, the PAH grew to become the largest Spanish movement since the Franco regime.

Organizing in the PAH are those who have been unable to pay back their loans since the financial crisis and are threatened by eviction. The platform negotiates with banks and officials to delay evictions or to prevent them through activist means, to attack the role of the banks, and to change the legal situation. So-called *mesas mixtas* have arisen in many sites: round tables at which the PAH looks together with the municipal governments for ways out of the housing shortage. The most important practices of the PAH, however, are its facilitation of dialogue among those affected by the evictions, its enabling of mutual empowerment and care, and its bursting open of the individualized suffering that hundreds of thousands in Spain were driven into by the crisis. Resisting the economic, social, and psychopathological individualization of the effects of the crisis, care is shared in the assemblies and actions of the platform in order to overcome both self-blame for indebtedness and the fear of eviction and loss of spaces for living and coexistence.

Unlike the PAH, in 2011 the many occupations of public squares dissolved after a month or so, in some cases after three months. In doing so, however, they did not simply disappear but took on new forms. The assemblies became decentralized. From 20 June to 23 July that year, the Marcha Popular Indignada to Madrid took place,

setting off from eight directions. The democracy movement continued while walking and bicycling through the rural areas of Spain.
Assemblies were organized at many sites, where people were able to
talk about their social, political, and economic problems and their
proposals for changes. Upon arrival in Madrid all aspects discussed
along the way were brought together in a large, common assembly
and – contrary to the movement's otherwise representation-critical
position – recorded in a document handed over to the congress of
parliamentarians several days later, although it received no response.[34]

In the cities where the central squares were occupied, the assemblies spread out to the surrounding neighbourhoods. Under the
slogan and hashtag #tomalasplazas (take the squares), thousands of
assemblies were established in the city districts, which were able to
focus more on their neighbourhoods and were more manageable in
terms of size. In addition to this spatial dispersion, concentrations
also emerged in various social fields: in 2012, under the concept of
the Mareas (tides), contexts took shape which – distinguished by
the various colours *marea verde*, *blanca*, *negra*, *roja*, and so on –
developed concrete concepts, demands, consultations, and actions
in various areas from education to law and health through to work.
These formations that developed on the basis of social sectors were
especially successful in the areas of health care and schools.[35]
Emerging at approximately the same time was the citizens' movement Yo Sí, Sanidad Universal, which has been fighting since the
state health reform in 2012 for public health care for all, including
migrants.[36]

Another movement that resumed the practices of the great march
from 2011 was the Movimiento por la Democracia, which became
active in the autumn of 2013 when it began to work out a 'Carta por la
democracia' at a workshop in Madrid. Twenty-eight further workshops followed in other Spanish cities, in which 200 people from
various groups and initiatives participated. They revised the document over and over again, before publishing it in March 2014 as a
brochure with a wealth of inventive illustrations.[37] The published
version of the Carta, however, continued to be understood as a draft,
not as a finished charter or document:

> We do not want it to end; a living document is, instead, one that is constantly discussed and worked out. We believe that this is a good summary of the most important demands that we have brought to the table as citizens over the past years. Our wishes and needs.[38]

The enduring process of constituting required that the document remain alive, that its demands not be established once and for all, but also that the positions of constituent and constituted power did not become fixed. The plan was to distribute the Carta everywhere, travelling across the country to hold as many assemblies and workshops as possible, through which the constituent process for a new democracy could be furthered and ever more people become involved.

By the early summer of 2014, however, at many sites less energy was being put into the Movimiento and further discussion of the charter. The country's election cycle had begun, and the focus shifted in various ways to the forms and rituals of representative democracy. In March came the founding of the Podemos (We Can) party, in which several activists from the PAH and the 15M movement became involved. Just a few weeks later, Podemos attained a respectable five seats in the European parliament election, and it has gone on to become a stable party – in the traditional sense – throughout Spain.[39] Encouraged by this success, an increasing number of activists began to discuss, outside of Podemos, whether the struggles for a different form of democracy could also be continued through participation in the established political system and begun anew in a different way. With the municipal elections in 2015 in view, they started working on im/possible strategies. 'The struggle for social change reaches the institutions.'[40] Municipalist projects set up by various Ganemos (We Win) platforms emerged, first in Barcelona, then in ever more cities and municipalities. Rather than forming a party like Podemos, they formed explicitly as sociopolitical movements that aimed to bring the practices of the PAH and the 15M movement, but also those of the Mareas and occupied social centres, to the city halls. These citizen platforms defined themselves as *confluencias*, emphasizing the confluence of heterogeneous streams. Yet without party alliances, their chances of winning were slight. In many municipalities the Ganemos platforms joined together with Podemos and the groupings of Anti-Capitalistas, for example in the Ahora Madrid (Madrid Now) alliance.[41] A comparable alliance was Barcelona En Comú, whose main candidate was the well-known PAH activist Ada Colau.

In the municipal elections of May 2015, something hardly antic-ipated was achieved: in both Madrid and Barcelona, the alliance was the strongest force. Ada Colau was elected mayor of Barcelona, and Manuela Carmena, a lawyer, took over the office in the capital. The alliances also participated in municipal governments in other cities. With their entry into the city halls, new forms of organization emerged for the *confluencias*, which saw themselves as spaces in which citizens and activists from social movements and other initia-tives were able to collaborate.[42] A new cycle had emerged, the cycle of the municipalist movement.

From the perspective of the Ganemos platforms, the aim was not to march through established political institutions to attain political power in a traditional sense. The goal of the *confluencias* was to transform those institutions through the practices used in the move-ments. These included new criteria for holding office, which was already evident in the instituting of Ganemos's lists of candidates: in contrast to how such lists are usually made in political parties, invit-ations to attend open assemblies in the individual constituencies were sent out.[43] From the beginning, efforts were made to break open the logic of politics as the business of a few representatives. The liberal political division of labour was opposed by the radical inclusion of the heterogeneous many who were not allied in interest groups. Rather than conceiving of politics as a profession, the idea was that 'politics can develop into yet another activity in the lives of everyone'.[44] Every-one should be able to participate in organizing social affairs in a way that accounts for mutual social relatedness and dependence in urban space. In contrast to the 'very weak social bond'[45] of voting in an election for representatives, the multiplicity of those involved gave the *confluencias* a solid social base which, with the help of social networks, enormously increased the distribution of information.[46] The integrative decision-making structures in open assemblies were no less effective than dirigiste practices. Yet they met with significant difficulties working within the established political systems. Due simply to the different political and social practices, tensions were present right from the start in the municipal alliances with Podemos. Mainly, however, the established political parties refused to accept decisions from the district assemblies, denying them legitimacy as non-elected organs. The heterogeneous many who cared about common affairs were not considered political actors by the representatives elected through parties.[47]

In contrast to this representationist understanding of politics, the Ganemos platforms argued that politics should again assume 'just management of collective problems'[48] – such as work, housing, health care, education, infrastructure, and the environment – which had been aggravated mainly since the financial crisis, rather than idly riding the crisis out, as the municipal governments were accused of doing. With the filtering of European austerity dictates through to the municipal level, and the related obligation to reduce debt, the realization of an alternative politics also met with massive budgetary restrictions.

Yet one of the greatest challenges lay in avoiding the self-perpetuation of the instituted in the newly instituting practices. Success in achieving this was mixed, not least due to the varied structuring and hierarchization of the municipal administrative apparatuses.[49] Entering the institutions and aspiring to transform them – such an enduring constituent process also affects the bodies. 'To resist this [institutional] conformity is hard work, since it requires finding heterodox ways of inhabiting and embodying power relations. Such embodying is the perhaps hardest social and psycho-somatic labour.'[50] For many things to do, there was a lack of time, while taking care of oneself and others was required to evade institutional constraints and give space to the becoming of the constituent force, which the 'masculine space[s]'[51] of the established political institutions generally did not allow.

What became most obvious as a result of these various challenges and blockages confronting the new political and social practices was the necessity of recurring experimenting in an enduring constituent process in order to reinvent the state apparatus, the administration, the bureaucracy, and, with that, to institutionalize coexistence and the kinds of subjectivation that can be lived therein. The alternating and coexisting cycles were underpinned by the desire to set off a democratic rebellion, beginning in the local, the neighbourhood, and the municipality, and creating a city that will enable a life of dignity for each and every person, where action can occur in sustainable and just ways.[52] The actualization of past practices, tried out at a municipal level, reveals what should be extended throughout the country, Europe, and beyond.[53]

The manifold democratic practices and new municipalisms emerged in the midst of a crisis of representative democracy which, in Europe and beyond, had generated a new form of authoritarian neoliberal governing through precarization and indebtedness.[54] Along with this political-economic transformation, the hegemonic liberal-capitalist understanding of time also collapsed, with still-unforeseeable consequences. In precarization, the future cannot be planned, and the linear narrative is lost; yet indebtedness paradoxically carries time forward into the future. The bursting of time in increasing precarization is crucial for enabling a break with the idea that political action must necessarily be tied to representation, and a revolutionary desire simultaneously emerges for a new form of democracy that can be tried out now, in now-time, rather than offering the empty promise of a permanently delayed future. The identity- and representation-critical stance that arises in the movements of the precarious is a now-time political practice that recognizes the deficits of representative democracy and the increasing impossibility of traditional means of organization in work relations. The heterogeneous precarious cannot be united or organized using identity logics. The heterogeneity of the socioeconomic modes of existence demands negotiation processes and decision-making structures that channel the multiplicity of positions without immobilizing them in the dual logic of inclusion and exclusion; it requires different forms of protection from insecurity, alternative economies, and an affective mutual relatedness that breaks open existing power relations and domination conditions.

From the start, the 15M movement used the term 'real democracy', most prominently expressed in the slogan '¡Democracia real ya!' This democracy is real, but not in the sense of being the only true democracy, the right democracy; as connoted by the Spanish word *ya*, it occurs materially in the now, mainly in the practice of assemblies and mutual relatedness. Ahora Madrid, Málaga Ahora – the Spanish *ahora* also means 'now'. The democracy movements that flow together and apart, including the new municipal politics of the citizen platforms, illustrate the present infinitive in which swarms of events interrupt and allow a constituent process to endure. The process is one of multiple starts and multiple durations all at once, at several sites, taking in many ways of instituting.

These movements turn the logic of liberal democracy, with its deferral of the impossible participation of all to the future, into a new democratic understanding of taking part as radical inclusion. This radical inclusion also means that more and more areas of society are being arranged by open assemblies, through modes of participation that are as egalitarian as possible, in order to self-organize common affairs in the municipalities, or in educational and health institutions, and to avert privatizations, especially of common goods such as water. Equality is not a deferred norm here, but is practised as the actualization of equality in assemblies. Consensual decisions are based not on unanimity or exclusion, but on expanding inclusion.

From the perspective of the municipalist movements in Spain, constituent processes must be broadly anchored in a desire from below, a desire coming from the movements, from everyday life. This is why transformation at the level of municipal politics is so important. Experiments and inventions beyond traditional forms of political representation are more likely at the municipal level, beyond the national context of classical party forms. These new democratic forms of instituting and constituting are not to be understood via a dichotomization of inefficient horizontality on the one side and efficient-hierarchical verticality on the other. Horizontal and vertical are not two axes at right angles to one another, with only a single crossing point where a decision must be made on which direction to take. Rather than axes, in a constituent process transversal vectors constantly emerge, emanating from micropolitical social movements which are not positioned as secondary to political parties. The vertical is thus not to be understood as an upright axis of organization, of party and government, but in the literal sense of the Latin *vertere*, as a dynamic 'turning' that allows the horizontality of social movements to reinvent the *form* of government. An alternative form of democracy does not emerge from above, but in and from the subjectivations, in and from the molecular pores of everyday life, enabling new socialities of the common for which forms of political action and concatenation must be found.

When new constituent, inclusive, and transversal forms of democracy are sought, the power in 'constituent power' is not one of domination. Power and existing institutions are not to be taken over, as though power were something that is primarily or even exclusively held in institutions. When relations of power are changed 'from below', through the ways that we live together every day, and are mutually related, then they may also be consolidated in new ways at the level of political organization and administration. Because we (re-)produce relations of power at every moment, the invention of new forms of democracy must begin here, with the invention of new institutions to replace and transform the existing ones.

Populist strategies are worthless for this type of empowerment coming from everyday life in Europe.[55] The growing orientation on a left populism, with its associated rhetoric, has no alternative but to once again refer to the 'nation' and 'people'; not necessarily to a people imagined in an identitarian way, as is the case on the authoritarian-populist and reactionary front, but to a people that, with its fears and anxieties, provides the key terms on the basis of which a party such as Podemos shapes its programme.[56] Simply wanting to channel the voices of the heterogeneous people is not enough. A possible transversal constellation of the constituent process can be seen, for example, in the multiplicity that emerged in Spain between the various molecular, micropolitical practices of the 15M movement, the PAH, Ganemos, and Podemos.

However, without a problematization of the gendered and racialized societal division of labour, a constituent process will not be able to break open the masculinist politics based on a separation of the political and the social. Along these lines, too, the democracy movements in Spain were increasingly shaped in terms of an exodus from masculinist political structures. From the very start of the movements, social reproduction and care were revalued and realigned. Feminist reflections on the reorganization of the division of labour, reproduction, and care achieved a new actuality.[57] At the same time, already during the occupation of the squares, there were many discussions on how feminism and queer practices could be understood in a non-identitarian way, and how sexism, homophobia, and transphobia arose not from social conditions of domination treated as secondary, but from the current effects of patriarchal, neoliberal conditions.[58] The specific type of activism that soon became established in the occupations, and which favoured such discussions, was one that distanced itself from a macho and exclusive militancy as well as the concomitant claims of dominance. In addition, no parties or organizations were allowed to advertise with flags or flyers. All practices and institutionalizations of representation were unwelcome. This largely non-masculinist politics had no interest in gathering a people in opposition to those 'up there'. It comprised practices beyond an understanding of political action within the framework of the autonomy of politics. In their practice of radical inclusion, the countless constituent singularities retrieve the multitude from the sphere of the private marked as apolitical. They invent new, non-representationist, solidarity-based ways of organizing and instituting that thwart the autonomy of the political and point to genealogies in feminist and queer movements since the 1970s, such as adopting more horizontal decision-making processes in order to counter the masculinist 'power at the top', or avoiding bellicose language in order to remain aware of and promote 'egalitarian forms of intervention'.[59]

Since the instituting of the new municipalisms, a reference to feminist practice has become self-evident in municipalist platforms and their translocal assemblies. In these contexts, the talk is increasingly of a 'feminization of politics'. For a new form of democracy that relies heavily on queer-feminist practices, however, this talk is misleading. At issue here is not that politics should become 'more feminine', in the sense that more women are present and occupy functions as representatives. The presence of large numbers of women will not by itself end the structural masculinist politics of neoliberal forms of governing. In the genealogy of feminist and queer practices, the new movements are not interested in further manifestations of dual genderism or other identitarian definitions. At the centre are mutual affections and relations of care. In breaking the division between the political and the social, rather than perpetuating an increasingly self-emptying politics of the 'empty signifier', feminist and queer positionings must be formulated just as clearly as an anti-racist stance,[60] especially in the face of the renewed staging of patriarchal 'white' masculinity and the ever new variants of 'fortress Europe'.[61]

6

Presentist Democracy

Care Practice and Queer Debt

By breaking the gendered division between public and private spheres, rejecting the autonomy of the political, releasing constituent power from the limitations of the law, and refusing the figure of a bourgeois capitalist, autonomous, identity-bound subject, a democracy detached from the primacy of representation can be practised. This is a democracy whose *demos* cannot be represented as a people, but instead unfolds as a manifold multitude. Multitudinous democracy bursts the taming, violent fetters of the private and allows everyday local practices to become political, practices which, in their relatedness to others and their dispersal, are not considered political in liberal logic. Such a democracy cannot be demanded or realized within a liberal political framework since its aim is to radically transform precisely this framework. This is a democracy that is not supported by autonomous individuals but emerges from connections and affections in their historical materializations. In countless beginnings and repetitions, it takes shape at a micropolitical level in subjectivations that are not a becoming of identitarian subjects, and in social relations that are able to condense and institute at administrative and organizational levels. It breaks with discrimination based on identitarian categories such as class, gender, sexuality, and 'race', and opposes the valorization of difference. It is a form of democracy that refuses the domination-securing and restabilizing processes of patriarchal-heteronormative and white gendering, and that counters neoliberal relations of exploitation. The manifold duration of the multitude enables new means of participation, of organizing and instituting.

All this is possible only in the course of a break with hegemonic liberal and capitalist understandings of time and history. Presentist democracy does not link reflection with the past, nor does it link the present with an identitarian presence or promise duration solely to a representation extended into the future for those not yet represented. The representation-critical democracy of the multitude knows of dis/continuities and simultaneities in the constellations and fabrics of relations in the present infinitive, within which the past actualizes and differentiates itself. In the present (tense) of the movement, this presentist democracy is already taking shape in revolutionary practices in the present.

Precarization and debt are the instruments of governing that the constituent power of the multitude currently uses to break open the masculinist autonomy of the political with the power of care relations, and to actualize and preserve the precariousness of life in a new form of democracy. Under neoliberal conditions, several dimensions of the precarious become manifest, dimensions which, more explicitly than under liberal Fordist conditions, enable new constellations of revolutionary practices capable of fundamentally transforming the gendered and racialized constructions of Western liberal-democratic modernity.

In bourgeois-capitalist society, the social bond is inseparably tied to a gendered and citizenship-based distribution of positions of in/dependence, care, and in/security. Such is the masculinist logic of domination with regard to protection and security, which, in the history of political dominance, theory, and economy, devalues fundamental precariousness – that is, mutual dependency, care, and relatedness – attempting to hide and fend it off as threatening.

Historically, the political idea of the individual independent from others, requiring protection against insecurities and threatening fellow human beings, stems primarily from the Hobbesian conception of the security state. In the twentieth century, ensuring protection from existential insecurity became the task of the Fordist social welfare state.[1] The patriarchal-heteronormative family with a male bread-winner was one of its central pillars, with a gender-specific division of labour consolidating this social security logic. Yet neither the social bond of Hobbes's *Leviathan* nor that of the Fordist welfare state was knotted in such a way that it eliminated the precarious from the world. On the contrary, each produced its own new historical forms of precarity, new insecurities, against which, once again, it was meant to protect. In contemporary neoliberal societies, social protection has been undergoing massive reconstruction for several decades; it has been dismantled, is less oriented on the family, and is being individualized once again.[2] Domination is legitimized less and less through social security; care and protection are privatized, while independence in combination with self-responsibility is transformed into an instrument of domination. How might we picture a social bond that does not devalue care and mutual dependencies, but instead starts from them – a bond that does not reproduce modern European security logics, but bursts them open sustainably and even conceives of law in a way that is guided by care?

As proposed in *State of Insecurity*, it is possible to distinguish three dimensions of the precarious:[3] precariousness, precarity, and governmental precarization. *Precariousness* identifies the socio-ontological dimension of bodies that always exist in relations with other living beings and environments. From birth onward, bodies are reliant on others for care and reproduction; they are dependent on social relations and are never entirely autonomous. Despite care and reproduction, bodies remain precarious: they can become ill, suffer accidents, and die. Precariousness is shared with others; it is the base of sociality and points to an ineluctable relatedness that is produced only in political and social acts, in its own specific way each time, as care (for) or also as violence. The second dimension of the precarious is that of *precarity*. This identifies the historical conditions of domination according to which protection, care, and safeguarding are divided up and distributed. The third dimension, *governmental precarization*, emphasizes the intertwining of state conduct and individualized self-government in a governing through insecurity, which enables a problematization of the complex interactions between instruments of government, economic conditions of exploitation, and modes of subjectivation in their ambivalence between subjugation and freedom.

The ambivalence between subjugation and freedom correlates with the constituent tensions of the modern figure of the autonomous individual. As a bearer of rights and freedom, the autonomous individual is the condition for liberal democracy, as well as for capitalist relations of production.[4] Hobbes delivered the first conceptions of this figure, granting the individual independent of social dependencies a central place in his political theory.[5] He connects the individual's fear of precariousness, of unprotected vulnerability, with the fear of a threatening, property-destroying other, and promises protection and security through law and the sovereign. In Hobbes's security state, the social bond wards off precariousness (which is construed as threatening), disaggregates mutual dependency, and juridically separates individuals from one another as bourgeois individuals, to then reunite them in the sovereign by means of representation. The first traces of the negative form of bourgeois freedom are already revealed here as freedom *from* the precariousness that is shared with others, a freedom which Hobbes, working in the absolutist tradition, theorizes in terms of a voluntary subjugation under the Leviathan, the sovereign, the state representative of all citizen-individuals. Representation and the law offer protection from a threatening precariousness and, at the same time, safeguard the property of propertied male individuals. The individual thus protected from (violent) redistribution (in the state of nature) is independent of others when no longer equal with them. With Hobbes, freedom from shared precariousness demands inequality, which becomes manifest in the contractual surrender of political freedom for the benefit of state representation. Relatively peaceful survival and the protection of property is possible here only at the price of inequality and subjugation under a patriarchal social contract, based on the bond of male citizens.[6]

In *De Cive*, interestingly, Hobbes proposes to view humans in the state of nature as 'men . . . sprung out of the earth, and suddainly (like Mushromes) come to full maturity without all kind of engagement to each other'.[7] In feminist theory, this early modern phantasma of independence is understood 'as [a] metaphor for an autonomous masculine subjectivity'[8] or as a 'denial of having been born of a woman'.[9] I would like to draw attention not only to the masculinist fantasy of being autonomous and unattached, but also to the fact that with his idea of mushrooms, Hobbes inadvertently chose an image of interrelatedness, ecology, and care that runs contrary to his intentions. Unknown in his day, but well established today, is the fact that mushrooms can in no way be viewed as isolated, independent growths; with their broadly branching underground mycelia they are among the largest cohesive organisms, constantly involved in a mutual exchange with their environments.[10] Thus, Hobbes's image of the fearful, vulnerable, isolated mushroom in the state of nature actually stands for his devaluation and denial of a dependency on others within a precariousness construed as threatening, a dependence on an unruly 'wilderness', on fabrics of relations of care, on the surround.

In many respects, John Locke delivered a counter-argument to Hobbes, yet still adopted his political-theoretical positioning of individualism. Locke, the founder of liberal thinking, derives the individual's right to self-determination from more than an idea of freedom and independence linked to property. Going beyond this, he conceives of labour as free labour in such a way that one's relationship to one's own body becomes one of property ownership. According to Locke, 'every Man has a *Property* in his own *Person* ... The *Labour* of his Body, and the *Work* of his Hands, we may say, are properly his.'[11] Adam Smith took up this idea a hundred years later when he declared that 'the property which every man has [is] his own labour, as it is the original foundation of all other property'.[12] Smith was convinced that the freedom of productive labour led to a situation in which the labourer, as a 'free man',[13] is able to feed not only himself but also his family, and is free of the charity of state or non-state institutions.[14]

The heterosexual, masculinist way of liberation from the subjugating bond of charity is central to the idea of the freedom of labour as independence from feudal conditions of coercion. At the same time, relations of care were not considered profitable spheres, and the reproduction of the labour force had to be guaranteed through heterosexual gender relations within the family. Independence from care is the basis of the idea of a liberal, capitalist masculinity that feminizes and devalues care. In the second half of the eighteenth century, this gender construction becomes entangled with the bourgeois idea of freedom as *voluntary* subjugation under the now self-made laws of political democracy. This is a social contract that justifies the legal equality of white, male, propertied, free citizens via the social and political bond of fraternity,[15] a masculinist bond that intertwines social independence and juridical subjection. But in its construction of liberal masculinity, the subjectivating ambivalence between freedom and obedience, between self-determination and control, is in no way transparent or obvious; instead, it appears as a paradox – one that can only appear on the ideological stage by suppressing its gendering and the patriarchal, heteronormative dual-gender system of the sexual contract required for that gendering. It is an arrangement of freedom and subjugation that rests decisively on the patriarchal subjugation of women in the private sphere.[16] In bourgeois-capitalist society, precariousness is tamed and contained in the private by means of a gender-specific division of social space. Care and reproduction are feminized, de-politicized, devalued, and structured through precarity based on gender, sexuality, and 'race'. Governmental body relations served the production of a class-specific and heterosexual, racialized dual-gender system, which, through gender segregation, not only guaranteed the maintenance of the labour force, but at the same time ensured generativity for strengthening the nation state.[17] On the basis of ideas of one's 'own' body and Christian practices of confession, biologistic and naturalized constructions of the disambiguation of gender and sexuality became manifest in the nineteenth century, as did constructions of a superior 'white race', which could not have arisen without the doctrine of 'possessive individualism'[18] and liberal ideas of freedom, self-determination, and civilized life. The social bond of bourgeois-capitalist society and its relation to the world are structured by conditions of domination and exploitation; mutual dependency is striated through precarity, through categorizations based on class, gender, 'race', and citizenship.

For eighteenth- and also nineteenth-century male workers, how-ever, individualization, the devaluation of the 'other', and the feminization of reproduction in the private sphere were not enough to tame precariousness. Smith's idea that the free labourer must be able to feed a family soon proved to be 'utopian capitalism'.[19] The social welfare state and the organizational structures of a (mainly masculine) workforce made it evident that individualization in lib-eral democracy was not possible without collective protection and insurance systems. Legal claims and solidarities led to a social com-promise that provided a welfare state complement to Fordist individualization which survived intact into the 1970s.[20] The idea of male freedom and independence through wage labour could thus be collectively supported and maintained, consolidating the gender-specific divisions between waged productive and unwaged reproductive labour as well as between a public and a private sphere. This welfare state bond of safeguarding was based on massive pre-carity in the form of structural relations of inequality in terms of origin, class, and gender.

In their examination of discourse on welfare mothers in the US in the 1980s and 1990s, Nancy Fraser and Linda Gordon showed why the ambivalence of bourgeois, juridical self-government between freedom and subjugation was adamantly perceived as a paradox, and thus, in its specific masculinity, could become economically exploitable. Accord-ing to Fraser and Gordon, white male workers' independence is based on their failure to perceive their own subjugation in relations of pro-duction. At the moment that white men were politically and legally equal, 'by definition', economic inequality among them 'no longer generated dependency ... Thus, *dependency* was redefined to refer exclusively to those noneconomic relations of subordination deemed suitable only for people of color and for white women.'[21] This male form of independence was based on the precarity of others, who were once again differentiated in their subordinate dependency into those who seemed worthy of being protected and those who did not – a '"good", household dependency, predicated of children and wives', on the one hand, and a '"bad" (or at least dubious) charity dependency'[22] on the other.

Still today, due to the liaison between capitalism and liberal democracy, the 'social question' begins as a question related to the worker.[23] The problem arising from this is not only that social democracy in Fordism concentrated primarily on the independence of the family breadwinner secured by the social welfare state, but that social rights with regard to health, education, housing, and residency continue to be significantly tied to wage labour. A social form of democracy that is structured differently is currently not capable of hegemony in Europe.

It has become obvious – at the latest since the financial and economic crisis that began in 2008 – that neoliberal governing no longer marginalizes the precarious only on the social periphery. With the individualizing reconstruction of the welfare state, the deregulation of the labour market, and the expansion of precarious employment, we are currently in a process of the normalization of precarization, which also affects large parts of the middle class.[24] In this normalization process, precarization has become a political and economic instrument of governing. At the same time, people continue to be legally, economically, and socially marginalized and excluded through structural inequality, through precarity, such that they are either less protected than others or are denied protection entirely.[25] This becomes clear in the systemic dismantling of borders related to finances and the strengthening of borders with regard to global migration. Within a 'global hierarchy of mobility' and of legal status, migrants are made highly precarious,[26] which enables a 'hyper-exploitation of these "others" in the post-Fordist labor markets', and not only for undocumented migrants.[27]

In the reconstructed neoliberal welfare state, governing through precarization is no longer based fundamentally on the gender-hierarchical and heteronormative dichotomy of autonomy and dependency, which was still traditional in the Fordist welfare state: the dichotomy between male individualization and female familization has been multiply broken open.[28] Beginning in the 1970s, social safeguarding constructed primarily on the basis of the Fordist family wage was seen as less and less financially viable. Women's precarious (additional) income not only facilitated the nascent flexibilization of the labour market, but also supported a neoliberally individualized social safeguarding linked to wage labour.[29] In the course of this process, rather than being expanded, collective social safeguarding systems were further altered or dismantled in favour of private insurance options. Social safeguarding was increasingly decollectivized and once again privatized, treated as the individual's self-responsibility and capitalized. As a result, for an increasing number of people, the only option when it comes to financing provisions for old age, health, and education is indebtedness.[30] This de-securing and indebting individualization has given rise to new inequalities.

However, patriarchal-heteronormative gender arrangements are not entirely ruptured by these transformations, but are, in part, merely shifted, as old inequalities simultaneously become manifest – for example in the still-devalued work of care and reproduction, which is further organized according to an international division of labour, and economically and ethnically differentiated and hierarchized.[31] In the internationalization of private households, the re-formation of the patriarchal in the area of care is particularly evident in the migration of women, who in global capitalism quite frequently move away from one 'patriarchal system' based on a gender-specific division of labour toward another.[32] In the neoliberal political economy, this internationalization of the private is based on a hierarchizing of rights, which conditions the extreme precarity of undocumented and illegalized women workers.[33]

Although for many EU citizens the neoliberal flexibilization of working relations means a flexibilization of family relations, it does not necessarily change the hierarchically organized gender division of labour. In places where social reproduction is not monetized through day care or care services, it is re-privatized through heteronormative re-familization.[34] Nonetheless, occurring parallel to that, there is an increasing dissolution of patriarchal gender relations, and an erosion of related hegemonic masculinities.[35] What has become evident is that neoliberal governing through precarization does not have to rely as heavily on a gender relation based on labour division and heteronormative generativity as was necessary for the formation of liberal capitalism and bourgeois society. Continued neoliberal governing through precarization appears not only to cause a conservative and internationalized restructuring of the private sphere as a heteronormative protected space for majority society; at the same time, the politico-economic function of 'family' increasingly also goes beyond heterosexual forms, leading to a further normalization of same-sex partnerships at social and legal levels. All that matters for neoliberal governmentality is the presence of supportive, protective, and reproductive private relationships, which, in this respect, take over the governmental function of the heteronormative family. This neoliberal valorization of the private culminates in the increasing assumption of state responsibilities for care by private and voluntary support networks, for example for refugees. Voluntary work becomes ever more useful in the context of what is in many places a much-weakened welfare state bond.[36]

In many sites in Europe, neoliberal governing through precarization demands specific forms of freedom and independence, which condense in the concept of self-responsibility. Social safeguarding is once again made the responsibility of the autonomous individual who, while no longer primarily gender-connoted, has genealogies in the era before the formation of European welfare states, which are now more clearly seen as historical exceptions.[37] This moralist understanding of freedom as self-responsibility enables a demeaning of precarization, poverty, and dependence on minimized social welfare provision as being solely self-inflicted. Wage labour continues to remain at the centre of the privatization of risks and their prevention within a now activating social welfare state, but under the paradigm of flexibility and competition, social rights are being dismantled, and obligations to conformist engagement and performance agreements structure the employment relationship in which complete time availability is demanded. When workers are unable to claim their rights, or lack knowledge of these rights, their precarious working and living conditions give rise to new dependencies on state institutions, employers, creditors, and banks. Conformism and fear increase, as does the acceptance of authoritarian-structured labour relations and institutions.

Precarious living and working conditions and the privatization of protection from precariousness are not the effects of economic crises, but the conditions of both a prospering global finance capitalism and the debt economy that is inseparably tied to it. These economies are predicated on an expansion of productivity, through which it is able to transform the forms of labour and dismantle industrial standards, because it is more interested in subjectivation than work in a traditional sense.[38] The debt economy requires a subjective figure who takes on (self-)responsibility and internalizes the risks in terms of both guilt and debt, becoming a doubly indebted personality that invests in and speculates with itself. This personality is key to the enabling and stabilizing of neoliberal governing through precarization and insecurity.

Two very different perspectives show that there is no escape from indebtedness; all are indebted in one way or another. Maurizio Lazzarato has formulated the first perspective, Stefano Harney and Fred Moten the second.

'If it is not individual debt, it is public debt that weighs, literally, on every individual's life, since every individual must take responsibility for it',[39] writes Lazzarato in *The Making of the Indebted Man*, in which he shows how Marx and Nietzsche, but also Deleuze and Guattari, explicitly connect the debt economy with morality, that is, with a particular form of subordinating subjectivation.[40]

In Christian genealogy, becoming indebted cannot be separated from burdening oneself with guilt. Moral guilt arises, according to Nietzsche, by way of the promise of repayment to the creditor.[41] The indebted person promises to behave in such a way that they are capable of giving back what has been given to them: they promise that they will pay back their guilt/debt. In the debt economy, the credit contract constitutes subjectivation. The obligation to give back what is owed corresponds with a disciplining self-governing that assures not only a subjectivating and social productivity, but also obedience. Placing behaviour at the service of repayment of debt means owing one's life and sociality and making oneself even more strongly (self-)governable. According to Lazzarato, in current politico-economic conditions, precarization leads to indebtedness, but it also actualizes paradigmatic social guilt/debt.[42] The social debt relation thus precedes precarization in employment relations. It means entering into an arrangement of domination as the loan contract guarantees the asymmetrical relationship between debtor and creditor, rather than arranging economic exchange relations between equal partners. For Nietzsche, the prerequisite for this debt relation is not dependency or bondage, but emancipation, freedom, autonomy, and responsibility. A person who is capable of making a promise must be a free 'sovereign individual', in order to have the 'extraordinary privilege of *responsibility*' and assert it for themselves. With that, 'this man who is now free, who actually *has* the *prerogative* to promise, this master of the *free* will, this sovereign', becomes an equal among equals.[43] This is the initial requirement for being able to conclude a contract in the first place. A loan or employment contract requires sovereign, autonomous individuals as legal persons. They have to be independent and autonomous, possess power over themselves, and thus the capacity for not only (self-)responsibility but also self-discipline.

For the production of the indebted subject, according to Nietzsche, a conscience is also necessary, an awareness of guilt. The indebted subject is furnished with a bad conscience that has no end.[44] 'The debt economy combines "work on the self" and labor, in its classical sense, such that ethics and economy function conjointly',[45] writes Lazzarato. This indebted self works endlessly on itself, in order to enter responsibly into a loan contract, in which it commits to a repayment of the debt obligation. Nietzsche speaks of a 'feeling of guilt, the personal obligation', that renders the relationship between debtor and creditor 'the oldest and most primitive personal relationship there is'.[46] He shows the (male) autonomous and sovereign subject to be one that is constituted by a bad conscience, because it imagines social relations and thereby care primarily as relations of guilt from which it must free itself. Precariousness shared with others must be devalued and feminized, which also implies – as we will see – aspects of the superiority construction of the 'white race'. The logic of the guilt/debt economy seems to be entangled in hegemonic Western white masculinity. In this logic, sociality always corresponds to a type of bondage, which nonetheless presupposes the autonomy and responsibility of the sovereign (male) individual, capable of concluding employment and loan contracts in capitalism. The social bond can then only be understood in terms of the moral guilt and bad conscience of male individuals who want to be autonomous and sovereign. Relations of care become solely guilt/debt obligations that burden the conscience. The guilt/debt of care leads to a devaluation of social ties and surrounds.

For this reason, too, the social relationship between debtor and creditor is an utterly asymmetrical one that forces the debtor's compliant behaviour in repaying their debt, not least in order to uphold the governmental linearity of time. For an understanding of the neoliberal governmental intertwining of time, precarization, and debt, it is necessary to comprehend that precarization means dealing with the unforeseeable, acting in the present without being able to predict what the near or the distant future will bring. The loan contract exploits precisely this condition, and, at the same time, prevents the creditor from being able to start something new, or even simply reject working under the existing conditions. The promise of the repayment of debt must continue, even when it demands something clearly paradoxical from the indebted person: in their precarization, they must estimate something that cannot be estimated, namely the future. 'To view the future as the present and anticipate it'[47] means not only controlling the future in the present, but also making the precarious predictable in the unpredictability of their lives through self-government and keeping them under control – this, however, is primarily for the purposes of the creditor. In the financial and debt economy, credit guarantees the linearity of the time of the victors.[48]

In neoliberal *self*-precarization,[49] this paradox of estimating something that cannot be estimated is nonetheless reversed. The temporality of the credit relation is turned around illusorily: through investments in what is allegedly one's 'own' future, the personality that is indebted in a dual sense consciously accepts precarization in the present. A loan is taken out with a view toward a fantasized better and more secure future. Self-precarization has become a widespread investment – mainly among the European middle classes – under the illusion that precarization in the present is only a passage to a better time to come. This type of affirmation of the linearity of time optimally upholds the loan relationship; breaking with the logic of credit is thus not possible. In this projection of the future, what is given up is the option of beginning something new in the present. This supposedly strategic self-precarization is in no way freely chosen, but is a servile form of self-government within the paradigm of the neoliberal loan economy.

In the relationship between borrower and lender, it becomes clear that the credit does not exploit labour, but social relations and ways of life.[50] In order to start anything at all, what is needed is not the force of labour but the power that emerges from sociality, care, precariousness, the reproductive and mutual dependencies, from trust in oneself and in others and thereby in the world. And it is precisely this trust, this ethical relationship, that is exploited by the credit. The logic of that economy is based on mistrust: 'Trust,' writes Lazzarato, 'the condition for action, becomes universal distrust, turning into a demand for "security".'[51]

Precarization and indebtedness are also woven together by the scarcity of time. The financial economy produces two central conditions: having no time and having no place in the present. Self-control and self-discipline, which make time seem scarce in the present and turn the future into something that can be anticipated, ensure the good behaviour of the borrower, their continuing to repay the loan – as though it were possible to be or to become entirely free of debt, as though a freedom from dependency were possible, and the autonomy and sovereignty of the masculinist, white, bourgeois idea of the subject beyond debt could be attained.

Given the scarcity of time, the present is rushed through, with an ever greater desire for a better future and, simultaneously, an increased fear that it may never arrive. This makes those who are governed more and more receptive to authoritarian political forms that promise security and control and offer a simple orientation. *Angst-Lust*, the pleasure of anxiety about the approaching catastrophe, grows. At the same time, in a present that is increasingly obsessed with the future, precarization as unpredictability is difficult to analyse, and the reflex of wanting to soon be rid of the insecurity becomes stronger and stronger.

What this normalization of precarization breaks are not only the post-war promises, but all 'Western' promises of progress: that – in spite of all the crises – things will always get better, that history progresses in a linear and continuous way. This broken promise for the future is supposedly restored through the linear temporal logic of credit and investment, but what they maintain is no more than a financialized future. Holding fast to the linearity of time, this future of credit means that workers and non-workers are needed only as financialized debtors in an endless capitalistic debt bondage, which cynically goes hand in hand with ever lower wages, as a profit can still be made from non-repayable debts and the debtors' bad loans.

However, what is the significance of this figure of a self-responsible individual legally competent to enter into a contract when borrowers not only will no longer pay back their debts, and will thus accumulate bad debt, but also are not even obliged to pay back their debts in full, since the creditors are able to secure their superior position precisely by upholding the debts? When they do not comply with their repayment obligations, borrowers are considered irresponsible. They have only a limited capacity to make the step toward becoming autonomous (white) subjects. They cannot become an equal among equals, or equal members of a debt community. This infantilizing and discriminatory asymmetry, rather than being a consequence of the economic-moral credit and debt contract, is already inscribed within it.

Denise Ferreira da Silva has analysed the historical forms of indebtedness that arose in the entanglement of capitalism and racism. The linear understanding of time, of progress and development, 'accounts for the obscuration of how the colonial participates in the creation of capital'.[52] The modern concept of freedom – as autonomy, self-responsibility, and sovereignty – was indeed part of the discourses on the abolition of slavery and the independence of the colonies, but there was no thematization of its racist implications. However, these implications alone can clarify the phenomenon of the 'unpayable debt'. According to Ferreira da Silva, racializing differentiation is not to be understood morally, socially, culturally, or biologically, but rather economically, as 'primitive accumulation', which, according to

Rosa Luxemburg, has no single origin but is continually re-incited.[53] As in the US subprime crisis, it is carried out through the shifting of debt/guilt in correspondence with the logic of white masculinist superiority.[54]

The borrowers in the subprime crisis lived mainly on low incomes and had taken out second-class (subprime) mortgages that they could hardly pay back to begin with. But for the creditors, these loans were nonetheless profitable because of their higher interest rates and extra fees.[55] In the 1990s, after a decades-long struggle for equality in relation to the right to own a home, the financial markets allowed many first-time buyers to obtain credit, estimating that, with the use of financial instruments such as derivates, there would be a continued growth in the profitability of the urban housing market.[56] With the reduction of social welfare services and public expenditures – in the interests of both the state and private capital – the home ownership that was now possible for low-wage workers and minorities was declared 'welfare for the masses'.[57] Now also non-whites and women – independent of the traditional white male family breadwinners who as a rule were considered first-class debtors – could be enticed with the prospect of propertied middle-class status and integrated into the financial market. Only they did not thereby become equal debtors, being considered from the outset as risky borrowers. Fifty years after having finally been allowed to acquire property in their own name, women, by virtue of their gender, were still viewed as not being worthy of loans granted on the best possible terms.[58]

Conditions of domination and exploitation that reach further into the past, however, are also extended into the present of bad debt through subprime loans that are difficult to repay.[59] Dispossession by slavery, and the prevention of ownership of property and other assets by 'freed people', remain at the root of the asymmetrical economic relations of debt in the present. A repetitive white moral discourse inculpates non-white borrowers as being responsible for their own plight and therefore 'not credit worthy', which was what caused them to (again) take on unpayable debts and live beyond the means allotted to them.[60] This unpayable guilt/debt is ascribed to debtors through sexist-racist constructions of subordination and lack, thus rendering invisible the entanglement of capitalism and racism in slavery and colonialism. In this discourse, the racially marked body is not allowed to fully cultivate the subjectivation that a loan contract demands. Endless indebtedness corresponds to the status of being not-yet-white; in the white ideology of superiority, work on the 'black' self always falls short of the white norm.[61] And this was precisely what allowed financial profit to be made from subprime loans.

Already with the end of slavery in the US in 1865, freedom and recognition as a self-responsible subject capable of entering into contracts was not an instant right, but something that freed people had to prove themselves worthy of. Corresponding to the Latin meaning of the word *emancipatio*, emancipation literally meant being discharged from the hand (*manus*) of the *pater familias*, the slave-holder, to be set free by him. In this logic, distinct from the logic of white self-liberation as a sovereign act, former slaves became freed people, but not free people.[62]

Even after 300 years of enslavement, whites still feared that black workers, supposedly characterized by sluggishness and laziness, would not comply with a capitalist production system based on free labour and possessive individualism. In *Scenes of Subjection*, Saidiya Hartman has shown how, by means of advice books first and foremost, freed slaves were to be trained and disciplined as free workers.[63] In order to counter the refusal to become a working subject capable of signing contracts, white discourse promoted a 'willingness to endure hardships, which alone guaranteed success, upward mobility and the privileges of citizenship'.[64] In fact, coercion and violence were the more usual means of compelling freed people to sign labour contracts and subject themselves to labour discipline, means that went far beyond those used in capitalist labour relations otherwise, and that were predicated on inequalities created by racist conditions of domination. The subordination demanded of the former enslaved workers marked the continuities between slavery and freedom. As emancipated persons made competent to sign contracts, of necessity they had to behave in accordance with liberal individualism as both dutiful subordinates and rational, self-responsible individuals.[65] Particular to the racist ambivalence of subordination and freedom,

however, was its basis in the construction of the guilt and debt of
emancipation, which meant that there was no prospect of freed
people ever achieving the ideal autonomy of white heterosexual masculinity. The freedom granted by the whites was seen as a gift from
the 'benefactors' to the enslaved, for which they needed to demon-
strate gratitude and worthiness, and which put them in debt to the
whites, making them guilty and increasing the compulsion to discipline. 'The burden of debt, duty and gratitude [was] foisted onto
the newly emancipated in exchange or repayment for their freedom.'[66] In the entanglement of autonomy and (self-)responsibility,
the white 'investment of faith' was viewed as moral debt to be paid
back, as an investment which the involuntary 'borrowers' had to
prove themselves worthy of through sustained repayment. 'To be
free was to be a debtor – that is, obliged and duty-bound to others.'[67]
This racist guilt/loan relationship is upheld by the linking of guilt/
debt and time. The freed were bound to the past by means of an
indebtedness for their freedom, because as free(d) autonomous
individuals they were now made responsible for the deeds attributed
to them, including ones from the past. Should they fail, the conces-
sions could be revoked. This temporality of guilt/debt is a linear time
that assures compliant behaviour. It binds the present to the past and
grafts a present full of deprivation onto the promise of becoming a
worthy and respected citizen some day in the future.[68] According to
this cynical logic, the 'freed people's' guilt/debt for emancipation
continues to bind them even today, in an inverted responsibility to
the past: the lasting individualized guilt/debt enables the construction of a white national innocence and widespread amnesia with
regard to slavery.[69] This racist bad-loan logic supports the construction of white superiority, for which repayment of the loan can never
end. For the whites, it is a necessarily non-returnable debt. The white
guilt/debt discourse demands of its others a double subjection:
self-discipline as a free(d) subject and the affirmation of eternal
guilt in relation to white superiority, driven by the promise of and
desire for future independence, for a freedom which releases one
from social connections. For this reason, too, credit is asocial and
uninterested in care.

An understanding of time that is not white in this sense, and not linear, and which is based on practices of care, attends to the 'existence of one's ancestors',[70] as Ferreira da Silva writes in reference to Benjamin. It knows of an underground fabric of relations, which, as a mode of living in space and time, is not morally but ethically obligated to past generations, to those who were silenced. It corresponds to an infinitive discontinuous understanding of now-time, to letting oneself be claimed by the ruled of past eras and tracking down the sparks of their militant energy.[71] In the transversal constellations of now-time, revolutionary practices can be actualized and white masculinist debt economies sustainably broken open. Care for the dispossessed evades the desire of wanting to become white. It searches for the impure, unfinished, in-sovereign, and precarious, and brings to an end what in the logic of white dominance can never end: the linearity of time in the service of an endless repayment for the credit of emancipation.

To oppose neoliberal capital's exploitation and increasing subservience and incorporation of the ability to relate into an exchange and debt logic, as well as the debt economy's ever more comprehensive access to social activities by means of measurement and evaluation, an extensive break with the capitalist management of time is required.[72] A time of rupture is needed, a time in which general access of capital can be stalled, a time that suspends the temporality of credit and exploitation. This break in time necessarily involves more than a subjective refusal of work or credit: it is another way to live time, one in which commonly produced social wealth is recaptured. However, to turn money back into available time, to transform welfare to possibilities, what are required are not only struggles but also new processes of subjectivation and new epistemologies.[73] With the normalization of precarization, and the ongoing crisis of the debt economy, it becomes apparent that there is no future in the sense of progress and growth. At the same time, this opens up a new present in which people can begin to care about how they want to live *now*.[74] This requires abandoning fantasies of the future rooted in capitalist understandings of time, and instead fostering a different understanding of the present, a queer-feminist reading of the debt-based paradigm of the social. It means conceiving of a debt without number or repayment, an infinite social debt emanating from a shared precariousness beyond morality and thereby conceived on the basis of mutual relatedness, dependencies, reproduction, and care.

When sociality is understood not as a relationship of guilt in Nietzsche's sense, but from a black and queer-feminist perspective as mutual dependency, in terms of endlessly indebted relations of care, then debts and time can be conceived differently. Shared precariousness in mutual dependency can be *preserved*, but never as an anthropological constant, as the restoration of an original vulnerability, or as the conservation of an ontological given. Retaining precariousness requires its preservation and actualization in the expanded present infinitive.

In their book *The Undercommons*, Stefano Harney and Fred Moten propose an alternative social understanding of bad, unpayable debt. The condition for this understanding is the separation of debt and credit. These unpayable debts, which in a social sense are bad, black, queer debts, are not tied to credit; they break with both credit and the debt economy. 'Credit is a means of privatization and debt a means of socialisation.'[75] As long as debts are locked up in a house, a home, a state, or a community, debt serves only credit, which needs it to keep running efficiently. 'But debt is social and credit is asocial. Debt is mutual. Credit runs only one way. But debt runs in every direction, scatters, escapes, seeks refuge.'[76] These bad debts are endlessly distributed and dispersed debts. They are debts that for social reasons – for reasons of being with each other, rather than for economic or moral reasons – cannot be repaid. They are without obligations, without demands, and fail to balance the balance sheets.[77] They are debts without a creditor – 'the black debt, the queer debt, the criminal debt'[78] – because they escape identity and do not refer back to a self. They lack autonomy but are full of affections. Practising bad debt corresponds with the ability to allow oneself to be affected by others, other people and other things; to be open, vulnerable, precarious: becoming-precarious as the ability to be affected. Only the bad debts preserve precariousness. Precarization and precarity, in contrast, serve credit and lead away from the social debts of care.

Bad care debts are debts arising from ties and mutual dependencies that refuse to pass as autonomous individual and yield to its isolating bonds of time and identity. Black, queer care debts burst open the white masculinist economy of credit and the identity of creditors. These debts move in the expansion of differences and multiplicities as each and every single person owes something different.[79] Taking queer social debts as the starting point leads to the fullness of social wealth, to excess in the now, not to a scarcity and lack that demands an accumulation of credit and doing things better in the future. Queer, black debtors seek mutual refuge, but not in the private, and not in a public realm differentiated from it. In the transversal fabrics of relations – the undercommons – which proliferate through time and space, a refuge is a site where precariousness is preserved, where the social, no longer separated from the political, creates 'fugitive publics'[80] that do not assign anyone a place, but allow the places to be occupied without categorizing them. Without borders or the debt of gratitude, the hospitality of radical inclusion lets debts proliferate. Seeking and granting refuge, moves, hides, and allows to begin anew. Becoming-precarious in the present, without a credit on the future, is not an individual undertaking. It is always a becoming-precarious together with others.

The common struggles in now-time are indebted; they have 'debt at a distance',[81] as Harney and Moten put it. They are debts that are tracked down via tigers' leaps. Debts at a distance are ties to revolutionary practices in the past in which the actual can be sensed. Such debts can be forgotten, remembered again, and actualized through leaps, but they cannot be forgiven or waived, as there are no grounds for that. They show themselves in the recurring, discontinuous ties between struggles, such as in the militance of post-operaism, which, as Harney and Moten point out, remembered the indebted ties to the black civil rights movement's radical tradition. Debts at a distance are ties that take care through space and time, spreading in revolutionary struggles of immanence, in practices of flight, exodus, and refusal, which do not flee to an outside as if there were an outside beyond bad social debts of care. 'The black radical tradition is the movement that works through this debt. The black radical tradition is debt work.'[82] Close by and at a distance.

The black radical tradition is also remembered in the queer-feminist care practices of Precarias a la Deriva. In the early 2000s they invented a practice of militance in which they tied/indebted themselves, at a distance, to practices of the Black Women's Club Movement.[83] After the Civil War and the abolition of slavery in the US, this grassroots movement emerged from the collaborative efforts of black women who supported women who had been freed from slavery, and developed practices of empowerment together with them.[84] It was these minor care practices, as well as also those of the civil rights movement of the 1950s and '60s, that the consciousness-raising groups of the radical US women's movement in the late 1960s and '70s tied/indebted themselves to, close by and at a distance.[85] Precarias a la Deriva also remember these fragmented, transversal practices of consciousness-raising in their militant research on neo-liberal precarization, care, and strike practices.

The militance of the Precarias begins precisely where the allegedly apolitical multitude finds its specific means of organizing in dispersal – contrary to the traditional perspective of organization that assesses the heterogeneous precarious as being hardly capable of organizing. In fact, it is necessary to collect the isolated heterogeneous knowledge of resistant practices. It is this gathering of practices opposing the impositions of precarized working and living conditions that enables a common constituting of the precarious.

Precarias a la Deriva – the name itself denotes a practice, a movement, which emerges from the dispersal of precarization: precarious women adrift through the city.[86] Dissatisfied with political action that avoided the issue of an increasingly fragmented everyday life, in the 2000s they embarked upon a path, indebted to the Zapatista movements of the 1990s, literally questioning while walking. Without starting from commonalities, from collective identities in precarity, militant research emerged when roaming through the city, visiting different precarious workplaces of the participants, and posing questions such as 'What is your precarity?' or 'What is your strike?' In the movement and on the way, in the practice that is both research and militance, knowledge accumulated of micropolitical refusals to maintain current governmentality.[87] As an exploration of the 'subterranean and frequently invisible thread(s) of unease and of day-to-day rebellions',[88] the queer-feminist practice of the Precarias begins from everyday life, from situatedness, from the fact that the personal is political and as something particular cannot be enclosed in the private. This militant research is empowering care practice as a 'critical weapon'[89] which, in the simultaneity of movement, knowledge production, and organization, refuses the phasal chrono-political logic according to which the movement comes first then the organization, but also refuses methods that could be replicated, or that could be used without situatedness and without indebted ties.[90]

How can presentist struggles, which are entangled in debts to black and queer-feminist care practices, entangled in practices of empowerment against racist and patriarchal classifications in global neoliberalism, develop in opposition to devalued care and precarization?

In several compositions and alliances, the Precarias have developed interrelated analyses, strategies, and practices. These are complex analyses beyond, and often preceding, those of the academic field, analyses that condense into the proposal for a new social formation based on care, and that lead to entirely new forms of strike. These are strategies and practices begun locally and micropolitically with the millennium, spread for years to come, again and again, and culminated most recently, at the end of the 2010s, in a major feminist strike wave across cities, countries, and oceans.

In 2002, migrant domestic workers, sex workers, lawyers, and others conducted militant research analysing the contexts of transnational care work and movements of migration.[91] Clearly emerging from the confluence of queer-feminist analyses of care was the masculinist-patriarchal paradigm of the self-care of free workers and citizens that has dominated market and profit logic since the start of capitalism, and which still positions those who carry out care work as dependants in the private realm and in the area of reproduction. In liberal individualism, emancipation is conceived in terms of an independence from care relations, and is tied to the civilizational idea of progress and growth, which tries to detach itself from care just as it tries to detach itself from the environment.[92]

But care is transversal. It traverses various times and spaces, and is not limited to either the household or women. Care is organized historically primarily through women's networks that traverse countries and borders and goes far beyond.[93] It is mutual and, although it is made invisible, it is a proliferous fabric of relations and dependencies. Care practices are everywhere, and envelop everything. Care is surround and environment. Not being tied to socially assigned positions, it is the binding element in shared precariousness.

How can something so transversal, so borderless, so surrounding as relations of care not be the basis of democracy? What might a social bond look like in which caring and the need for care are no longer devalued, privatized, and hierarchized through the cutting of rights? For this, a fundamental break with the dominant liberal understanding of the social bond is necessary, a break with that bond in which some are protected and others are denied protection. The proposal of Precarias a la Deriva for a social formation based on care is not only a break, but at the same time a breach. The Spanish neologism *cuidadanía* captures the multiplicity of relations of care. *Cuidadanía* does not mean a type of social or political community, as a community cannot be conceived beyond belongings.[94] *Cuidadanía* joins citizenship (*ciudadanía*) and care (*cuidado*) to create a concept of a new form of coexistence in which mutual dependency is not devalued or shifted into the private. In the midst of the neoliberal 'crisis of care' and its inseparable 'precarization of existence', Precarias's political and social strategy is to sustainably break through the masculinist logic of security and insecurity. Caring as well as the need for care are valued and become the starting point for politico-economic contemplations.[95] Regardless of how extensive the use of capitalized and technologized self-care is, a human body needs a roof over its head, nutrition, sexuality, and work and education opportunities, as well as support when ill. Not only at the start of life, but throughout an entire lifetime, and particularly in old age, human bodies remain in need of care, and are dependent on the care given by others, usually precarious others, who are increasingly migrants.[96] Care is no longer a

one-dimensional and individualized relationship between dependants and independents, and emancipation is no longer freedom from
precariousness. But first and foremost, this understanding of care is
free of moral components.[97] Care is no longer dependent on private,
contingent, gratitude-owing behaviour toward others. What is necessary is a general 'right to take care, and to be cared for',[98] which at the
same time includes not being obliged to do care work by virtue of
one's social position. The *cuidadanía* is based on this right, in which
individuals are not understood as separate from one another, but
rather as manifold, mutually affected singularities. It is a right that
recognizes the precariousness shared with others and breaks through
the autonomy of the political.

In general, care rights in the *cuidadanía* can be determined in a
way that withdraws the foundation of the ideal male-bourgeois
subject of a nation state, a subject that stabilizes its superior position
by outsourcing its own precariousness and shifting it as a deficit onto
the precarity of the depreciated, subordinate 'others' who are excluded
as threatening and made invisible. The (neo-)liberal governmental
interplay of control, regulation, and government, which grants civil
rights according to the logic of the need for workers and their 'suit-
ability as consumers',[99] is broken open when the *cuidadanía* is
conceived beyond (nation-)state border regimes.[100]

A potential practice of *cuidadanía* is the strike as care strike.[101]
Traditionally, the strike is understood as a suspension of work, in order
to fight for better working conditions and strengthen the labour unions
and the working class generally. With a care strike, on the contrary, the
idea is not to suspend care, but to make visible at many sites, in many
relationships, and on days such as 8 March, together with many others,
the extensive dependence on care; to give care in abundance, while
inventing new relations of care and experimenting with them.

> The strike is always interruption and visibilization and care is the
> continuous and invisible line whose interruption would be devas-
> tating. But all that is lacking is a change of perspective to see that
> there is no paradox: the care strike would be nothing other than
> the interruption of the order that is ineluctably produced in the

moment in which we place the truth of care in the center and politicize it.[102]

On 8 March 2018, the care strike became visible in demonstrations throughout Spain, in which 6 million people, nearly 13 per cent of the Spanish population, participated. The mobilization and organization took place over many months, in countless local consciousness-raising contexts, as well as in regional assemblies. Alliances among feminist movements in Latin America, Italy, Poland, Turkey, and the US organize against femicide, against gendered and racialized conditions of ownership, against exploitation and extractivism, and against the impositions of neoliberal conditions, joining together in everyday life and on the streets.[103] In Spain, the strengthening of the feminist movement means a further cycle, a new phase in the constituent process for a new form of democracy.

The care strike is a situated and international political strategy to make precariousness, the dependence of every living being on care and reproduction, the starting point of struggles in now-time.[104] This does not occur simply by making the need for care visible and exhibiting the vulnerability and mortality of bodies. Placing relations of care at the centre means, rather, creating manifold forms of empowerment through mutual social ties/indebtedness, through queer, black, bad debts. The abundance of care is brought out of the homes onto the streets, over the borders, and into the assemblies to become the starting point for any change in the world that reduces precarization and precarity and preserves precariousness in a becoming-precarious – in non-linear interrelatedness, in transversal constellations, and in the movements of a new form of democracy.

Presentist democracy is a democracy of care and indebtedness. Its irregular contours are shaped by the six components of the present infinitive.[105]

(1) Presentist democracy does not have to be postponed to the future. Its present is not a point on a timeline; it expands in a grammar of the present tense and exposes itself to what is to come as refuge. It is

grounded in care, connections, affections. It is supported by the multi-plicities of singularities, which prevent the *demos* from becoming a national *Volk* as they are always already interrelated beyond the borders of space and time. This mutual dependency in presentist democracy is what facilitates not having to become a subject in the logic of liberal representative democracy and be bound to an identity. The present infinitive's situatedness in care enables de-subjectivation, not as a denial of the rights of subjects, but in order to discover new ways of subjectivation that emerge from the affections of surrounding bodies and things.[106]

(2) Presentist democracy receives its durations from the multiplicity of the multitude, from the multiplicity of times and spaces, from their dis/continuities and new beginnings. It is becoming, a constant becoming-democratic in the now-time of constituent processes. The affecting relations of power also multiply themselves in the countless folds of duration. There is no outside of power, only immanence, because there is no outside of time and no outside of care and debts. In the present infinitive, time is never beyond power, and vice versa. The plurality of the present (tense) allows the transversal return and concatenation of struggles and events, the simultaneity of many environments. The duration of presentist democracy itself is therefore multiply ecological, because it unfolds in becoming and supplies all being with change, acting, and experimenting.

(3) Presentist democracy emerges from the measureless difference that cannot be tamed in representation. It is shaped by radical inclusion and the affirmation of dispersion, without uniting it in an organization. Presentist democracy is the indefinite form that emerges from the constituent power of the multitude. To be heard, it does not demand any representation of its interests. Different experiences at different sites do not have to be homogenized in order to be tied to each other. Presentist democracy draws its force from the dynamics of open, heterogeneous assemblages.

(4) Presentist democracy is indebted to a swarm of events that cannot be represented by one single event. Events emerge in the intensity of

affections that in their contagion do not require any mediation. The swarm of events expands through infections of revolutionary practices, such as that of the recurring, multiplying feminist strikes. Their repetition in time and space is transversal return. Starting from the affecting relations of power, leaps and dances of resistance, transversal constellations, and indebtedness at a distance repeat and differentiate. Every phase of organizing and instituting becomes indebted elsewhere, to other practices, other struggles, in other times and spaces.

(5) Presentist democracy emerges from relations of debt and care. It is deeply indebted, beyond shame and morals. Accordingly, it is aware of the power of memory for shaping the discontinuous, constantly differentiating now-time and for the forgetting, that cares that nothing is lost. Without believing in reconstruction and recovery, in their transversal return, presentist democratic practices enable the preservation of debts from precariousness and relations of care. They are creative acts of actualization and differentiation in now-time. Presentist democracy itself is composed of transversal constellations of space and time. It is aware of the defeated, the ruled, in the linear time of the victors. In revolutionary tigers' leaps, it breaks with patriarchal, racist, and capitalist conditions of domination and exploitation.

(6) Presentist democracy does not divide the movement from instituting and organizing, the social from the political. Its goal is not to make the many converge into a one but to organize the multiplicity in dispersal. Without identitarian references, presentist democracy always supports situated forms of transnationalization. Its instituting practices are local and transnational all at once, recomposition of sociality and space, constellation of various times. In this way, organization takes place in the leaps from past and present, in the polyphony of long-silenced voices and the voices of today. This is how democracy in the present tense emerges.

Notes

Democracy in the Present Tense: An Introduction

1. Stuart Hall, 'Popular-Democratic vs Authoritarian Populism', in *Marxism and Democracy*, ed. Alan Hunt, London: Lawrence & Wishart, 1980, 157–80. For an actualization, see also Alex Demirović, 'Autoritärer Populismus als neoliberale Krisenbewältigungsstrategie', *PROKLA: Zeitschrift für kritische Sozialwissenschaft* 190 (2018), 27–42.

2. Stuart Hall, 'Authoritarian Populism: A Reply to Jessop et al.', *New Left Review* 1:151 (1985), 115–24, here 116.

3. See Birgit Sauer, 'Authoritarian Right-Wing Populism as Masculinist Identity Politics: The Role of Affects', in *Right-Wing Populism and Gender: European Perspectives and Beyond*, ed. Gabriele Dietze and Julia Roth, Bielefeld: transcript, 2020, 25–44. Authoritarian populism, like liberalism, is, according to Sauer, genuinely gendered.

4. 'Anti-Genderism' is one instance of a 'moral panic'. See, among others, Agnieszka Graff, Ratna Kapur, and Suzanna Danuta Walters, 'Introduction: Gender and the Rise of the Global Right', *Signs: Journal of Women in Culture and Society* 44:3 (2019), 541–60, here 551.

5. See Gabriele Dietze, *Sexueller Exzeptionalismus: Überlegenheitsnarrative in Migrationsabwehr und Rechtspopulismus*, Bielefeld: transcript, 2019, 115–40; and Elzbieta Korolczuk and Agnieszka Graff, 'Gender as "Ebola from Brussels": The Anticolonial Frame and the Rise of Illiberal Populism', *Signs: Journal of Women in Culture and Society* 43:4 (2018), 797–821.

6. Sara R. Ferris, *In the Name of Women's Rights: The Rise of Femonationalism*, Durham, NC: Duke University Press, 2017.

7. See Sabine Hark and Paula-Irene Villa, *The Future of Difference: Beyond the Toxic Entanglement of Racism, Sexism and Feminism*, London: Verso, 2020. On the colonial dimensions of patriarchal gender relations, see Rita Laura Segato, 'A Manifesto in Four Themes', *Critical Times* 1:1 (2018), 198–211.

8. See Raewyn Connell and James W. Messerschmidt, 'Hegemonic Masculinity: Re-thinking the Concept', *Gender & Society* 19:6 (2005), 829–59.

9. Gabriele Dietze writes in the context of the concomitant superiority discourse of 'sexual exceptionalism-based rejection of migration' (Dietze, *Sexueller Exzeptionalismus*, 31).

10. See Sauer, 'Authoritarian Right-Wing Populism'.

11. See Michel Foucault, *Society Must Be Defended: Lectures at the Collège de France 1975–1976*, New York: Picador, 2003.

12. Jan-Werner Müller, *What Is Populism?*, Philadelphia: University of Pennsylvania Press, 2016, 23 and 41; Chantal Mouffe, *The Democratic Paradox*, London: Verso, 2000, Chapter 4.

13. See Graff et al., 'Introduction', 550, with special focus on Poland, India, and the US. See also Joan W. Scott, 'The Uses and Abuses of Gender', *Tijdschrift voor Genderstudies* 16:1 (2013), 63–77.

14. Already in 2001, Pope John Paul II spoke of 'specific ideologies of "gender"'. See Elizabeth S. Corredor, 'Unpacking "Gender Ideology" and the Global Right's Anti-Gender Countermovement', *Signs: Journal of Women in Culture and Society* 44:3 (2019), 613–38, here 615; see also Mary Anne Case, 'Trans Formations in the Vatican's War on "Gender Ideology"', ibid., 639–64). Pope Francis spoke firmly on 'Gender Ideology' in his Encyclical Letter, *Laudato Si' – On Care for Our Common Home*, 24 May 2015, para. 155. In his speech before Polish bishops on World Youth Day in Krakow in 2016, he called for the rescue of humanity from gender ideology. In March 2019, the Vatican's UN representative, Filipino archbishop Bernardito Auza, further emphasized the 'danger' of 'gender ideology' in his talk in New York, describing it as a 'threat for the future', primarily that of the children, and as a 'step back for humanity'. See Salvatore Cernuzio, 'The Holy See against Gender Ideology: A Danger to Humanity. Sex is Not a Subjective Choice', *La Stampa*, 22

March 2019. This campaign was taken up by many right-wing politicians with and without connections to the Catholic Church.

15. On femicides in a European comparison in 2017, see europeandatajour nalism.eu. Deadly violence against trans*women does not appear in any police statistics. All of these femicides are political murders and not crimes in the private sphere.

16. See Klaus Dörre, 'Die national-soziale Gefahr: Pegida, Neue Rechte und der Verteilungskonflikt – sechs Thesen', in *PEGIDA – Rechtspopulismus zwischen Fremdenangst und 'Wende'-Enttäuschung?*, ed. Karl-Siegbert Rehberg et al., Bielefeld: transcript, 2016, 259–74; Thomas Piketty, *Capital in the Twenty-First Century*, Cambridge, MA: Harvard University Press, 2017; Didier Eribon, *Returning to Reims*, Los Angeles: Semiotext(e), 2013.

17. Pierre Bourdieu, 'Job Insecurity Is Everywhere Now', in *Acts of Resistance: Against the New Myths of Our Time*, Cambridge: Polity Press, 1999, 81–7. The first transnational movement of the precarious opposing these political-economic transformations arose already at the start of the 2000s with the EuroMayDay movement. See Gerald Raunig, *A Thousand Machines: A Concise Philosophy of the Machine as Social Movement*, Los Angeles: Semiotext(e), 2010.

18. See Isabell Lorey, *State of Insecurity: Government of the Precarious*, London: Verso, 2015.

19. See Andrea Maihofer, 'Pluralisierung familialer Lebensformen: Zerfall der Gesellschaft oder neoliberal passgerecht?', in *Kapitalismuskritische Gesellschaftsanalyse: Queer-feministische Positionen*, ed. Katharina Pühl and Birgit Sauer, Münster: Westfälisches Dampfboot, 2018, 113–38; Gundula Ludwig, 'Desiring Neoliberalism', *Sexuality Research and Social Policy* 13 (2016), 417–27; see also Isabell Lorey, Gundula Ludwig, and Ruth Sonderegger, *Foucaults Gegenwart: Sexualität – Sorge – Revolution*, Vienna: transversal texts, 2016.

20. See Demirović, 'Autoritärer Populismus', 30–4.

21. See The Invisible Committee, *Now*, Los Angeles: Semiotext(e), 2017, 8.

22. Ibid., 9.

23. See also Segato, 'A Manifesto in Four Themes'.

24. The first protests by the Argentinian movement NiUnaMenos took place in March 2015 in Buenos Aires. See, among others, Verónica Gago et al., 'How Would You Go to Strike? The Women's Strike and Beyond', special

issue, *South Atlantic Quarterly* 117:3 (2018), as well as *Critical Times* 1:1 (2018). See also Isabell Lorey, '8M – The Great Feminist Strike', *transversal*, March 2019.

25. In Italy, the increasingly strong movement spread under the slogan 'Non Una di Meno', and is active everywhere where the rights of women are restricted. See Non Una di Meno, *Abbiamo un Piano: Piano femminista contro la violenza maschile sulle donne e la violenza de genere*, 2017, nonunadimeno.files.wordpress.com.

26. See Linda Martín Alcoff et al., 'Women of America: We're Going on Strike. Join Us so Trump Will See Our Power', *Guardian*, 6 February 2017. See also Cinzia Arruzza, Tithi Bhattacharya, and Nancy Fraser, *Feminism for the 99%: A Manifesto*, London: Verso, 2019.

27. One book inspiring this is Silvia Federici, *Caliban and the Witch: Women, the Body and Primitive Accumulation*, New York: Autonomedia, 2004. The discontinuous timelines of this resistance update Rosa Luxemburg's strike theory from the early twentieth century, in which the mass strike is presented as a revolutionary force that changes its direction and movement, but never stops, instead always beginning again and starting afresh. See Rosa Luxemburg, *The Mass Strike, the Political Party and the Trade Unions*, Detroit, MI: Marxist Educational Society of Detroit, 1925, 32. There are also numerous references, primarily in Latin America and Spain, to Madrid's activist-theoretical collective Precarias a la Deriva, which in 2002–3 called for an anti-capitalist care strike – a new form of political strike referring 'to all practices that unravel the politically radical character of care . . . that place the sustainability of shared life at the centre, and challenge capitalist accumulation logic at its very core'. See Precarias a la Deriva, 'Precarización de la existencia y huelga de cuidados', in *Estudios sobre génerro y economía*, ed. María Jesús Vara, Madrid: Akal, 2006, 104–34, here 127; and Precarias a la Deriva, *Was ist dein Streik?*, Vienna: transversal texts, 2014, 109.

28. References to past strikes include, for example, the women's strike in Iceland in 1975, when 90 per cent of women stopped working for twenty-four hours in the struggle for equal pay. Twenty-five years later, in 2000, the first international campaign for a worldwide women's strike appeared, in which all care work would be halted to demand pay for household labour, and for money to be spent on care rather than the

military. In Germany, appreciation of the 1994 women's strike offers another reference. See Gisela Notz, 'Wir wollen Brot und Rosen', *Ada Magazin*, 23 September 2018.

  On the critique of the liberal emancipation concept, see Isabell Lorey, 'Emancipation and Debt', presentation at the Emancipation Conference, Technical University, Berlin, 27 May 2018.

29. InfoSex, 'If Women Are Becoming a Multitude All Around the World', *Dinamo Press*, 14 December 2016.

30. Verónica Gago, '#WeStrike: Notes toward a Political Theory of the Feminist Strike', *South Atlantic Quarterly* 117:3 (2018), 660–9, here 665.

1. Rousseau: Assembly, Not Representation

1. The constitution as a constituted power is differentiated from the constitutional power, the juridical constituent power.

2. Alexander Hamilton, James Madison, and John Jay, *The Federalist Papers (1787–1788)*, New York: Bantam, 2003.

3. See Olympe de Gouges, 'Declaration of the Rights of Woman and the Female Citizen', olympedegouges.eu.

4. As restitution for expropriated plantations and failed military operations, France demanded a sum that was impossible to repay. An embargo was imposed against Haiti, with the approval of the US, among others, until these debts were repaid, which forced the young black state into persistent debt slavery. See David Graeber, *Debt: The First 5,000 Years*, New York: Melville House, 2011, 6; on non-repayable black debts, see also the final chapter of this book.

5. Although many enslaved women took part in the revolutionary struggle, women's suffrage was not introduced in Haiti until 1950.

6. Michel-Rolph Trouillot, 'Unthinkable History: The Haitian Revolution as a Non-Event', in *Silencing the Past: Power and the Production of History*, Boston: Beacon Press, 2015.

7. See, among many others, Paul Nolte, *Was ist Demokratie? Geschichte und Gegenwart*, Munich: C.H. Beck, 2012.

8. The clarification of who belongs to the *demos* cannot be separated from disputes over the appropriate forms of bourgeois masculinity.

9. Thomas Hobbes, *Leviathan – or the Matter, Forme, and Power of a Common-Wealth, Ecclesiastical and Civill* (1651), London: Ely, 1909, XVI, 126; XVII, 129–32; and XIV. See also Thomas Hobbes, *De Cive: Philosophical Rudiments Concerning Government and Society* (1651), 1.X–XI and 13.XV.

10. Hobbes, *Leviathan*, I, 8.

11. Ibid., XXII, 181.

12. The liberal idea of a negative individual freedom is already shown in the concomitant form of bourgeois freedom as freedom *from* a precariousness shared with others. See Quentin Skinner, *Hobbes and Republican Liberty*, Cambridge: Cambridge University Press, 2008.

13. See Hobbes, *De Cive*, 1.III.

14. See Carole Pateman, *The Sexual Contract*, Stanford: Stanford University Press, 1988, 43–7. Hobbes lays the normative cornerstones for this contract, which a short time later also support John Locke's liberalist 'possessive individualism'. See C.B. Macpherson, *The Political Theory of Possessive Individualism: Hobbes to Locke*, Oxford: Oxford University Press, 2011; John Locke, *Two Treatises of Government*, Cambridge: Cambridge University Press, 1994. For Immanuel Kant, too, only free, independent men who own property could be citizens forming the people who sovereignly unite to make laws for themselves. Excluded from this juridical masculinity are not only all women, but all house and shop employees, as well as day labourers. See Immanuel Kant, 'On the Common Saying: "This May Be True in Theory, but It Does Not Apply in Practice"' (1793), in *Kant: Political Writings*, ed. H.S. Reiss, Cambridge: Cambridge University Press, 1991, 78. Kant calls the Others of the people – those who are not citizens and therefore cannot participate in the formation of the whole of the nation – the 'unruly crowd', or the '*rabble* (*vulgus*)', whose illegal association is *the mob* (*agere per turbas*) – conduct that excludes them from the quality of a citizen'. Immanuel Kant, *Anthropology from a Pragmatic Point of View* (1798), Cambridge: Cambridge University Press, 2006, 213 (emphasis in original). Kant uses the old verb *rottiren*, which means 'to connect', as in 'to connect in mobs (gangs)'. A '*Rottirer*' was a heretic, a mutineer, an insurgent, one who plots together with others.

15. See Isabell Lorey, *Figuren des Immunen: Elemente einer politischen Theorie*, Zurich: Diaphanes, 2011.

16. Among other things, there was no consensus on how large a republic can be to ensure freedom and political rationality, whether there have to be dependent or independent mandates, or how plural or homogeneous those to be represented have to be. See, among others, Dirk Jörke, 'Demokratie in neuen Räumen: Ein theoriegeschichtlicher Vergleich', *Österreichische Zeitschrift für Politikwissenschaft* 40:1 (2011), 7–19.

17. See Hamilton, Madison, and Jay, *Federalist Papers*, Articles 9 and 10. Madison argued for a conceptual differentiation between a Republic and a Democracy, whereby the latter stood for a negatively connoted form of direct democracy, and the Republic for a positively connoted form of representative democracy.

18. Jean-Jacques Rousseau, *The Social Contract: Or, the Principles of Political Rights* (1762), New York: G.P. Putnam's Sons, 1893, II.6, 56–7.

19. Ibid., III.12, 138.

20. Those who did not belong to the upper class of a conquered community, as a rule received only limited Roman citizenship, which mandated military service for the men, but did not offer any voting rights (*civitates sine suffragio*). Freed slaves also received only limited citizenship rights. See Hans Wieling, *Die Begründung des Sklavenstatus nach ius gentium und ius civile*, Stuttgart: Steiner, 1999; and Jane F. Gardner, *Being a Roman Citizen*, New York: Routledge, 2010, 7–10.

21. Rousseau, *Social Contract*, III.12, 138. Rousseau devoted a separate section to 'slavery' at the beginning of his text.

22. Rousseau's writings, especially *The Social Contract*, provoked extreme controversies. Liberal critics have argued that his reference to antiquity is anachronistic (see Catherine Colliot-Thélène, *Democracy and Subjective Rights: Democracy without Demos*, London: Rowman & Littlefield, 2018, 34), without, of course, problematizing the tradition that the multitude does not count politically; that democracy without representation was not possible even in Geneva during Rousseau's lifetime (see Robert A. Dahl, *Democracy and Its Critics*, New Haven, CT: Yale University Press, 1991); that Rousseau argued vulgar-democratically (see Ernst Fraenkel, *Deutschland und die westlichen Demokratien*, Frankfurt am Main: Suhrkamp, 1991, 307); that his concept of popular sovereignty is totalizing and negates the individual person (see Iring Fetscher, *Rousseaus politische Philosophie: Zur Geschichte des demokratischen*

Freiheitsbegriffs, Frankfurt am Main: Suhrkamp, 1975). Others have welcomed precisely this conception of popular sovereignty. See, for example, Carl Schmitt, *The Crisis of Parliamentary Democracy*, Cambridge, MA: MIT Press, 1988; Johannes Agnoli and Peter Brückner, *Die Transformation der Demokratie*, Berlin: Voltaire, 1967; Benjamin Barber, *Strong Democracy: Participatory Politics for a New Age*, Berkeley: University of California Press, 2003; Giorgio Agamben, 'Introductory Note on the Concept of Democracy', *Theory & Event* 13:1 (2010). For the critics of sovereignty, on the other hand, Rousseau is an important creative mind in the context of a participatory and emancipatory democracy. See Carole Pateman, *Participation and Democratic Theory*, Cambridge: Cambridge University Press, 1970; and Ingeborg Maus, *Über Volkssouveränität: Elemente einer Demokratietheorie*, Frankfurt am Main: Suhrkamp, 2011.

23. To cite only a few of the feminist positions: Linda Zerilli, *Signifying Woman: Culture and Chaos in Rousseau, Burke, and Mill*, Ithaca, NY: Cornell University Press, 1994; Lori Jo Marso, *(Un)manly Citizens: Jean-Jacques Rousseau's and Germaine de Staël's Subversive Women*, Baltimore: Johns Hopkins University Press, 1999; Melissa Matthes, *The Rape of Lucretia and the Founding of Republics: Readings in Livy, Machiavelli and Rousseau*, University Park: Pennsylvania State University Press, 2000; Elizabeth Rose Wingrove, *Rousseau's Republican Romance*, Princeton: Princeton University Press, 2000; Lynda Lange (ed.), *Feminist Interpretations of Jean-Jacques Rousseau*, University Park: Pennsylvania State University Press, 2002; Friederike Kuster, *Rousseau – Die Konstitution des Private: Zur Genealogie der bürgerlichen Familie*, Berlin: Akademie, 2005; Juliane Rebentisch, *The Art of Freedom: On the Dialectics of Democratic Existence*, Cambridge: Polity, 2016; Magdalena Scherl, *Ersehnte Einheit, unheilbare Spaltung: Geschlechterordnung und Republik bei Rousseau*, Bielefeld: transcript, 2016.

24. See Cornelia Klinger, '"Für den Staat ist das Weib die Nacht": Die Ordnung der Geschlechter und ihr Verhältnis zur Politik', in *Geschlechterdifferenz: Texte, Theorien, Positionen*, ed. Doris Ruhe, Würzburg: Königshausen & Neumann, 2000, 61–100.

25. I am not speaking of the state here, as state institutions can be instituted as administrations beyond national borders.

26. Josiah Ober, 'The Original Meaning of "Democracy": Capacity to Do Things, Not Majority Rules', *Constellations* 15:1 (2008), 3–9, here 3.

27. See ibid., 7.

28. Rousseau, *Social Contract*, III.4, 101, see also II.3, 40–1.

29. Ibid., III.4, 102.

30. Rebentisch interprets Rousseau in this way, defending liberal representative democracy. See Rebentisch, *The Art of Freedom*, 183–224.

31. Rousseau, *Social Contract*, III.12, 137.

32. Ibid., III.15, 145.

33. Just a few decades after the publication of *The Social Contract*, Emmanuel Sieyès presented the opposite view of representation on the eve of the French Revolution: the nation cannot assemble; it is not comprised of 'a small number of individuals'. The 'common will' must therefore be entrusted to 'extraordinary representatives': representatives 'with a special mandate to frame the constitution' in the National Assembly (Emmanuel-Joseph Sieyès, 'What Is the Third Estate?' [1789], in *Political Writings*, Indianapolis: Hackett, 2003, 92–162, here 139–40). The representatives are assigned the *pouvoir constituant*, the legislative constituent power, which is distinguished from the constituted and executing power, the *pouvoir constitué*.

34. For a constitutional theory interpretation of Rousseau, see Maus, *Volkssouveränität*, 329–35; on the performative aspects in Rousseau, see, among others, Claire R. Snyder, *Citizen-Soldiers and Manly Warriors: Military Service and Gender in the Civic Republic Tradition*, Lanham: Rowman & Littlefield, 1999.

35. The original *corps moral et collectif* is not the mythical and moral collective for which it is often mistaken, but rather – in the same way that the legal person is called *personne morale* in French today – a collective legal person, which is made up of contractually associated members, and is capable of common decisions. See Maus, *Volkssouveränität*, 329.

36. Rousseau, *Social Contract*, I.6, 22.

37. Ibid.

38. Ibid.

39. See Maus, *Volkssouveränität*, 329–31.

40. Rousseau, *Social Contract*, II.3, 40 (trans. modified).

41. Ibid., II.3, 41 (trans. modified).

42. Ibid., II.6, 56–7.

43. Ibid., II.7, 59–60. The first part of the quote corresponds to Marx's translation of it in his text 'On the Jewish Question' (1843), in *The Marx-Engels Reader*, ed. Robert Tucker, New York: Norton & Company, 1978, 26–46, here 46.

44. Melissa Butler also speaks of the state as 'the family writ large', in her 'Rousseau and the Politics of Care', in Lange, *Feminist Interpretations of Rousseau*, 212–82, here 224.

45. Louis Althusser criticized Rousseau, arguing that the social contract is not at all a contract, or at least is a 'paradoxical structure', because the contractual partners do not all exist at the moment of conclusion. No contract can be made with the sovereign or the public, because they first arise through the contract. See Althusser, 'Rousseau: *Social Contract*', in *Politics and History: Montesquieu – Rousseau – Marx*, London: Verso, 2007, 113–60, here 126 and 130.

46. Rousseau, *Social Contract*, I.7, 23.

47. Ibid.

48. Ibid., I.6, 19–22.

49. Ibid., III.13, 140.

50. For Rousseau, without the ambivalence of freedom and subjugation, a contract that forces a person to renounce his freedom and subjugate himself entirely to another is not a legal contract, but rather slavery: 'Thus, from whatever direction the subject is regarded, the right of slavery is null; not only because it is illegitimate, but because it is absurd and signifies nothing. The words *slave* and *right* are contradictory – they mutually exclude each other' (ibid., I.4, 17). This is clarified very early on in the *Social Contract*, in the chapter 'Slavery'.

51. On the ambivalence of freedom and subjugation under neoliberal conditions, see Lorey, *State of Insecurity*, 31–6.

52. Although Rousseau acknowledged that England had the oldest parliamentary tradition, the *peuple* is only free there when it elects the parliament; however, it does not exist in the parliament as the representative institution. For Rousseau, representation corresponds with a form of government emanating from the 'feudal governments, from that iniquitous and absurd government under which the human race was degraded, and where the name of man was a dishonor' (Rousseau, *Social Contract*, III.15, 145).

53. Ibid., II.12, 81 as well as III.15, 145. The *pouvoir législatif* also does not correspond with a constituent assembly of representatives, like the one that a few decades later would work out the constitution during the French Revolution over a longer time period, and then dissolve again.

54. Ibid., III.15, 143–4.

55. 'Power can transmit itself, but not will' (ibid., II.1, 35). Contrary to my interpretation, Rousseau's popular sovereignty has been understood as incompatible with a constitutional division of powers, among other reasons due to its indivisibility (for a critique of this, see Maus, *Volkssouveränität*, 333).

56. Rousseau, *Social Contract*, II.2, 36.

57. See ibid., II.6; as well as Colliot-Thélène, *Democracy and Subjective Rights*, 38.

58. See Rousseau, *Social Contract*, II.2, 36.

59. However, the constituted power of the government, which Rousseau treats as an administrative act, also conceals a special twist. Rousseau has in mind the Roman republic in the fifth to third centuries BC. The plebeians' own tribunes, hard won from the patricians, serve as his role model for a republic without representation. Rousseau falsely calls the plebeians '*le Peuple romain*' (ibid., III.15, 147) and, with his equation of the Latin word *populus* with the plebeians or the plebs, repeats a misunderstanding that has run throughout the history of political thought. In fact, the patrician men, along with the plebeian men, are part of the *populus*; in the Roman republic, both belong to the assembly of the *populus*, initially with different voting rights. See Jochen Bleicken, *Die Verfassung der Römischen Republik: Grundlagen und Entwicklung*, Paderborn: Schöningh, 1995, 120–33; and Lorey, *Figuren des Immunen*, 30–1 and 56–7.

  The plebeians gave themselves their own laws at the end of the fifth century, after their first exodus from Rome. These laws were not considered legal in the political domain of the patricians for quite some time. In order to establish them, the plebeians also elected tribunes, which enforced their interests in the political order dominated by the patricians. Although the plebeian tribunes were not part of the executive, they were equipped with a veto right. Rousseau emphasized that the tribunes never dared represent the plebeians. No one in Rome ever imagined that the tribunes could 'usurp the functions of the people', and 'in the midst of so great a multitude they never tried to pass of themselves a single plebiscite' (Rousseau, *Social Contract*, III.15, 146). In this section, Rousseau brings in the multitude in a role that they had otherwise not had in the *Social Contract*, namely when speaking of the plebs who cannot simply be represented by the tribunes, which as a 'force applied by power' can only represent the plebeian constituted power but never the constituent power of the plebeian *multitude*. On the constituent power of the plebeians, and for a detailed depiction of the Roman struggle of the orders, see Lorey, *Figuren des Immunen*, 25–82.

60. Rousseau, *Social Contract*, II.9, 70.

61. Ibid., III.16, 149.

62. Ibid. (trans. modified). The separation of powers is also recommended because the *peuple* of male citizens, which expresses the general will, 'always desires the good; but of itself it does not always see what is good' (ibid., II.6, 57). There is a further reason why permanent assemblies of the *peuple* are not possible: Rousseau establishes that it also has to do with the climate: 'among the Greeks', the people were constantly assembled at the marketplace; 'Your more rigorous climates give you more needs; six months of the year the public square is not habitable' (ibid., III.15, 147).

63. See ibid., III.14, 142.

64. Ibid., III.4, 101.

65. The *form* of government played no role for the executive: the government does not have to be democratic; it can also be aristocratic or monarchic (see ibid., III.2, 94), as it always simply executes the 'laws that have been passed democratically' (Maus, *Volkssouveränität*, 327). Rousseau recommends the government form of democracy only once, for Corsica. In his constitutional draft for the island, he proposes democracy for financial reasons. The Corsicans are poor, and in his eyes, democracy is the least expensive form of government. However, it does not satisfy his normative demands for an ideal republic. See Jean-Jacques Rousseau, 'Plan for a Constitution for Corsica' (1766), in *The Plan for Perpetual Peace, On the Government of Poland, and Other Writings on History and Politics: The Collected Writings of Jean-Jacques Rousseau*, vol. 2, Hanover, NH: University Press of New England, 2005, 123–55, here 126–7; see also Maus, *Volkssouveränität*, 328–9.

66. See Rousseau, *Social Contract*, III.10, 133.

67. Ibid., III.10, 134 (emphasis in original).

68. Daniel Bensaïd, 'Permanent Scandal', in Giorgio Agamben et al., *Democracy in What State?*, New York: Columbia University Press, 2012, 16–43, here 29.

69. Rousseau, *Social Contract*, II.12, 82.

70. Ibid., III.12, 137.

71. Ibid., I.5, 17; II.6, 56; III.5, 146; IV.4, 185. 'Multitude' is also used for a bunch of 'special decrees' (II.4, 45), a 'multitude of causes' (III.1, 90), and a 'multitude of gods and religions' (IV.8, 206).

72. Ibid., I.7, 24.

73. What Rousseau grasps as multitude is mistakenly identified in many debates in political theory as the 'real people'. See Colliot-Thélène, *Democracy*, 38–46.

74. See Jean-Jacques Rousseau, *Émile, or Education* (1762), London: Dent, 1921, Book V.

75. With reference to Rousseau's *Social Contract*, Karl Marx explained that part of the function of the bourgeois society was to dissolve social life into its component parts and thereby naturalize them. The bourgeois political revolution, by means of which citizens achieve control, does not revolutionize their conditions in the social: 'Human emancipation will only be complete when the real, individual man . . . has recognized and organized his own powers (*forces propres*) as *social* powers so that he no longer separates this social power from himself as *political power*.' Marx, 'Jewish Question', 46 (emphasis in original).

76. Rousseau, *Social Contract*, I.2, 3.

77. Ibid., I.5, 17–18.

78. It is no coincidence that when referring to the dispersed many, Rousseau also uses a different term. In the section 'The People' he does not write about the citizens who form the legislative, but, rather, about the relationship between the 'extent of its territory, and . . . the number of its people' (ibid., II.10, 72). The word he uses when writing about the interplay of climate, fertile country, and the 'fecundity of women' is 'population' (ibid., II.10, 74). Concretized in such a biologistic way, the undefined *multitude* becomes a defined population. This recalls, naturally, the new political economy that Foucault identified as biopolitics. Rousseau,

however, is not concerned in the *Social Contract* with biopolitics, but rather with the special relationship of freedom and subjugation, which when specifically related to sex is very differently pronounced. When it is about the dimension of governing, Rousseau speaks less of the government of a population than of the government of a society.

79. Rousseau, *Émile*, V, 321.

80. Ibid.: 'Yet where sex is concerned man and woman are unlike; each is the complement of the other; the difficulty in comparing them lies in our inability to decide, in either case, what is a matter of sex, and what is not . . . How far such differences may extend we cannot tell; all we know for certain is that where man and woman are alike we have to do with the characteristics of the species; where they are unlike, we have to do with the characteristics of sex.'

81. See on this Scherl, *Ersehnte Einheit*.

82. See Marion Heinz, 'Zur Konstitution geschlechtlicher Subjekte bei Rousseau', in *Geschlechterordnung und Staat: Legitimationsfiguren der politischen Philosophie (1600–1850)*, ed. Marion Heinz and Sabine Doyé, Berlin: Akademie, 2012, 163–80, here 168–9.

83. Rousseau, *Émile*, V, 323: 'Woman is also endowed with boundless passions; God has given her modesty to restrain them.'

84. See Jean-Jacques Rousseau, *Politics and the Arts: Letter to M. d'Alembert on the Theatre* (1758), Ithaca, NY: Cornell University Press, 1968; on this, see also Kuster, *Rousseau*, 197–8, and Rebentisch, *Art of Freedom*.

85. See Rousseau, *Émile*, V, 323. 'Man is dependent on woman through his desires; woman is dependent on man through her desires and also through her needs . . . A man has no one but himself to consider, and so long as he does right he may defy public opinion' (ibid., 328).

86. Ibid., 324: 'or at least all her youth; everything reminds her of her sex'.

87. See ibid., 328.

88. Ibid., 324–5. Already in his article published in 1755, Rousseau writes, 'in exchange for the provision he makes for them', the husband ought 'to be able to superintend his wife's conduct, because it is of importance for him to be assured that the children, whom he is obliged to acknowledge and maintain, belong to no-one but himself'. Jean-Jacques Rousseau, 'Discourse on Political Economy' (1755), in *The Social Contract and Discourses by Jean-Jacques Rousseau*, London: Dent, 1923, 249–87, here 250.

89. Rousseau, *Social Contract*, I.7, 26.

90. See Rousseau, *Émile*, IV, 212. Shown here is a specifically bourgeois genealogy of the current authoritarian populism elaborated in the introduction. The imagined threat of the other man, which drives Rousseau's concept of masculinity and reproduction, is updated as reactionary migration politics.

91. Ibid., V, 324. Also informative for the contemporary diversity of gender stagings are Rousseau's negative remarks on salons and the theatre. See Rousseau, *Politics and the Arts*, 87–92.

92. Rousseau, *Émile*, V, 325.

93. Ibid.

94. See Jean-Jacques Rousseau, 'Economy [abridged]' (1755), in *The Encyclopedia of Diderot and d'Alembert Collaborative Translation Project*, Ann Arbor: University of Michigan Library, 2009.

95. Michel Foucault recognizes the significance of this turn of political economy for the formation of modern biopolitical governmentality when he writes: 'The family will change from being a model to being an instrument . . . a privileged instrument for the government of the population.' Michel Foucault, *Security, Territory, Population: Lectures at the Collège de France 1977–78*, ed. Michel Senellart, New York: Palgrave Macmillan, 2009, 141; and also the reference to Rousseau, 142–3.

96. 'In fact, if the voice of nature is the best counsellor to which a father can listen in the discharge of his duty . . . nor should he follow any rule other than the public reason, which is the law . . . From all that has just been said, it follows that *public* economy, which is my subject, has been rightly distinguished from *private* economy, and that, the State having nothing in common with the family except the obligations which their heads lie under of making both of them happy.' Rousseau, 'Discourse on Political Economy', 251–2 (emphasis in original).

97. Foucault, *Security, Territory, Population*, 106.

98. Michel Foucault, 'Meshes of Power' (1981), in *Space, Knowledge and Power: Foucault and Geography*, ed. Jeremy W. Crampton and Stuart Elden, London: Routledge, 2016, 158.

99. Ibid., 161; see also Michel Foucault, '*Omnes et Singulatim*: Towards a Criticism of "Political Reason"' (1981), in *Power: Essential Works of Michel Foucault 1954–1984*, vol. 3., New York: New Press, 2000, 298–325.

100. Michel Foucault, *The History of Sexuality*, vol. 1., *The Will to Knowledge* (1978), New York: Vintage, 1990, 152–7.

101. See Chapter 5 for more detail on this.

102. As Jacques Derrida suggests in his book *De la grammatologie* from 1967. See also the next chapter on this.

103. Rousseau, *Politics and the Arts*, 125. Here, too, Rousseau insists on a 'moral' heteronormative gender order and vilifies all gender practices that undermine this order. He polemicizes that seen on the stage are much too passionate stagings: such 'heroes all gotten up, so mawkish, so tender', who are prime examples of the 'effeminate' man, and 'mitigate his taste for his real duties' (ibid., 117). He accused women actors of 'divesting of modesty' and 'dissoluteness' (ibid., 91; on Rousseau's vilifying of gender parodies, see also Rebentisch, *Art of Freedom*, 193–6).

104. Rousseau, *Politics and the Arts*, 125–6.

105. Ibid., 126.

106. Ibid., 93.

107. Ibid.

108. Ibid., 99.

109. See ibid.

110. See ibid., 108.

111. Ibid., 120.

112. See ibid., 111 and 122.

113. Gilles Deleuze, *Difference and Repetition*, New York: Columbia University Press, 1994, 10; instead, the references are Nietzsche and Kierkegaard.

114. Rousseau, *Politics and the Arts*, 125.

115. See ibid., 124.

116. Ibid., 125.

117. Deleuze, *Difference and Repetition*, 8.

118. Rousseau, *Politics and the Arts*, 125–6. It seems the republican-societal festival unfolds what Rousseau thought it was necessary to inhibit in the political realm in the *Social Contract*. But it is not a boundless festival, not one that welcomes all without limits. It is, first and foremost, for people from the city, for the population (see ibid., 132). Rousseau does not imagine an unclosed hospitality. See on this Derrida's considerations in the following chapter.

119. Ibid., 127.

120. Ibid.

121. Ibid., 129.

122. Ibid., 126.

2. Derrida: Democracy to Come

1. Jacques Derrida, *Of Grammatology* (1974), Baltimore: Johns Hopkins University Press, 1998, 262.

2. Ibid., 246.

3. Ibid.

4. Ibid., 262.

5. See Heinz Kimmerle, *Derrida zur Einführung*, Hamburg: Junius, 1988, 51.

6. Derrida, *Grammatology*, 246.

7. G.W.F. Hegel, *Elements of the Philosophy of Right* (1821), Mineola, NY: Dover, 2005, xix.

8. G.W.F. Hegel, *Philosophy of Nature, Part Two of The Encyclopedia of the Philosophical Sciences (1830)*, vol. 2, Oxford: Clarendon, 2004, 15 (§ 247).

9. Ibid., 39 (§ 259).

10. Ibid.

11. Ibid., 36 (§ 258) (emphasis in original).

12. Ibid., 39 (§ 259).

13. See Pierre Macherey, *In a Materialist Way: Selected Essays*, London: Verso, 1998, 151.

14. Hegel, *Philosophy of Nature*, 39 (§ 259).

15. Ibid., 37 (§ 259).

16. Ibid. (emphasis in original).

17. See G.W.F. Hegel, *The Phenomenology of Spirit*, Oxford: Oxford University Press, 1977, 60–3, para. 97–106.

18. Hegel, *Philosophy of Nature*, 36 (§ 258) (emphasis in original).

19. Ibid., 37 (§ 259) (emphasis in original).

20. G.W.F. Hegel, *Jenaer Systementwürfe III: Naturphilosophie und Philosophie des Geistes. Vorlesungsmanuskript zur Realphilosophie* (1805–6), ed. Rolf P. Horstmann, Hamburg: Meiner, 1987, 11.

21. Hegel, *Phenomenology of Spirit*, 62, para. 104.

22. Hegel, too, differentiates the form of rule of the state from *oikos*, among other reasons because he distinguishes the dynamics of progress from naturalized kinship relations. See, for example, G.W.F. Hegel, *Lectures on the History of Philosophy* (1857), Aalton: WordBridge, 2011, 38–9; see also Eva Bockenheimer, 'Georg Wilhelm Friedrich Hegel: Von der natürlichen Bestimmtheit der Geschlechter zu ihrer intellektuellen und sittlichen Bedeutung in der bürgerlichen Ehe und Familie', in Heinz and Doyé, *Geschlechterordnung und Staat*, 305–40, here 313–16.

23. See Hegel, *Elements of the Philosophy of Right*, 82–96. Marx accused Hegel of conceiving of an autonomy of the political and thereby a 'separation of actual life from political life'. Karl Marx, *Critique of Hegel's Philosophy of Right* (1843), Cambridge: Cambridge University Press, 1970.

24. See Hegel, *Elements of the Philosophy of Right*, 181 and 183–4.

25. See Hegel, *Phenomenology of Spirit*.

26. Hegel, *Elements of the Philosophy of Right*, xx (emphasis in original).

27. Ibid.

28. Ibid.

29. Ibid. (emphasis in original).

30. Ibid. (emphasis in original).

31. Derrida, *Grammatology*, 137.

32. Ibid.

33. See Hegel, *The Phenomenology of Spirit*. Negative associations of terms such as 'presence' or 'presentist' with 'immediate', 'authentic', and 'corporal' make vestiges of Hegel's philosophy of history evident still today.

34. Derrida, *Grammatology*, 306.

35. Ibid.

36. Ibid.

37. Rousseau, *Social Contract*, III.12 and III.15 as well as IV.4.

38. See Jacques Derrida, *Rogues: Two Essays on Reason*, Stanford: Stanford University Press, 2005, xii.

39. See also Chapter 5 in the present book.

40. See Derrida, *Rogues*, 37 and 114. 'Democracy could not gather itself around the presence of an axial and univocal meaning that does not destroy itself and get carried away with itself' (ibid., 40).

41. See ibid., 33.

42. Ibid., 30.

43. I have identified this dynamic as 'biopolitical immunization' (Lorey, *Figuren des Immunen*, 260–81).

44. Derrida, *Rogues*, 9–10.

45. Émile Benveniste, *Dictionary of Indo-European Concepts and Society*, Chicago: Hau Books, 2016, 366. Josiah Ober, whom I referred to in the previous chapter, reads the Greek word *krátos* without gender as the capacity to do things; he underscores a not-inevitably self-referential etymological meaning (see Ober, 'Original Meaning of "Democracy" ').

46. See Benveniste, 'Hospitality', in *Dictionary of Indo-European Concepts*, 61–74.

47. Derrida, *Rogues*, 11.

48. Ibid., 17. For a further critique of patrilinear paternal logic, see Jacques Derrida, *The Politics of Friendship*, London: Verso, 1997.

49. Derrida, *Rogues*, 12.

50. The perpetual phallocentric return to oneself is also inscribed in the Greek word *autos* contained in 'autonomy' (see ibid., 14).

51. See ibid., 18.

52. See ibid., 36–7.

53. Ibid., 34.

54. Ibid., 14–15.

55. Ibid., 73.

56. Ibid., 74.

57. Ibid.

58. Rousseau, *Social Contract*, III.4, 104.

59. Ibid., 102.

60. See ibid., III.15.

61. Ibid., III.4, 104, see also Derrida, *Rogues*, 75.

62. The title of the fourth chapter of Book III is 'Democracy'.

63. Derrida, *Rogues*, 75.

64. See ibid., 53–5; and Jean-Luc Nancy, *The Experience of Freedom*, Stanford: Stanford University Press, 1993, 102.

65. See Chapter 1, p. 22 of this volume.

66. See Derrida, *Politics of Friendship*, 104.

67. See Derrida, *Rogues*, 63; for the distinction between conditional and absolute hospitality, see also Jacques Derrida, *Of Hospitality*, Stanford: Stanford University Press, 2000.

68. See Benveniste, *Dictionary of Indo-European Concepts*, 67; for detail on various dominance-securing strategies of juridical immunity and of biopolitical immunization, see Lorey, *Figuren des Immunen*, 236–59 and 260–80.

69. Derrida, *Politics of Friendship*, 105. At another point, he speaks of 'the heterogeneity of a *pre-*'. See Jacques Derrida, *Specters of Marx: The State of the Debt, the Work of Mourning, and the New International*, New York: Routledge, 2006, 33 (emphasis in original).

70. Derrida, *Specters of Marx*, 20.

71. See Derrida, *Rogues*, 142.

72. See ibid., xv.

73. Derrida, *Specters of Marx*, xix.

74. See Derrida, *Rogues*, xi. 'A foreseen event is already present, already presentable; it has already arrived or happened and is thus neutralized in its irruption' (ibid., 143).

75. Derrida, *Hospitality*, 25. Translation altered.

76. Ibid., 51.

77. Paolo Virno, *A Grammar of the Multitude: For an Analysis of Contemporary Forms of Life*, Los Angeles: Semiotext(e), 2004, 31.

78. The gift of hospitality must be given without requirement, it must be presented as a gift. See Derrida, *Hospitality*, 29 and 83; see also Derrida, *Specters of Marx*, 211–12.

79. This takes up an argument pursued in the last chapter of this book that separates credit from social debt, based on Stefano Harney and Fred Moten, *The Undercommons: Fugitive Planning and Black Study*, London: Minor Compositions, 2013. On this, see also Jacques Derrida, 'The Madness of Economic Reason: A Gift without Present', in *Given Time I: Counterfeit Money*, Chicago: Chicago University Press, 1992, 34–70; as well as my text dealing with this, Isabell Lorey, 'Precarisation, Indebtedness, Giving Time', in *Maria Eichhorn: 5 Weeks, 25 Days, 175 Hours*, ed. Chisenhale Gallery, London: Chisenhale, 2016, 38–49.

80. On the concept of 'radical inclusion' in the context of the practices of the Spanish democracy movement, see Isabell Lorey, 'Präsentische Demokratie: Radikale Inklusion – Jetztzeit – Konstituierender Prozess', in *Transformationen der Demokratie – Demokratische Transformationen*,

ed. Alex Demirović, Münster: Westfälisches Dampfboot, 2016, 265–77; as well as Chapter 5 of the present book.

81. 'De-Munisierung' is a term I have already developed in *Figuren des Immunen* in the context of the resistant figure of the 'constituent immunization': 'The collective composition, the recomposition, emerges in a movement of evading [*Entziehen*] and depositing [*Ent-Setzen*], which can be described as de-munization. It moves away from every *munus*. De-munization does not comprise the *munus* being removed as a punishment, but on the contrary, evading the *munus*: in this political context refusing the *munus* signifies the ability to act politically' (ibid., 290–1).

82. Here there are links to Benveniste's etymological unfolding of the Greek word *hostis* as guest and foreigner. He emphasizes that hospitality in the context of the *potlatch* as festival 'is founded on the idea that one man is bound to another' (Benveniste, *Dictionary of Indo-European Concepts*, 67). See, on the *potlatch*, where the exchange of gifts is not suspended, Marcel Mauss, who in the 1950s still spoke of 'primitive' or 'archaic' forms of exchange among the US-American indigenous people. Marcel Mauss, *The Gift: The Form and Reason for Exchange in Archaic Societies* (1925), New York: Routledge, 2001.

83. See also Isabell Lorey, 'Sorge im Präsens: Verbundenheit, Sorge, _Mit_', in *Ökologien der Sorge*, ed. Tobias Bärtsch et al., Vienna: transversal texts, 2017, 113–22.

84. Derrida, *Rogues*, 38.

85. Jacques Derrida, 'Ich mißtraue der Utopie, ich will das Un-Mögliche', interview, *Die Zeit*, 8 March 1998. On 'thinking of impossible possible, possible as impossible, an impossible-possible', see also Jacques Derrida, 'The Future of the Profession or the Unconditional University', in *Without Alibi*, Stanford: Stanford University Press, 2002, 234–7, here 234.

86. Derrida, *Rogues*, 29.

87. Ibid., 84.

88. Ibid., xiv.

89. See the next chapter of the present book.

90. Derrida, *Specters of Marx*, 211. For more on 'messianicity is . . . anything but utopian' and 'messianic without messianism', see also Jacques

Derrida, 'Marx and Sons', in *Ghostly Demarcations: A Symposium on Jacques Derrida's* Specters of Marx, ed. Michael Sprinker, London: Verso, 1999, 213–69, here 248.

91. Derrida, *Politics of Friendship*, 105.

3. Benjamin: Leaps of Now-Time

1. Walter Benjamin, 'On the Concept of History', in *Selected Writings, 4: 1938–1940*, ed. Howard Eiland and Michael W. Jennings, Cambridge, MA: Belknap, 2006, 389–400. The Roman numerals after quotations in the following indicate the relevant theses in Benjamin's text. Many aspects of my interpretation of Benjamin were the result of discussions with and inspiration from the participants in the trilingual Benjamin reading group in Málaga from autumn 2017 until the end of 2018. At each meeting, while enjoying tapas and wine, we discussed in German, English, and Spanish, a thesis from Benjamin's text 'On the Concept of History'. Inputs have been contributed by Ruth Sonderegger, Leticia Sabsay, Curro Machuca Prieto, Rosa Fernández Gómez, Gerald Raunig, Astrid Deuber-Mankowsky and Stefan Nowotny.

2. In the subtitle for the introduction to his bestseller, *The Ancient City: A Study on the Religion, Laws, and Institutions of Greece and Rome* (1864), Baltimore: Johns Hopkins University Press, 1980, Numa Denis Fustel de Coulanges (1830–89) recorded his ongoing scholarly interest: 'the necessity of understanding the oldest Beliefs of the Ancients in order to understand their Institutions'. Fustel had exceptional influence on the estimation of religion for the constitution of societies.

3. With the accusation of *acedia*, Benjamin concentrates his critique pursuant to the historical epochs represented by Fustel academically.

4. Walter Benjamin, 'Resümee des Fragments N9a8', quoted by Willi Bolle, 'Geschichte', in *Benjamins Begriffe*, ed. Michael Opitz and Erdmut Wizisla, vol. 1, Frankfurt am Main: Suhrkamp, 2000, 399–442, here 439. See Walter Benjamin, *The Arcades Project*, Cambridge, MA: Belknap, 1999, 474.

5. Alex Demirović, 'Der Tigersprung: Überlegungen zur Verteidigung der "Gegenwart"', *PROKLA: Zeitschrift für kritische Sozialwissenschaft* 183 (2016), 307–16, here 312–13.

6. Stéphane Mosès, *The Angel of History: Rosenzweig, Benjamin, Scholem*, Stanford: Stanford University Press, 2009, 113.

7. Karl Marx, 'The Eighteenth Brumaire of Louis Bonaparte', in *The Marx-Engels Reader*, 594–617. See also, Demirović, 'Tigersprung', 313–15.

8. Marx, 'Eighteenth Brumaire', 596.

9. Ibid., 597.

10. Ibid.

11. Ibid., 597–8. 'Hier ist die Rose, hier tanze!' (Here is the rose, dance here) is kept in the original German.

12. Hegel, *Elements of the Philosophy of Right*, xx. See the detailed discussion of this passage in Hegel in the previous chapter.

13. And not to the future, as Brunkhorst claims in his detailed commentary on Marx: Hauke Brunkhorst, 'Kommentar', in Karl Marx, *Der achtzehnte Brumaire des Louis Bonaparte*, Frankfurt am Main: Suhrkamp, 2007, 133–329, here 297.

14. Karl Marx, 'The Civil War in France', in *The Marx-Engels Reader*, 618–52, here 633.

15. Karl Marx, 'First and Second Drafts to *The Civil War in France*', in *The Civil War in France*, Peking: Foreign Languages Press, 1966, 121 (emphasis added).

16. See Roger V. Gould, *Insurgent Identities: Class, Community, and Protest in Paris from 1848 to the Commune*, Chicago: Chicago University Press, 1995, 165.

17. On the interpretation of the Commune as an insurrection, see Michael Hardt and Antonio Negri, *Multitude: War and Democracy in the Age of Empire*, New York: Penguin, 2004, 69.

18. See, on the following interpretation of the Paris Commune and its feminist reading, mainly the second and third chapters of Gerald Raunig's *Art and Revolution: Transversal Activism in the Long Twentieth Century*, Los Angeles: Semiotext(e), 2007.

19. See Prosper Olivier Lissagaray, *History of the Paris Commune of 1871* (1876), St Petersburg, FL: Red and Black, 2007, 72; Louise Michel, *The Red Virgin: The Memoirs of Louise Michel* (1886), ed. Lowry Bullit and Elizabeth Ellington Gunter, Tuscaloosa, AL: University of Alabama Press, 1981, 63; Antje Schrupp, *Nicht Marxistin und auch nicht Anarchistin: Frauen in der ersten Internationale*, Königstein: Helmer, 1999, 125.

20. 'At the same pace at which the progress of modern industry developed, widened, intensified the class antagonism between capital and labour, the State power assumed more and more the character of the national power of capital over labour, of a public force organised for social enslavement, of an engine of class despotism.' Marx, 'Civil War in France', 630.

21. See in Gould's *Insurgent Identities* the chapter 'Public Meetings and Popular Clubs, 1968–70', 121–52.

22. Marian Leighton, 'Der Anarchofeminismus und Louise Michel', in *Louise Michel: Ihr Leben – Ihr Kampf – Ihre Ideen. Frauen in der Revolution*, ed. Renate Sami, Berlin: Kramer, 1976, 17–56, here 32–3; Schrupp, *Nicht Marxistin*, 124. On the reorganization of women's work, see the chapter on Elisabeth Dmitrieff and the 'Frauenunion', in Schrupp, *Nicht Marxistin*, 100–50.

23. See Lissagaray, *History of the Paris Commune*, 48; Raunig, *Art and Revolution*, 75.

24. See Lissagaray, *History of the Paris Commune*, 25–8.

25. Raunig, *Art and Revolution*, 73.

26. Ibid.

27. See Leighton, 'Anarchofeminismus', 35 and 38; on professional schools as training sites for women of 'all social levels', see Michel, *Red Virgin*, 104.

28. See Kristin Ross, *The Emergence of Social Space: Rimbaud and the Paris Commune*, London: Verso, 2008, 137.

29. Raunig, *Art and Revolution*, 75 (emphasis in original).

30. Marx, 'First and Second Drafts to *The Civil War in France*', 125 (emphasis in original).

31. Marx, 'The Civil War in France', 632.

32. Marx, 'First and Second Drafts to *The Civil War in France*', 146.

33. Women first attained suffrage in France in 1944.

34. See Louise Michel, 'Die Frau in der Freimaurerloge' (1904), in *Louise Michel: Texte und Reden*, ed. Eva Geber, Vienna: bahoe, 2019, 27–31, here 30.

35. Walter Benjamin, 'Paris, Capital of the Nineteenth Century', in *The Arcades Project*, 1–14, here 13.

36. See Kristin Ross, *Communal Luxury: The Political Imaginary of the Paris Commune*, London: Verso, 2015, 15; Leighton, 'Anarchofeminismus', 34–5. Louise Michel, one of the most well-known women of the Commune, wrote in her memoirs: 'The issue of political rights is dead. Equal education, equal trades, so that prostitution would not be the only lucrative profession open to a woman – that is what was real in our program.' Michel, *Red Virgin*, 59.

37. See Ross, *Communal Luxury*, 37; Eva Geber, 'Zur Einführung', in *Louise Michel: Texte und Reden*, 7–26, here 15–16.

38. See Schrupp, *Nicht Marxistin*, 148. Louise Michel was a member of the National Guard, commander of the 61st Montmartre battalion, and head of the vigilance committee, to which women as well as men belonged. During the peak phase of the Commune, on 11 April 1871, the Union des femmes pour la défense de Paris et les soins aux blessés (Union of the women for the defence of Paris and the care of the wounded) was formed by, among others, Elisabeth Dmitrieff, a Russian intellectual who at the time was working with Marx.

39. See ibid., 126–8; Leighton, 'Anarchofeminismus', 27 and 35.

40. Henri Lefebvre, *La Proclamation de la Commune, 26 Mars 1871*, Paris: Gallimard, 1965, 21.

41. See Raunig, *Art and Revolution*, 78. On celebratory thoughts of the Commune subsequent to the events, see Ann Rigney, 'Remembering Hope, Transnational Activism beyond the Traumatic', *Memory Studies* 11:3 (2018), 368–80.

42. See Marx, 'Eighteenth Brumaire'; Marx, 'The Civil War in France'; and Ross, *The Emergence of Social Space*. Louise Michel: 'the Commune wanted more than anything else the social revolution' (quoted by Leighton, 'Anarchofeminismus', 27).

43. Raunig speaks of a '*militant* festival'. *Art and Revolution*, 79 (emphasis in original).

4. Foucault: Present Infinitive

1. Michel Foucault, 'Power and Sex', an interview by Bernard-Henri Levy, *Telos* 32 (1977), 152–61, here 159 (trans. modified). Foucault says in French 'historien du présent'. Michel Foucault, 'Non au sexe roi', in *Dits et écrits II: 1976–1988*, ed. Daniel Defert, François Ewald, and Jacques Lagrange, Paris: Gallimard, 2001, 256–69, here 265.

2. Ibid., 160.

3. See Michel Foucault, 'Space, Knowledge, and Power', in *The Foucault Reader*, ed. Paul Rabinow, New York: Pantheon, 1984, 239–56, here 250. Foucault uses the concept of the return or recurrence, one of Nietzsche's concepts. From the 1960s, he refers to Nietzsche again and again. In an interview with Paul Rabinow he even describes himself as 'Nietzschean' (*The Foucault Reader*, 6). On Foucault's references to Nietzsche, see Daniel Defert, 'Course Context', in Michel Foucault, *Lectures on the Will to Know and Oedipal Knowledge*, ed. Daniel Defert, François Ewald, and Andrea Fontana, London: Palgrave Macmillan, 2003, 262–86.

4. Foucault, 'Power and Sex', 160.

5. Foucault formulated this understanding of reversible power relations in *The Will to Knowledge*, 94–7. On Foucault's conceptions of power, transformed over the years, see my text, 'Das Gefüge der Macht', in *Gouvernementalität und Geschlecht: Politische Theorie im Anschluss an Michel Foucault*, ed. Brigitte Bargetz et al., Frankfurt am Main: Campus, 2015, 31–61.

6. Foucault, 'Space, Knowledge, and Power', 250.

7. On the question of the *actualité* and the present, see Foucault's confrontation with Kant in two of his final texts: 'What Is Enlightenment? (Qu'est-ce que les Lumières?)', in *Dits et écrits II: 1976–1988*, 1381–97, here 1386–7 and 1393–4 ('What Is Enlightenment?', in *The Foucault Reader*, 32–50), and 'Qu'est-ce que les Lumières?', in *Dits et écrits II*, 1498–1507, here 1498–1501 and 1505–6 ('Kant on Enlightenment and Revolution', *Economy and Society* 15:1 [1986], 88–96).

8. Michel Foucault, 'The Subject and Power', *Critical Inquiry* 8:4 (1982), 777–95, here 785 (trans. slightly modified).

9. Ibid.

10. Ibid., 780.

11. Ibid., 785.

12. This thinking is also inspired by Maurice Blanchot and Georges Bataille. See Michel Foucault, *Remarks on Marx: Conversations with Duccio Trombadori*, New York: Semiotext(e), 1991, 46–7.

13. Michel Foucault, 'Nietzsche, Genealogy, History', in *Language, Counter-Memory, Practice: Selected Interviews and Essays*, ed. D.F. Bouchard, Ithaca, NY: Cornell University Press, 1977, 139–64, here 139–40. This text was written around the same time as the lectures in 1970/71 on 'The Will to Know' (see Defert, 'Course Context', 273).

14. Foucault, 'Nietzsche, Genealogy, History', 139–40.

15. See ibid., 142.

16. Friedrich Nietzsche, 'On the Uses and Disadvantages of History for Life', in *Untimely Meditations* (1874), ed. Daniel Breazale, Cambridge: Cambridge University Press, 1997, 57–124, here 62 (emphasis in original). 'With the word "unhistorical" I designate the art and power of *forgetting* and of enclosing oneself within a bounded *horizon*' (ibid., 120, emphasis in original).

17. Ibid., 62. 'If you are to venture to interpret the past you can do so only out of the fullest exertion of the vigour of the present' (ibid., 94).

18. Ibid., 65. 'I call "suprahistorical" the powers which lead the eye away from becoming towards that which bestows upon existence the character of the eternal and stable, towards *art* and *religion*' (ibid., 120, emphasis in original).
    Ibid., 62 (emphasis in original). The plastic power is 'the capacity to develop out of oneself in one's own way, to transform and incorporate into oneself what is past and foreign'.

19. Ibid., 63.

20. Foucault, 'Nietzsche, Genealogy, History', 146.

21. See ibid., and 162.

22. See Friedrich Nietzsche, *Thus Spoke Zarathustra* (1883–85), London: Penguin, 1974.

23. Foucault, 'Nietzsche, Genealogy, History', 153 (trans. modified).

24. Ibid., 158.

25. Ibid., 157.

26. Ibid.

27. Michel Foucault, 'Theatrum Philosophicum', in *Language, Counter-Memory, Practice*, 167–96.

28. Ibid., 176.

29. Ibid.

30. Deleuze and Guattari speak of an 'infinite Now'. See Gilles Deleuze and Félix Guattari, *What Is Philosophy?*, New York: Columbia University Press, 1994, 112.

31. See Foucault, 'Theatrum Philosophicum', 175. Foucault uses the notion of *événement-sens*, referring to Gilles Deleuze's *Logique du sens* (1969) (*The Logic of Sense*, New York: Columbia University Press, 1990, 181–5). As an alternative to the English translation as 'meaning-sense' in Foucault's 'Theatrum Philosophicum', we use 'event-sense', which is closer to the French original.

32. See also Deleuze, *Logic of Sense*, 21–5.

33. Foucault, 'Theatrum Philosophicum', 174. The French original says: 'Le sens-événement est toujours à la fois la pointe déplacée du présent et l'éternelle repetition de l'infinitif.' See Michel Foucault, *Dits et écrits I, 1954–1975*, ed. Daniel Defert, François Ewald, and Jacques Lagrange, Paris: Gallimard, 2001, 943–67, here 950.

34. Foucault, 'Theatrum Philosophicum', 174 (trans. slightly modified).

35. Ibid., 175 (trans. slightly modified).

36. Foucault, *Remarks on Marx*, 31.

37. See Deleuze, *Difference and Repetition*; Jean-Luc Nancy, *Being Singular Plural*, Stanford: Stanford University Press, 2000; François Jullien, *The Philosophy of Living*, Kolkata: Seagull, 2016, 107–17; Jullien's interest, based on the example of Chinese thinking, is in the processual aspect of change, but not the event (see ibid., 118–24).

38. Foucault, 'Theatrum Philosophicum', 173.

39. Deleuze, *Logic of Sense*, 181.

40. See, on the concept of the ecstatic in this context, with reference to Spinoza and Deleuze: Judith Butler, 'Bodily Vulnerability, Coalitions, and Street Politics', in *The State of Things*, ed. Marta Kuzma, Pablo Lafuente, and Peter Osborne, London: Koenig, 2012, 163–97, here 180; see also Isabell Lorey, 'Ekstatische Sozialität', *engagée: philosophisch-politische einmischungen* 2 (2015/16), 20–3; for an understanding of indebtedness, see Harney and Moten, *The Undercommons*, as well as the last chapter of the present book.

41. Gilles Deleuze, *Foucault* (1986), London: Continuum, 1999, 60, see overall 59–77.

42. See ibid., 76. See also Foucault's lecture in *Security, Territory, Population*, 87–114.

43. In his lecture 'What Is Critique?', Foucault emphasizes that it is about turning effects into events, about the common resistance of singularities, based on the decision not to be thus governed, and therefore not to be thus affected. See Michel Foucault, *The Politics of Truth*, Los Angeles: Semiotext(e), 2007, 41–82, here 66–7.

44. With this manifoldness, Bergson has Hegel and the dialectical method in mind. See Henri Bergson, *Time and Free Will: An Essay on the Immediate Data of Consciousness* (1889), London: Allen & Unwin, 1950, Chapter 2, 75–139, and Chapter 3, 140–221; see also Gilles Deleuze, *Bergsonism*, New York: Zone Books, 1991, 38. In the following I conceptualize this first type of multiplicity as manifoldness.

45. See also Henri Bergson, *The Creative Mind: An Introduction to Metaphysics* (1934), Mineola, NY: Dover, 2007, 139–40; see also Deleuze, *Bergsonism*, 44.

46. Deleuze, *Bergsonism*, 40–9. On the concept of the fold, see also Gilles Deleuze, *The Fold: Leibniz and the Baroque*, Minneapolis: University of Minnesota Press, 1992.

47. Henri Bergson, *Duration and Simultaneity: With Reference to Einstein's Theory* (1922), New York: Bobbs Merrill, 1965, 52; see also Deleuze, *Bergsonism*, 80.

48. Deleuze, *Bergsonism*, 81.

49. Bergson, *Duration and Simultaneity*, 52.

50. Compatible here are the contemplations on decolonial multiple understandings of time by Johannes Fabian, *Time and the Other: How Anthropology Makes Its Objects* (1983), New York: Columbia University Press, 2014; and also Brigitta Kuster, *Choix d'un passé: Transnationale Vergegenwärtigungen kolonialer Hinterlassenschaften*, Vienna: transversal texts, 2016, as well as the understanding of present and ecology in Donna Haraway, *Staying with the Trouble: Making Kin in the Chthulucene*, Durham, NC: Duke University Press, 2016, and Anna Lowenhaupt Tsing, *The Mushroom at the End of the World: On the Possibility of Life in Capitalist Ruins*, Princeton: Princeton University Press, 2015.

51. Isabell Lorey, 'Maßlose Differenz', in *Inventionen 2: Exodus. Reale Demokratie. Territorium. Immanenz. Maßlose Differenz. Biopolitik*, ed. Isabell Lorey et al., Zurich: Diaphanes, 2012, 154–7.

52. On the concept of the hierarchized difference in precarity in contrast to the relational difference of precariousness, see Lorey, *State of Insecurity*, 17–22.

53. Deleuze, *Difference and Repetition*, 262.

54. Ibid., 263.

55. Ibid., 29 and 34–5.

56. Ibid., 42.

57. Ibid., 29.

58. 'Since things are said to repeat when they differ even though their concept is *absolutely* the same' (ibid., 270, emphasis in original). Hegel's dialectic does not correspond with a method of static determination; nonetheless the movement between identity and difference is that of a determining movement of identity, 'in which difference remains cursed and deficient' (Raunig, *Art and Revolution*, 138).

59. See Harney and Moten, *Undercommons*, 19–20.

60. Referring to the final sentence in Deleuze, *Difference and Repetition*: 'the difference which displaces and disguises them [each drop and each voice] and, in turning upon its mobile cusp, causes them to return' (304). On the affirmation of differences, see, for example, 267.

61. The term 'untimely' is from Nietzsche and is directed against normalized and unquestioned predominant understandings of time: 'untimely – that is to say, acting counter to our time, and thereby acting on our time, and, let us hope, for the benefit of a time to come' (Nietzsche, 'Uses and Disadvantages of History for Life', 60). The time to come can be understood in the sense of Derrida, not as future, but as expanded present (see Chapter 2).

62. See Deleuze, *Difference and Repetition*, 10–11.

63. Ibid., 11.

64. Foucault, 'Theatrum Philosophicum', 194; see also Deleuze, *Difference and Repetition*, 300: 'Repetition in the eternal return appears . . . as the peculiar power of difference . . . The eternal return affirms difference, it affirms dissemblance and disparateness, chance, multiplicity and becoming.'

65. Foucault, 'Theatrum Philosophicum', 177.

66. Stefan Nowotny, 'Swarm of Events: What Is New in History and the Politics of Enunciation', trans. Aileen Derieg, *transversal: multilingual webjournal*: 'inventions' (January 2011), transversal.at. According to Nowotny, an event thinking, in opposition to Alain Badiou, is 'reaching an understanding about a historical space *and* event space, which is permeated by multiplicities and contingencies, by openings and closures, by the emergence of the new and by irreversibilities, and in which the task cannot be to cleanly "separate" event and counter-event from one another, but rather to create *new* plasticities in the midst of all that, even where the social and political terrain appears to be hopelessly rigidified' (ibid., emphasis in original).

67. Ibid.

68. Ibid.

69. Félix Guattari proposed the term 'transversality' as the line of flight out of the either-or of verticality and horizontality that 'tries to overcome both the impasse of pure verticality and that of mere horizontality'. Félix Guattari, 'Transversality' (1972), in *Psychoanalysis and Transversality: Texts and Interviews 1955–1971*, Los Angeles: Semiotext(e), 2015, 102–20, here 113; see also Roberto Nigro and Gerald Raunig, 'Transversalität', in *Inventionen 1: Gemeinsam, prekär, potentia, Kon-/Disjunktion, Ereignis, Transversalität, Queere Assemblagen*, ed. Isabell Lorey et al., Zurich: Diaphanes, 2011, 194–6.

70. See Deleuze, *Logic of Sense*, 169–76.

71. See Deleuze, *Bergsonism*, 56: 'We place ourselves *at once* in the past; we leap into the past as in a proper element' (emphasis in original).

72. Henri Bergson, *Mind-Energy: Lectures and Essays* (1920), Westport, CT: Greenwood, 1975, 175.

73. Henri Bergson, *Matter and Memory* (1896), London: Dover, 2004, 73; see also Deleuze, *Bergsonism*, 56.

74. See Henri Bergson, *Creative Evolution*, New York: Holt & Co., 1911, 199–201, and Macpherson, *Political Theory of Possessive Individualism*.

75. Bergson, *Matter and Memory*, 74; Deleuze, *Bergsonism*, 57.

76. Benjamin, 'Concept of History', thesis V, 390.

77. See Deleuze, *Bergsonism*, 64–5.

78. Ibid., 58.

79. Ibid., 100.
80. Ibid., 104.
81. See ibid., 56–8.
82. See ibid., 106.
83. See ibid., 38. Unfortunately, Deleuze did not elaborate on this aspect in his book on Bergson.
84. On the concept of instituent practices, see Gerald Raunig, 'Instituent Practices: Fleeing, Instituting, Transforming', *transversal: multilingual webjournal*: 'do you remember institutional critique?' (January 2006); Gerald Raunig, 'Instituent Practices, No. 2: Institutional Critique, Constituent Power, and the Persistence of Instituting', *transversal: multilingual webjournal*: 'extradisciplinaire' (January 2007); Stefan Nowotny and Gerald Raunig, 'Instituent Practices: New Introduction to the Revised Edition', *transversal*, May 2016, transversal.at/blog.
85. See Michel Foucault, 'Revolutionary Action: "Until Now" ', in *Language, Counter-Memory, Practice*, 218–33, here 231.
86. Ibid., 232.
87. Ibid.
88. Ibid., 232–3.
89. Ibid., 233.
90. I refer here to the essay titled in English 'Kant on Enlightenment and Revolution'. See on the genealogy of Foucault's thinking about the Kantian question 'What Is Enlightenment?', as in the title of this essay in the French original 'Qu'est-ce que les Lumières?' (1984), Foucault's lecture 'What Is Critique?' from 1978; Isabell Lorey, 'Die Wiederkehr revolutionärer Praxen in der infinitiven Gegenwart', in Lorey et al., *Foucaults Gegenwart*, 77–103.
91. See Immanuel Kant, *The Conflict of the Faculties* (1798), Lincoln: University of Nebraska Press, 1992; Foucault, 'Kant on Enlightenment and Revolution', 90–1.
92. Foucault, 'Kant on Enlightenment and Revolution', 93.
93. Ibid. Foucault speaks of it, following Kant, as 'at once as a singular event . . . and as a permanent process' (ibid., 95).
94. Ibid., 94 (first emphasis added).
95. Ibid., 95.
96. Ibid. (trans. slightly modified).

5. Negri: Democracy and Constituent Power

1. Foucault, 'Power and Sex', 159–60.
2. Through the indispensable fact of political representation, which is always exclusionary, equality is made impossible. As feminist and postcolonial theories especially have demonstrated, inequality is constitutive.
3. See Alex Demirović, *Demokratie und Herrschaft: Aspekte kritischer Gesellschaftstheorie*, Münster: Westfälisches Dampfboot, 1997, 83. Difficulties of participation are not easily resolved in the liberal, bourgeois form of democracy as they are among its aporias. Representative democracy is not to be separated from the logic of the state, and in a Hegelian sense is considered a 'political democracy', which is separate from society, from *all*, who should be represented (see Marx, *Critique of Hegel's Philosophy of Right*).
4. Parties that (at times) consider themselves to be movement-parties, such as Syriza in Greece, Die Linke in Germany, or Podemos in Spain, also give priority to the party form.
5. See Antonio Negri, 'The Constitution of Strength', in *Insurgencies: Constituent Power and the Modern State*, Minneapolis: University of Minnesota Press, 1999, 303–36; Antonio Negri and Raúl Sánchez Cedillo, 'For a Constituent Initiative in Europe', *transversal*, January 2015; see also Isabell Lorey and Gerald Raunig, 'Das gespenstische Potenzial des potere costituente: Vorbemerkungen zu einem europäischen konstituierenden Prozess', in Antonio Negri and Raúl Sánchez Cedillo, *Für einen konstituierenden Prozess in Europa: Demokratische Radikalität und die Regierung der Multituden*, Vienna: transversal texts, 2015, 9–36.
6. Negri, *Insurgencies*, 321; see also Gilles Deleuze, 'Control and Becoming', in *Negotiations, 1972–1990*, New York : Columbia University Press, 1995, 169–76, here 171.
7. See Foucault, *Will to Knowledge*, 135–44.
8. See Foucault, *Society Must Be Defended*, 37; see also Brigitte Bargetz et al. (eds), *Gouvernementalität und Geschlecht: Politische Theorie im Anschluss an Michel Foucault*, Frankfurt am Main: Campus, 2015.
9. See the first components of the 'present infinitive' in the last chapter.

10. See the first chapter. The demarcation to those who do not count, who do not belong and are not part of all, is constitutive of the idea of the represented people/*Volk*.

11. Hermann Heller, 'Die Souveränität: Ein Beitrag zur Theorie des Staats- und Völkerrechts' (1927), in *Collected Works*, vol. 2, ed. Martin Draht et al., Leiden: Sijthoff, 1971, 31–202, here 97. The originally sovereign constituent power of the many is, with Heller, inhibited and restrained by dividing the people by means of representation: 'the people as unity' is present in parliament, and through the rule of the heterogeneous many, it is the sovereign. In contrast to Heller, his contemporary antipode Carl Schmitt concedes the *Volk* the force that makes the constitution and creates the law and therewith the juridically constituent power (see Maus, *Volkssouveränität*, 105). However, Schmitt distinguishes between a sovereignty that creates laws and a sovereignty that makes decisions. He considers the 'real people' a community of beings that are not organizable and not formable (Carl Schmitt, *Constitutional Theory* [1928], Durham, NC: Duke University Press, 2008, 128): as an 'unorganized mass' (ibid., 271) it is the 'origin of all political happening' (ibid., 128). Nonetheless, the sovereign people, as essentially identical and unified, remains an idea that has to be represented through the one sovereign who decides for the *Volk* (see ibid., 240). In the Weimar Republic, the president of the German Reich, as head of the executive, is the one who decides alone in the state of exception (see Carl Schmitt, *Political Theology: Four Chapters on the Concept of Sovereignty* [1922], Chicago: Chicago University Press, 2005, 7). In Schmitt's opinion, the parliament is clearly not sufficiently capable of this representation due to the plurality of the positions represented in it. Schmitt shifts the democratic (popular-) sovereignty of the legislative to the executive, and in doing so does not perform the modern transfer of sovereignty from absolutist prince to the people as sovereign legislative authority of a democracy that decides in parliament, representatively. He leaves the key sovereignty with the executive and thus conceives of a 'dictatorship with a democratic foundation' (Maus, *Volkssouveränität*, 108; see also 105–10). Like Schmitt, Giorgio Agamben also reverses the competences in his thesis on the state of exception. Agamben also belongs among those who, contrary to Antonio Negri, consider it 'unthinkable' to distinguish constituent power from

sovereignty. See Giorgio Agamben, *Homo Sacer: Sovereign Power and Bare Life*, Stanford: Stanford University Press, 1998, 44.

This control of the heterogeneous many through the construction of the *Volk* actualizes itself through to leftist debates about an always divided people. Representation, which is always exclusionary, makes it necessary, in a widespread argumentation of left-liberal political theory, to distinguish between those represented and the allegedly 'real people'. This division should be constitutive and is to be affirmed as it makes clear that there can never be a unity, that 'one true people' can never exist. See on this, for example, the various texts in Alain Badiou et al., *What Is a People?*, New York: Columbia University Press, 2016, as well as Colliot-Thélène, *Democracy*, 36–40.

12. Virno, *Grammar of the Multitude*, 24. Here, Virno echoes the thoughts of Jacques Rancière, who nonetheless does not speak of the multitude when referring to those who do not count, do not have a voice, or who stammer, speaking instead of 'the part of those who have no part' (Jacques Rancière, *Disagreement: Politics and Philosophy*, Minneapolis: University of Minnesota Press, 1999). For Rancière, the many are anyone and everyone (see Isabell Lorey, 'The 2011 Occupy Movements: Rancière and the Crisis of Democracy', *Theory, Culture & Society* 31:7–8 [2014], 43–65). But it is not simply that the voices of the many *individuals* are not heard in the established order of the constituted power. Even more so, the ears of the rulers are not capable of perceiving the polyphony of the many who are not divided into autonomous, separate individuals; the cacophony of the countless who are bound with one another.

13. Virno, *Grammar of the Multitude*, 24.

14. On a political concept of class that does start from heterogeneity, see Isabell Lorey, 'Lucha de clases', in 'Conceptos para comprender la sociedad contemporánea', *Cuadernos de Teoría Social* 4:8 (2018), 126–8.

15. Negri, *Insurgencies*, 306.

16. Ibid., 307.

17. Ibid.

18. Ibid.

19. Michael Hardt and Antonio Negri, *Assembly*, Oxford: Oxford University Press, 2017, 42–6.

20. See Negri, *Insurgencies*, 308–9.

21. Ibid., 310.

22. Ibid., 311.

23. Ibid., 321.

24. See Antonio Negri, 'Constituent Republic', in *Revolutionary Writing: Common Sense Essays in Post-Political Politics*, ed. Werner Bonefeld, New York: Autonomedia, 2003, 243–53.

25. See Alex Demirović and Andrea Maihofer, 'Vielfachkrise und die Krise der Geschlechterverhältnisse', in *Krise, Alltag, Allianzen: Arbeits- und geschlechtersoziologische Perspektiven*, ed. Hildegard Maria Nickel and Andreas Heilmann, Weinheim: Beltz, 2013, 30–48; Alex Demirović, 'Democracy in Times of Crisis', *transform! European Journal for Alternative Thinking and Political Dialogue* 11 (2012); Alex Demirović et al. (eds), *VielfachKrise im finanzmarktdominierten Kapitalismus*, Münster: Westfälisches Dampfboot, 2011.

26. See Sabine Lang and Birgit Sauer, 'Hat die europäische Krise ein Geschlecht? Feministische und staatstheoretische Überlegungen', in *Europäische Staatlichkeit: Zwischen Krise und Integration*, ed. Hans-Jürgen Bieling and Martin Große Hüttmann, Wiesbaden: Springer, 2016, 241–58.

27. See David Stuckler and Sanjay Basu, *The Body Economic: Why Austerity Kills*, New York: Basic, 2013; Niki Kubaczek and Gerald Raunig, 'The Political Reinvention of the City', *transversal*, November 2017, transversal.at/blog; as well as Lorey and Raunig, 'Das gespenstische Potenzial'.

28. See Raúl Sánchez Cedillo, 'Rajoynato, municipalismos, sistema de contrapoder', *transversal: multilingual webjournal*: 'monster municipalisms' (September 2017).

29. Kubaczek and Raunig, 'Political Reinvention of the City'.

30. See Raúl Sánchez Cedillo, '15M: Something Constituent This Way Comes', *South Atlantic Quarterly* 113:3 (2012), 573–84, as well as Montserrat Galcerán Huguet, 'Demokratie, Gouvernementalität und das "Gemeinsame" in der spanischen 15M-Bewegung', in *Inventionen 2*, 62–75.

31. On the MayDay movements of the precarious, see Lorey, *State of Insecurity*, 99–111.

32. On this, see, for example, the Wikipedia entry on 'Movimiento por una vivienda digna en España', es.wikipedia.org.

33. See La PAH, afectadosporlahipoteca.com, as well as Ada Colau and Adrià Alemany, *¡Sí se puede! Crónica de una pequeña gran Victoria*, Barcelona: Destino, 2013.

34. See marchapopularindignada.wordpress.com, and on the *Documento problematicas pueblos*, see marchapopularindignada.wordpress.com/category/documento-problematicas-pueblos. Neither the social democratic government of José Luis Zapatero, which was in office until December 2011, nor the conservative successor government under Mariano Rajoy, which held office until June 2018, was interested in talks with the democracy movements.

35. See the listed colours and working areas of the various Mareas at 15mpedia.org/wiki/Lista_de_mareas.

36. See yosisanidaduniversal.net.

37. See the brochure *Carta por la Democracia* by Movimiento por la Democracia, Madrid, 2014; see also Movimiento por la democracia, Madrid, 'El Movimiento por la Democracia, en la nueva coyuntura', *Diagonal*, 25 June 2014, diagonalperiodico.net.

38. Movimiento por la Democracia, *Carta*.

39. On the history of Podemos, see Raul Zelik, 'Podemos and the "Democratic Revolution" in Spain', *Global Research*, May 2015; Emmanuel Rodriguez López, *La política en el ocaso de la clase media: El ciclo 15M-Podemos*, Madrid: Traficantes de sueños, 2016. The party likewise founded for this EU election, Partido X – in which people from the 15M movement were also involved, and which in addition to the usual election tours by the candidates was heavily supported by an online voting process – failed by only a narrow margin to gain a seat. Partido X also campaigned primarily for new forms of democracy and promised to deploy against the corruption running throughout the established Spanish system (see partidox.org). Several of the candidates from Partido X were subsequently involved in Barcelona En Comú.

40. Montserrat Galcerán Huguet, 'The Struggle for Social Change Reaches the Institutions', *transversal: multilingual webjournal*: 'monster municipalisms' (September 2016). Montserrat Galcerán Huguet, professor of political philosophy at Complutense Universität in Madrid, entered the

Madrid municipal government in 2015 and became a city councillor (consejal) for the districts of Moncloa-Aravaca and Tetuán.

41. Further alliances bear the names Málaga Ahora, Participa Sevilla, Compromís per Valéncia, and so on.

42. See Gerald Raunig, 'Confluences: The Molecular-Revolutionary Force of the New Municipalismos in Spain', *transversal: multilingual webjournal*: 'monster municipalisms' (September 2016).

43. On the method of creating the lists, see Galcerán Huguet, 'Struggle for Social Change', as well as Montserrat Galcerán Huguet and Pablo Carmona Pascual, 'Los futuros del municipalismo: Feminización de la política y radicalización democrática', *transversal: multilingual webjournal*: 'monster municipalisms' (September 2016). Like Galcerán Huguet, Carmona Pascual belonged to the platform Ganemos within the alliance Ahora Madrid, and became city councillor for the Madrid districts of Salamanca and Moratalaz.

44. Galcerán Huguet, 'Struggle for Social Change'. At the same time, a code for political ethics was introduced to end the politicians' privileges and corruption. See, for example, for Barcelona En Comú: barcelonaencomu.cat/sites/default/files/pdf/codi-etic-eng.pdf.

45. Galcerán Huguet, 'Struggle for Social Change'.

46. It was not necessary for all to be physically present at the assemblies; communication media were part of the horizontal decision-making structures. 'Decisions are made together and respected, but priority is given to caring for multiplicity, the active search for consensus and the identification of dissent so that it can be worked through and resolved' (ibid., trans. modified).

47. 'This rejection', according to Montserrat Galcerán Huguet, 'is very strong with respect to participative budgets and the new forums of district-level participation' (ibid.). In the logic of representation, the practice of radical inclusion was a strong threat to the politicians' privileges, which accrue from the liberal understanding of representative democracy.

48. Ibid.

49. In Madrid, for example, contrary to Ganemos's demands, with the taking over of the government by Ahora Madrid, the hierarchical structures of the administration were maintained, which greatly inhibited a transformation

from within. The administration in Barcelona was already organized in a more decentralized way when Barcelona En Comú entered the government, which facilitated the restructuring. On the militant research in the city administration of Barcelona during the election campaign of 2015, see Raunig, 'Confluences'.

50. Manuela Zechner, 'Let's Play? Citizenship, Subjectivity and Becoming in Municipalism', *transversal: multilingual webjournal*: 'monster municipalisms' (September 2016).

51. Ibid.

52. See, for example, Málaga Ahora (facebook.com/malagaahora) and Barcelona En Comú (barcelonaencomu.cat).

53. On this, see Negri and Sánchez Cedillo, 'For a Constituent Initiative'; see also the network of Fearless Cities, co-initiated by fearlesscities.com, whose first meeting took place as the 'International Municipalist Summit' from 9 to 11 June 2017 in Barcelona. But not only did new municipalisms emerge within the established political system, they also formed as a municipalist movement, to which the biannual *mac*-meetings are testimony. The first *mac*-meeting took place from 1 to 3 July 2016 in Málaga; *mac* stands for *municipalismo* (municipalism), *autogobierno* (self-government), and *contrapoder* (counter-power) (see mac1.uno). See the manifesto that was developed at that meeting: 'The Municipalist Manifesto', *transversal: multilingual webjournal*: 'monster municipalisms' (September 2016). The second meeting, *mac2* (mac2.uno/en), took place from 20 to 22 January 2017 in Pamplona; *mac3* (mac3.uno/) from 12 to 15 October 2017 in A Coruña; and *mac4* (elsaltodiario.com/palabras-en-movimiento/mac4-de-municipalismo-y-contrapoder) from 22 to 24 June 2018 in Madrid. On municipalism, see relevant publications such as Observatorio Metropolitano, *La apuesta municipalista: La democracia empieza por lo cercano*, Madrid: Traficantes de sueños, 2014; Angel Calle Collado and Ricard Vilaregut Sáez, *Territorios en democracia: El municipalismo a debate*, Barcelona: Icaria, 2015; Fundación de los Comunes, *Hacia nuevas instituciones democráticas*, Madrid: Traficantes de sueños, 2016; Rodríguez López, *La política en el ocaso de la clase media*. For discussion available in English see the special issue of *transversal: multilingual webjournal*: 'monster municipalisms' (September 2016).

54. See also the next chapter.

55. See Negri and Sánchez Cedillo, 'For a Constituent Initiative'.

56. See Pablo Iglesias Turrión, 'Understanding Podemos', *New Left Review* 93 (2015), 7–22; Pablo Iglesias Turrión, 'Spain on Edge', *New Left Review* 93 (2015), 23–42; see also Iñigo Errejón and Chantal Mouffe, *Construir Pueblo, Hegemonía y radicalización de la democracia*, Barcelona: Icaria, 2015, which argues for a left populism following from Ernesto Laclau and discusses the ideological strategies of the first years of Podemos; see also Chantal Mouffe, *For a Left Populism*, New York: Verso 2018.

57. For example, that of the Madrid collective Precarias a la Deriva on *cuidadanía*, a citizenship based on care. See Precarias a la Deriva, *Was ist dein Streik?*; for Greece, see, for example, the special section of *Social Anthropology* 24:2 (2016) on solidarity, 'The Other Side of the Crisis: Solidarity Networks in Greece'.

58. See the *Dossier de la Comisión de Feminismos Sol*, madrid.tomalaplaza. net; the manifesto of the transsexual network Transmaricabollo, 'Manifesto del orgullo indignado 2011', madrid.tomalaplaza.net; as well as Gracia Trujillo Barbadillo, 'La protesta dentro de la protesta: Activismos queer/cuir y feminista en el 15M', *Encrucijadas: Revista Crítica de Ciencias Sociales* 12 (2016), 1–18; Galcerán Huguet, 'Demokratie'; and Sánchez Cedillo, '15M'.

59. Galcerán Huguet, 'Struggle for Social Change'.

60. Ernesto Laclau, *On Populist Reason*, London: Verso, 2005, 232.

61. See Étienne Balibar, 'How Can the Aporia of the "European People" Be Resolved?', *Radical Philosophy* 181 (September/October 2013), 13–17.

6. Presentist Democracy: Care Practice and Queer Debt

1. See Robert Castel, *L'insécurité sociale: Qu'est-ce qu'être protégé?*, Paris: Éditions du Seuil, 2003.

2. See Brett Neilson and Ned Rossiter, 'Precarity as a Political Concept, or, Fordism as Exception', *Theory, Culture & Society* 25:7–8 (2008), 51–72.

3. See Lorey, *State of Insecurity*.

4. On Rousseau's ambivalence regarding freedom and subjection differing according to gender, see Chapter 1 of this book.

5. See Hobbes, *Leviathan*.

6. Hobbes, *De Cive*, 1.III.

7. Ibid., VIII, I.

8. Eva Kreisky and Birgit Sauer, *Feministische Standpunkte in der Politik-wissenschaft: Eine Einführung*, Frankfurt am Main: Campus, 1995, 136.

9. Seyla Benhabib and Linda Nicholson, 'Politische Philosophie und die Frauenfrage', in *Pipers Handbuch der politischen Ideen*, vol. 5, ed. Iring Fetscher and Herfried Münkler, Munich: Piper, 1987, 513–62, here 533.

10. On the interweaving of precarious living conditions with precarious environments, see Tsing, *Mushroom at the End of the World*, 29.

11. John Locke, *Second Treatise of Government* (1689), in *The Founders' Constitution*, Chicago: University of Chicago Press, 1986, vol. 1, Ch. 16, Doc. 3, lines 123–6 (emphasis in original).

12. Adam Smith, *An Inquiry into the Nature and Causes of the Wealth of Nations* (1776), London: Methuen, 1904, Book 1, Ch. 10, Part II.

13. Ibid., 1.10, I.

14. Ibid.

15. For a critique of this fraternalism, see Derrida, *Politics of Friendship*, 93–101.

16. See Pateman, *Sexual Contract*, 93–4.

17. See Silvia Federici, *Revolution at Point Zero: Housework, Reproduction, and Feminist Struggle*, New York: Autonomedia, 2012; Ann Laura Stoler, *Race and the Education of Desire: Foucault's History of Sexuality and the Colonial Order of Things*, Durham, NC: Duke University Press, 1995; Foucault, *Will to Knowledge*, 136–42.

18. Macpherson, *Political Theory of Possessive Individualism*.

19. Pierre Rosanvallon, *Le capitalisme utopique: Critique de l'idéologie économique*, Paris: Points, 1999.

20. See Robert Castel, *From Manual Workers to Wage Laborers: Transformation of the Social Question*, New York: Routledge, 2017.

21. Nancy Fraser and Linda Gordon, 'A Genealogy of *Dependency*: Tracing a Keyword of the U.S. Welfare State', *Signs: Journal of Women in Culture and Society* 19:2 (1994), 309–36, here 319 (emphasis in original).

22. Ibid., 320.

23. See Birgit Sauer, 'Krise des Wohlfahrtsstaates: Eine Männerinstitution unter Globalisierungsdruck?', in *Globale Gerechtigkeit? Feministische*

Debatte zur Krise des Sozialstaats, ed. Helga Braun and Dörthe Jung, Hamburg: Konkret Literatur, 1997, 113–47.

24. See also Christoph Butterwegge, *Hartz IV und die Folgen: Auf dem Weg in eine andere Republik?*, Weinheim: Beltz, 2015.

25. See Judith Butler, *Frames of War: When Is Life Grievable?*, New York: Verso, 2009.

26. Zygmunt Bauman, *Globalization: The Human Consequences*, New York: Columbia University Press, 1998, 69.

27. Alessandro De Giorgi, 'Immigration Control, Post-Fordism, and Less Eligibility: A Materialist Critique of the Criminalization of Immigration across Europe', *Punishment & Society* 12:2 (2010), 147–67, here 152.

28. See, among others, Sabine Hark and Mike Laufenberg, 'Sexualität in der Krise: Heteronormativität im Neoliberalismus', in *Gesellschaft: Feministische Krisendiagnosen*, ed. Erna Appelt et al., Münster: Westfälisches Dampfboot, 2013, 227–45, here 235; Alexandra Scheele, 'Widersprüchliche Anerkennung des Privaten: Eine Kritik aktueller Entwicklungen wohlfahrtsstaatlicher Politik', in *Staat und Geschlecht: Grundlagen der aktuellen Herausforderungen feministischer Staatstheorie*, ed. Gundula Ludwig et al., Baden-Baden: Nomos, 2009, 167–82.

29. This is particularly evident among single mothers, most of whom, in Germany, are dependent on welfare and live in poverty. See the study published by the Bertelsmann Stiftung: Anne Lenze and Antje Funcke, *Alleinerziehende unter Druck: Rechtliche Rahmenbedingungen, finanzielle Lage und Reformbedarf*, Gütersloh: Bertelsmann, 2016.

30. See Maurizio Lazzarato, *The Making of the Indebted Man: An Essay on the Neoliberal Condition*, Los Angeles: Semiotext(e), 2012.

31. On global chains of affect and care, see Arlie Russell Hochschild, 'Global Care Chains and Emotional Surplus Value', in *On the Edge: Living with Global Capitalism*, ed. Anthony Giddens and Will Hutton, London: Jonathan Cape, 2000, 130–46; Luzenir Caixeta et al., *Hogares, Cuidados y Fronteras/Homes, Care and Borders/Haushalte, Sorge und Grenzen*, Madrid: Traficantes de Sueños, 2004; Encarnación Gutiérrez Rodríguez, *Migration, Domestic Work and Affect: A Decolonial Approach on Value and the Feminization of Labour*, New York: Routledge, 2010; Precarias a la Deriva, 'Cuidados globalizados', in *A la deriva: Por los circuitos de la precariedad feminista*, Madrid: Traficantes de Sueños, 2004, 217–48.

32. Rhacel Salazar Parreñas, *Servants of Globalization: Women, Migration, and Domestic Work*, Stanford: Stanford University Press, 2001, 78.

33. Helma Lutz, 'Life in the Twilight Zone: Migration, Transnationality and Gender in the Private Household', *Journal of Contemporary European Studies* 12:1 (2004), 47–55; Alex Knoll et al., *Wisch und Weg! Sans-Papier-Hausarbeiterinnen zwischen Prekarität und Selbstbestimmung*, Zurich: Seismo, 2012. Other than in private households, such informal employment conditions are primarily found in labour-intensive rural agriculture, in the building industry, and in other low-qualification jobs.

34. See Hark and Laufenberg, 'Sexualität in der Krise', 236–8.

35. See Andrea Maihofer, 'Familiale Lebensformen zwischen Wandel und Persistenz: Eine zeitdiagnostische Zwischenbetrachtung', in *Wissen – Methode – Geschlecht: Erfassen des fraglos Gegebenen*, ed. Cornelia Behnke et al., Wiesbaden: VS, 2014, 313–34.

36. See Serhat Karakayali, 'Volunteers: From Solidarity to Integration', *South Atlantic Quarterly* 117:2 (2018), 313–31. For the UK, see Emma Dowling and David Harvie, 'Harnessing the Social: State, Crisis and the (Big) Society', *Sociology* 48:5 (2014), 869–86.

37. See Neilson and Rossiter, 'Precarity as a Political Concept'.

38. Lazzarato, *Making of the Indebted Man*, 51–2.

39. Ibid., 38.

40. See Karl Marx, *Comments on James Mill, Éléments D'Économie Politique*, at marxists.org; Gilles Deleuze and Félix Guattari, *Anti-Oedipus: Capitalism and Schizophrenia*, London: Athlone, 1984.

41. Friedrich Wilhelm Nietzsche, *On the Genealogy of Morality* (1887), Cambridge: Cambridge University Press, 2007, 36–7 (second essay, aph. 2).

42. Lazzarato, *Making of the Indebted Man*, 11.

43. Nietzsche, *Genealogy of Morality*, 37 (second essay, aph. 2) (emphasis in original).

44. See ibid., 39–40 (second essay, aph. 4).

45. Lazzarato, *Making of the Indebted Man*, 11.

46. Nietzsche, *Genealogy of Morality*, 45 (second essay, aph. 8).

47. Ibid., 36 (second essay, aph. 1).

48. See Benjamin, 'Concept of History', theses IV and VII.

49. On the development of this concept, see Isabell Lorey, 'Governmentality and Self-Precarization: On the Normalization of Cultural Producers',

transversal: multilingual webjournal: 'machines and subjectivation' (November 2006).

50. See Marx, *Comments on James Mill*; Lazzarato, *Making of the Indebted Man*, 55–61.

51. Ibid., 57.

52. Denise Ferreira da Silva, 'Unpayable Debt: Reflections on Value and Violence', in *The documenta 14 Reader*, ed. Quinn Latimer and Adam Szymczyk, Munich: Prestel, 2017, 81–112, here 94.

53. See ibid., 99–109.

54. The EU's austerity policies were long accompanied by the construction of a racialized southern Europe of guilt and debt: the financial crisis created a 'new' European South: 'The South is not an existing, given place, but a gendered, sexualised and racialised myth. Within Western hegemonic epistemology, the South is animalistic, feminine, childish, queer and black. The South is potentially sick, weak, disabled, shallow, stupid, lazy and poor. The South is portrayed as lacking sovereignty, knowledge, wealth and therefore fundamentally indebted to the North', writes Paul B. Preciado in 'Let Your South Walk, Dance, Listen and Decide', *documenta 14 Public Paper* 2 (2017), 2. On medial defamation of Greece as part of a gendered and racialized European South, see also Lorey and Raunig, 'Das gespenstische Potenzial', 11–20.

55. The huge increase in housing foreclosures in 2006 in the US did not set off any alarms. Those affected had low incomes, and many of them were Afro-Americans, Hispanic migrants, and single mothers. Panic first spread when the white middle class was also threatened by forced evictions in 2007; in September 2008 Lehman Brothers collapsed and triggered the global financial and economic crisis. The crisis was able to reach global dimensions due to the long ignorance of the effects on those first affected. Banks were, in part, able to immunize themselves from bankruptcy with state aid, while the risks were socialized. See David Harvey, *The Enigma of Capital: And the Crises of Capitalism*, London: Profile, 2010, 5; as well as Paula Chakravartty and Denise Ferreira da Silva, 'Accumulation, Dispossession, and Debt: The Racial Logic of Global Capitalism – An Introduction', *American Quarterly* 64:3 (2012), 361–85, here 365–6.

56. See David Harvey, 'The Urban Roots of Financial Crises: Reclaiming the City for Anti-Capitalist Struggle', *Socialist Register: The Crisis and the Left* 48 (2012); Randy Martin, *Knowledge Ltd: Toward a Social Logic of the Derivative*, Philadelphia: University of Pennsylvania Press, 2015.

57. As Angela Mitropoulos suggests, it can be assumed on the part of the borrowers that the financial risk was consciously chosen by some, as a strategy for exiting the confining conditions of a 'monetarised, racialised and gendered housing regime', in order to live deliberately beyond one's means and generate 'surplus in the most unproductive ways'. Angela Mitropoulos, *Contact and Contagion: From Biopolitics to Oikonomia*, London: Minor Compositions, 2012, 216.

58. See Brigitte Young, 'Gendered Dimensions of Money, Finance, and the Subprime Crisis', in *Gender and Economics: Feministische Kritik der politischen Ökonomie*, ed. Christine Bauhardt and Gülay Çağlar, Wiesbaden: VS, 2010, 258–77, here 268–9.

59. On diverse colonialist dispossession, see Brenna Bhandar, *Colonial Lives of Property: Law, Land, and Racial Regimes of Ownership*, Durham, NC: Duke University Press, 2018.

60. See Ferreira da Silva, 'Unpayable Debt', 89; Young, 'Gendered Dimensions', 273–4.

61. 'Black' is not understood in an identitarian way here. It refers to the refusal of the possibility of becoming a normative, autarkic subject. The full achievement of this autonomous subject is, indeed, not possible for anyone, but in discriminatory conditions of domination it is denied in different ways to those who are not white and male, and the agreement is that it can only be approximated.

62. For a critical look at the concept of emancipation, see Lorey, 'Emancipation and Debt'.

63. See Saidiya V. Hartman, *Scenes of Subjection: Terror, Slavery, and Self-Making in Nineteenth-Century America*, Oxford: Oxford University Press, 1997, 127. There are many indications that the liberal-capitalist opportunity of becoming an autonomous individual owning their own labour and selling it was not very attractive for some of those emancipated. They began to move around, to become mobile; they refused to enter into contractual ties with former slave owners, and due to their minimal needs were capable of surviving outside of wage labour. 'In

effect, by refusing to stay in their place, the emancipated insisted that freedom was a departure, literally and figuratively, from their former condition' (ibid., 128). In their mobility, which was no longer a running away but the practising of freedom of movement, they evaded, at times, the new constraints and limitations, an evasion which was considered, rightly so, subversive and dangerous for the existing white social and economic order.

64. Ibid., 129.

65. See ibid., 129–30.

66. Ibid., 130.

67. Ibid., 131.

68. See ibid., 133.

69. See ibid., 132.

70. Ferreira da Silva, 'Unpayable Debt', 85.

71. See Benjamin, 'Concept of History', theses II, VI, and XIV in particular. For more on Benjamin, see Chapter 3.

72. See Tiziana Terranova, 'Red Stack Attack! Algorithms, Capital and the Automation of the Commons', *EuroNomade: Inventare il comune sovvertire il presente*, 9 March 2014.

73. See Maurizio Lazzarato, *Governing by Debt*, Los Angeles: Semiotext(e), 2015, 251 and 88–90.

74. See Valentina Desideri and Stefano Harney, 'Fate Work: A Conversation', *ephemera: theory and politics in organization* 13:1 (2013), 159–76, here 168.

75. Harney and Moten, *Undercommons*, 61.

76. Ibid.

77. See ibid., 63–4.

78. Ibid., 61.

79. See Desideri and Harney, 'Fate Work', 169.

80. Harney and Moten, *Undercommons*, 64.

81. Ibid.

82. Ibid.

83. See Marta Malo de Molina, 'Common Motions, Part 1: Workers-Inquiry, Co-research, Consciousness-Raising', *transversal: multilingual webjournal*: 'militant research' (April 2006).

84. See Anne Firor Scott, 'Most Invisible of All: Black Women's Voluntary Associations', *Journal of Southern History* 56:1 (1990), 3–22; Wanda A.

Hendicks, *Gender, Race, and Politics in the Midwest: Black Club Women in Illinois*, Bloomington, IN: Indiana University Press, 1998.

85. See Kathie Sarachild, 'Consciousness-Raising: A Radical Weapon', in *Feminist Revolution*, ed. Kathie Sarachild, New York: Redstockings, 1975, 44–150, here 145. On the radical black feminist movement and consciousness-raising groups, see also the interview with Barbara Smith in Keeanga-Yamahtta Taylor (ed.), *How We Get Free: Black Feminism and the Combahee River Collective*, Chicago: Haymarket Books, 2017, 29–69.

86. See Precarias a la Deriva, 'Adrift Through the Circuits of Feminized Precarious Work', *transversal: multilingual webjournal*: 'Prekariat' (July 2004); Precarias a la Deriva, 'A Very Careful Strike: Four Hypotheses', *The Commoner* 11 (2006), 33–45; Precarias a la Deriva, 'Die Prekari-sierung der Existenz: Ein Gespräch', in Renate Lorenz and Brigitta Kuster, *Sexuell arbeiten: Eine queere Perspektive auf Arbeit und prekäres Leben*, Berlin: b_books, 2007, 259–72; Precarias a la Deriva, 'Projekt und Methode einer "militanten Untersuchung": Das Reflektieren der Multitude in Actu' (2005), in *Empire und die biopolitische Wende: Die internationale Debatte im Anschluss an Hardt und Negri*, ed. Marianne Pieper et al., Frankfurt am Main: Campus, 2007, 85–108.

87. During the derives, audio and video recordings were made and then exchanged in open workshops and shared text reading. See Precarias a la Deriva, 'Of Questions, Illusions, Swarms and Deserts: Notes on Research and Activism from Precarias a la Deriva' (2004), crash course666.wordpress.com.

Malo de Molina, 'Common Notions, Part 1'. Such militant research is indebted and tied to the various kinds of (self-)research conducted by (women) workers: the workers' research examined by Karl Marx in 1880; by Käthe Leichter in Vienna in 1931 (who, shortly after the financial crisis in 1928, carried out the first feminist crisis analysis, not only inter-viewing women workers in the factory, but also investigating household and reproduction work and leisure time); by the group Socialisme ou Barbarie in the 1950s in France; or the workers' investigation in the context of the operaist journal *Quaderni Rossi* in Italy in the 1960s and 1970s, which Antonio Negri was also a part of. The militant research of Precarias emerges, however, mainly from actualized splinters of queer-feminist and black-empowerment care practices. See ibid., as well as Käthe Knittler, 'Wissensarbeit und militante Untersuchung: Zwischen Produktion und Rebellion. Über Möglichkeiten widerständiger Wissens-produktion', *Kurswechsel* 1 (2013), 74–83.

88. A modification of Sarachild's term 'radical weapon' in 'Consciousness-Raising: A Radical Weapon'; see also Malo de Molina, 'Common Notions, Part 1'.

89. This is an actualization of political positions from the radical US wom-en's movement of the 1970s: 'Consciousness-raising was seen as both a method for arriving at the truth and a means for action and organizing. It was a means for the organizers themselves to make an analysis of the situation, and also a means to be used by the people they were organizing and who were in turn organizing more people. Similarly, it wasn't seen as merely a stage in feminist development which would then lead to another phase, an action phase, but as an essential part of the overall feminist strategy.' Sarachild, 'Consciousness-Raising', 147.

90. The text production resulting from this is part of the militant research that, together with the term 'Precarias a la deriva', comprises a 'poly-phonic we' of care workers who also generate 'transnational alliances'. Precarias, 'Cuidados globalizados', 217.

91. See ibid., 222–4.

92. See ibid., 224–5.

93. See Precarias, 'Precarización de la existencia y huelga de cuidado', 122–6; Precarias, *Was ist dein Streik?*, 98–108. On the problematic of right- and left-wing conceptions of community, see Lorey, *Figuren des Immunen*, 199–227.

94. See Precarias, 'Precarización', 113–17; Precarias, *Was ist dein Streik?*, 76–86.

95. See Precarias, 'Cuidados globalizados', 235–40; Precarias, 'Precar-ización', 112–13, and Precarias, *Was ist dein Streik?*, 74–5. The concept of care includes all areas of social reproduction: household and care work as well as jobs in health and education. This understanding of care likewise takes into account new forms of communicative and affective work, such as sex work. See Precarias, 'Precarización', 105–9, and Precarias, *Was ist dein Streik?*, 57–67.

96. The actualization of feminist debates from the 1980s and 1990s with a moral of care – following from, among others, Carol Gilligan, *In a Different*

Voice: Psychological Theory and Women's Development, Cambridge, MA: Harvard University Press, 1982 – is rejected. See, among others, Precarias, 'Cuidados globalizados', 220–1.

97. Precarias, 'Precarización', 126; Precarias, *Was ist dein Streik?*, 107.

98. Precarias, 'Precarización', 124; Precarias, *Was ist dein Streik?*, 102.

99. See also Sabine Hess and Bernd Kasparek (eds), *Grenzregime: Diskurse, Praktiken, Institutionen in Europa*, Berlin: Assoziation A, 2010; Lisa-Marie Heimeshoff et al. (eds), *Grenzregime II: Migration – Kontrolle – Wissen. Transnationale Perspektiven*, Berlin: Assoziation A, 2014; Sabine Hess et al. (eds), *Der lange Sommer der Migration: Grenzregime III*, Berlin: Assoziation A, 2016.

100. See Precarias, 'Precarización', 126–32; Precarias, *Was ist dein Streik?*, 109–22.

101. Precarias, 'A Very Careful Strike', 42 (trans. slightly modified).

102. See Verónica Gago (ed.), 'How Would You Go to Strike? The Women's Strike and Beyond', *South Atlantic Quarterly* 117:3 (2018); see also *Critical Times* 1:1 (2018).

103. On a situated internationalism in the context of the feminist strike movements, see Verónica Gago and Marta Malo (eds), 'Against the Day: The New Feminist International', *South Atlantic Quarterly* 119:3 (2020); Verónica Gago, *Feminist International: How to Change Everything*, London: Verso, 2020.

104. See Chapter 4 for details on the six components of the present infinitive.

105. On this, see also Haraway, *Staying with the Trouble*, as well as Tsing, *Mushroom at the End of the World*.

Bibliography

Literature

Agamben, Giorgio, *Homo Sacer: Sovereign Power and Bare Life* (1995), trans. Daniel Heller-Roazen (Stanford: Stanford University Press, 1998).

—, 'Introductory Note on the Concept of Democracy', trans. Nicholas Heron, *Theory & Event* 13:1 (2010).

Agnoli, Johannes, and Peter Brückner, *Die Transformation der Demokratie* (Berlin: Voltaire, 1967).

Alcoff, Linda Martín, Cinzia Arruzza, Tithi Bhattacharya, Nancy Fraser, Barbara Ransby, Keeanga-Yamahtta Taylor, Rasmea Yousef Odeh, and Angela Davis, 'Women of America: We're Going on Strike. Join Us so Trump Will See Our Power', *Guardian*, 6 February 2017.

Althusser, Louis, 'Rousseau: *Social Contract*', in *Politics and History: Montesquieu – Rousseau – Marx* (London: Verso, 2007), 113–60.

Arruzza, Cinzia, Tithi Bhattacharya, and Nancy Fraser, *Feminism for the 99%: A Manifesto* (London: Verso, 2019).

Badiou, Alain, Pierre Bourdieu, Judith Butler, Georges Didi-Huberman, Sadri Khiari, and Jacques Rancière, *What Is a People?*, trans. Jody Gladding (New York: Columbia University Press, 2016).

Balibar, Étienne, 'How Can the Aporia of the "European People" Be Resolved?', *Radical Philosophy* 181 (September/October 2013), 13–17.

Barber, Benjamin, *Strong Democracy: Participatory Politics for a New Age* (1984; Berkeley: University of California Press, 2003).

Bargetz, Brigitte, Gundula Ludwig, and Birgit Sauer, eds, *Gouvernemen-talität und Geschlecht: Politische Theorie im Anschluss an Michel Foucault* (Frankfurt am Main: Campus, 2015).

Bauman, Zygmunt, *Globalization: The Human Consequences* (New York: Columbia University Press, 1998).

Benhabib, Seyla, and Linda Nicholson, 'Politische Philosophie und die Frauenfrage', in *Pipers Handbuch der politischen Ideen*, vol. 5, ed. Iring Fetscher and Herfried Münkler (Munich: Piper, 1987), 513–62.

Benjamin, Walter, 'On the Concept of History', in *Selected Writings, 4: 1938–1940*, ed. Howard Eiland and Michael W. Jennings, trans. Edmund Jephcott et al. (1940; Cambridge, MA: Belknap, 2006), 389–400.

—, *The Arcades Project*, transl. Howard Eiland and Kevin Mclaughlin (1927–40; Cambridge, MA: Belknap, 1999).

—, 'Paris, Capital of the Nineteenth Century', in *The Arcades Project*, trans. Howard Eiland and Kevin Mclaughlin (Cambridge, MA: Belknap, 1999), 1–14.

Bensaïd, Daniel, 'Permanent Scandal', in Giorgio Agamben et al., *Democracy in What State?*, trans. William McCuaig (New York: Columbia University Press, 2012), 16–43.

Benveniste, Émile, *Dictionary of Indo-European Concepts and Society*, trans. Elizabeth Palmer, intro. Giorgio Agamben (Chicago: Hau Books, 2016).

Bergson, Henri, *Time and Free Will: An Essay on the Immediate Data of Consciousness*, trans. Frank L. Pogson (1889; London: Allen & Unwin, 1950).

—, *Matter and Memory*, trans. Nancy Margaret Paul and W. Scott Palmer (1896; London: Dover, 2004).

—, *Creative Evolution*, trans. Arthur Mitchell (New York: Holt & Co., 1911).

—, *Mind-energy: Lectures and Essays*, trans. H. Wildon Carr (1920; Westport, CT: Greenwood, 1975).

—, *Duration and Simultaneity: With Reference to Einstein's Theory* (1922), trans. Leon Jacobson (New York: Bobbs Merrill, 1965).

—, *The Creative Mind: An Introduction to Metaphysics*, trans. Mabelle L. Andison (1934; Mineola, NY: Dover, 2007).

Bhandar, Brenna, *Colonial Lives of Property: Law, Land, and Racial Regimes of Ownership* (Durham, NC: Duke University Press, 2018).

Bleicken, Jochen, *Die Verfassung der Römischen Republik: Grundlagen und Entwicklung* (Paderborn: Schöningh/UTB, 1995).

Bockenheimer, Eva, 'Georg Wilhelm Friedrich Hegel: Von der natürlichen Bestimmtheit der Geschlechter zu ihrer intellektuellen und sittlichen Bedeutung in der bürgerlichen Ehe und Familie', in *Geschlechterordnung und Staat: Legitimationsfiguren der politischen Philosophie (1600–1850)*, ed. Marion Heinz and Sabine Doyé (Berlin: De Gruyter, 2012), 305–40.

Bolle, Willi, 'Geschichte', in *Benjamins Begriffe*, vol. 1, ed. Michael Opitz and Erdmut Wizisla (Frankfurt am Main: Suhrkamp, 2000), 399–442.

Brunkhorst, Hauke, 'Kommentar', in Karl Marx, *Der achtzehnte Brumaire des Louis Bonaparte* (Frankfurt am Main: Suhrkamp, 2007), 133–329.

Bourdieu, Pierre, 'Job Insecurity Is Everywhere Now', in *Acts of Resistance: Against the New Myths of Our Time*, trans. Richard Nice (Cambridge: Polity, 1999), 81–7.

Butler, Judith, *Frames of War: When Is Life Grievable?* (New York: Verso, 2009).

—, 'Bodily Vulnerability, Coalitions, and Street Politics', in *The State of Things*, ed. Marta Kuzma, Pablo Lafuente, and Peter Osborne (London: Koenig, 2012), 163–97.

Butler, Melissa, 'Rousseau and the Politics of Care', in *Feminist Interpretations of Rousseau*, ed. Lynda Lange (University Park: Pennsylvania State University Press, 2002), 212–82.

Butterwegge, Christoph, *Hartz IV und die Folgen: Auf dem Weg in eine andere Republik?* (Weinheim: Beltz, 2015).

Caixeta, Luzenir et al., *Hogares, Cuidados y Fronteras/Homes, Care and Borders/ Haushalte, Sorge und Grenzen* (Madrid: Traficantes de Sueños, 2004).

Calle Collado, Angel, and Ricard Vilaregut Sáez, *Territorios en democracia: El municipalismo a debate* (Barcelona: Icaria editorial, 2015).

Case, Mary Anne, 'Trans Formations in the Vatican's War on "Gender Ideology" ', *Signs: Journal of Women in Culture and Society* 44:3 (2019), 639–64.

Castel, Robert, *From Manual Workers to Wage Laborers: Transformation of the Social Question*, trans. Richard Boyd (1995; New York: Routledge, 2017).

—, *L'insécurité sociale: qu'est-ce qu'être protégé?* (Paris: Éditions du Seuil, 2003).

Cernuzio, Salvatore, 'The Holy See against Gender Ideology: A Danger to Humanity. Sex Is Not a Subjective Choice', *La Stampa*, 22 March 2019.

Chakravartty, Paula, and Denise Ferreira da Silva, 'Accumulation, Dispossession, and Debt: The Racial Logic of Global Capitalism – An Introduction', *American Quarterly* 64:3 (2012), 361–85.

Colau, Ada, and Adrià Alemany, *¡Sí se puede! Crónica de una pequeña gran victoria* (Barcelona: Destino, 2013).

Colliot-Thélène, Catherine, *Democracy and Subjective Rights: Democracy without Demos* (London: Rowman & Littlefield, 2018).

Connell, Raewyn, and James W. Messerschmidt, 'Hegemonic Masculinity: Re-thinking the Concept', *Gender & Society* 19:6 (2005), 829–59.

Corredor, Elizabeth S., 'Unpacking "Gender Ideology" and the Global Right's Anti-Gender Countermovement', *Signs: Journal of Women in Culture and Society* 44:3 (2019), 613–38.

Critical Times 1:1 (2018).

Dahl, Robert A., *Democracy and Its Critics* (New Haven, CT: Yale University Press, 1991).

De Giorgi, Alessandro, 'Immigration Control, Post-Fordism, and Less Eligibility: A Materialist Critique of the Criminalization of Immigration across Europe', *Punishment & Society* 12:2 (2010), 147–67.

De Gouges, Olympe, 'Declaration of the Rights of Woman and the Female Citizen' (1791), olympedegouges.eu.

Defert, Daniel, 'Course Context', in *Michel Foucault, Lectures on the Will to Know and Oedipal Knowledge: Michel Foucault, Lectures at the Collège de France*, ed. Daniel Defert, François Ewald, and Andrea Fontana (London: Palgrave Macmillan, 2003), 262–86.

Deleuze, Gilles, *Bergsonism*, trans. Hugh Tomlinson and Barbara Habberjam (1966; New York: Zone Books, 1991).

—, *Difference and Repetition*, trans. Paul Patton (1968; New York: Columbia University Press, 1994).

—, *Logique du sens* (Paris: Éditions de Minuit, 1969).

—, *Logic of Sense*, ed. Constantin V. Boundas, trans. Mark Lester and Charles Stivale (1969; New York: Columbia University Press, 1990).

—, Félix Guattari, *Anti-Oedipus: Capitalism and Schizophrenia*, preface Michel Foucault, trans. Robert Hurley, Mark Seem, and Helen R. Lane (1972; London: Athlone, 1984).

—, *Foucault*, ed. and trans. Seán Hand (1986; London: Continuum, 1999).

—, *The Fold: Leibniz and the Baroque*, trans. Tom Conley (1988; Minneapolis: University of Minnesota Press, 1992).

—, 'Control and Becoming', in *Negotiations, 1972–1990*, trans. Martin Joughin (1990; New York: Columbia University Press, 1995), 169–76.

—, and Felix Guattari, *What Is Philosophy?*, trans. Hugh Tomlinson and Graham Burchell (1991; New York: Columbia University Press, 1994).

Demirović, Alex, *Demokratie und Herrschaft: Aspekte kritischer Gesellschaftstheorie* (Münster: Westfälisches Dampfboot, 1997).

—, 'Democracy in Times of Crisis', *transform! European Journal for Alternative Thinking and Political Dialogue* 11 (2012).

—, 'Der Tigersprung: Überlegungen zur Verteidigung der "Gegenwart" ', *PROKLA: Zeitschrift für kritische Sozialwissenschaft* 46:183 (2016), 307–16.

—, 'Autoritärer Populismus als neoliberale Krisenbewältigungsstrategie', *PROKLA: Zeitschrift für kritische Sozialwissenschaft* 48:190 (2018), 27–42.

—, and Andrea Maihofer, 'VielfachKrise und die Krise der Geschlechterverhältnisse', in *Krise, Alltag, Allianzen: Arbeits- und geschlechtersoziologische Perspektiven*, ed. Hildegard Maria Nickel and Andreas Heilmann (Weinheim: Beltz, 2013), 30–48.

—, Julia Dück, Florian Becker, and Pauline Bader (eds.), *Vielfach Krise im finanzmarktdominierten Kapitalismus* (Münster: Westfälisches Dampfboot, 2011).

Derrida, Jacques, *Of Grammatology*, trans. Gayatri Chakravorty Spivak, introd. Judith Butler (1967; Baltimore: Johns Hopkins University Press, 2016).

—, *Specters of Marx: The State of the Debt, the Work of Mourning, and the New International*, trans. Peggy Kamuf (1993; New York: Routledge, 2006).

—, *The Politics of Friendship*, trans. George Collins (1994; London: Verso, 1997).

—, *Of Hospitality*, trans. Rachel Bowlby (1997; Stanford: Stanford University Press, 2000).

—, 'The Madness of Economic Reason: A Gift without Present', in *Given Time I: Counterfeit Money*, trans. Peggy Kamuf (1991; Chicago: University of Chicago Press, 1992), 34–70.

—, 'Ich mißtraue der Utopie, ich will das Un-Mögliche', interview, *Die Zeit*, 8 March 1998.

—, 'Marx & Sons', in *Ghostly Demarcations: A Symposium on Jacques Derrida's Specters of Marx*, ed. Michael Sprinker, trans. Kelly Barry (London: Verso, 1999), 213–69.

—, 'The Future of the Profession or the Unconditional University', in *Without Alibi*, trans. Peggy Kamuf (2001; Stanford: Stanford University Press, 2002), 234–7.

—, *Rogues: Two Essays on Reason*, trans. Pascale-Anne Brault and Michael Naas (2003; Stanford: Stanford University Press, 2005).

Desideri, Valentina, and Stefano Harney, 'Fate Work: A Conversation', *ephemera: theory and politics in organization* 13:1 (2013), 159–76.

Dietze, Gabriele, *Sexueller Exzeptionalismus: Überlegenheitsnarrative in Migrationsabwehr und Rechtspopulismus* (Bielefeld: transcript, 2019).

Dörre, Klaus, 'Die national-soziale Gefahr: Pegida, Neue Rechte und der Verteilungskonflikt – sechs Thesen', in *PEGIDA – Rechtspopulismus zwischen Fremdenangst und "Wende"-Enttäuschung?*, ed. Karl-Siegbert Rehberg, Franziska Kunz, and Tino Schlinzig (Bielefeld: transcript, 2016), 259–74.

Dowling, Emma, and David Harvie, 'Harnessing the Social: State, Crisis and the (Big) Society', *Sociology* 48:5 (2014), 869–86.

Eribon, Didier, *Returning to Reims* (2009), trans. Michael Lucey (Los Angeles: Semiotext(e), 2013).

Errejón, Iñigo, and Chantal Mouffe, *Construir Pueblo, Hegemonía y radicalización de la democracia* (Barcelona: Icaria editorial, 2015).

Fabian, Johannes, *Time and the Other: How Anthropology Makes Its Objects* (1983; New York: Columbia University Press, 2014).

Federici, Silvia, *Caliban and the Witch: Women, the Body and Primitive Accumulation* (New York: Autonomedia, 2004).

—, *Revolution at Point Zero: Housework, Reproduction, and Feminist Struggle* (New York: Autonomedia, 2012).

Ferreira da Silva, Denise, 'Unpayable Debt: Reflections on Value and Violence', in *The documenta 14 Reader*, ed. Quinn Latimer and Adam Szymczyk (Munich: Prestel 2017), 81–112.

Ferris, Sara R., *In the Name of Women's Rights: The Rise of Femonationalism* (Durham, NC: Duke University Press, 2017).

Fetscher, Iring, *Rousseaus politische Philosophie: Zur Geschichte des demokratischen Freiheitsbegriffs* (Frankfurt am Main: Suhrkamp, 1975).

Foucault, Michel, 'Revolutionary Action: "Until Now" ', in *Language, Counter-Memory, Practice Selected Essays and Interviews*, ed. D.F. Bouchard, trans. Donald F. Bouchard and Sherry Simon (1970; Ithaca, NY: Cornell University Press, 1977), 218–33.

—, 'Theatrum philosophicum', in *Dits et écrits I, 1954–1975*, ed. Daniel Defert, François Ewald, and Jacques Lagrange (1970; Paris: Gallimard, 2001), 943–67.

—, 'Theatrum Philosophicum', in *Language, Counter-Memory, Practice: Selected Interviews and Essays*, ed. D.F. Bouchard, trans. Donald F. Bouchard and Sherry Simon (1970; Ithaca, NY: Cornell University Press, 1977), 167–96.

—, 'Nietzsche, Genealogy, History', in *Language, Counter-Memory, Practice: Selected Interviews and Essays*, ed. D.F. Bouchard, trans. Donald F. Bouchard and Sherry Simon (1971; Ithaca, NY: Cornell University Press, 1977), 139–64.

—, *Society Must Be Defended: Lectures at the Collège de France 1975–1976*, ed. François Ewald, trans. David Macey (New York: Picador, 2003).

—, 'Power and Sex: An Interview by Bernard-Henri Levy', trans. David J. Parent, *Telos* 32 (1977), 152–61.

—, 'Non au sexe roi', in *Dits et écrits II: 1976–1988*, ed. Daniel Defert, François Ewald, and Jacques Lagrange (1977; Paris: Gallimard 2001), 256–69.

—, *Security, Territory, Population: Lectures at the Collège de France 1977–78*, ed. Michel Senellart, François Ewald, and Alessandro Fontana, trans. Graham Burchell (New York: Palgrave Macmillan, 2009).

—, *The History of Sexuality*, vol. 1., *The Will to Knowledge*, trans. Robert Hurley (1978; New York: Vintage, 1990).

—, 'What Is Critique?', in *The Politics of Truth*, ed. Sylvère Lotringer, introd. John Rajchman (1978; Los Angeles: Semiotext(e), 2007), 41–82.

—, *Remarks on Marx: Conversations with Duccio Trombadori*, trans. R. James Goldstein, James Cascaito (1978/1980; New York: Semiotext(e), 1991).

—, 'Meshes of Power', in *Space, Knowledge and Power: Foucault and Geography*, ed. Jeremy W. Crampton and Stuart Elden, trans. Gerald Moore (1981; London: Routledge, 2016).

—, '*Omnes et Singulatim*: Towards a Criticism of "Political Reason" ', in *Power: Essential Works of Michel Foucault 1954–1984*, vol. 3 (1981; New York: New Press, 2000), 298–325.

—, 'Space, Knowledge, and Power', in *The Foucault Reader*, ed. Paul Rabinow, trans. Christian Hubert (1982; New York: Pantheon, 1984), 239–56.

—, 'The Subject and Power', *Critical Inquiry* 8:4 (1982), 777–95.

—, 'What Is Enlightenment? (Qu'est-ce que les Lumières?)', in *Dits et écrits II: 1976–1988*, ed. Daniel Defert, François Ewald, and Jacques Lagrange (1984; Paris: Gallimard, 2001), 1381–97.

—, 'What Is Enlightenment?', trans. Catherine Porter, in *The Foucault Reader*, ed. Paul Rabinow, trans. Christian Hubert (New York: Pantheon 1984), 32–50.

—, 'Qu'est-ce que les Lumières?', in *Dits et écrits II*, ed. Daniel Defert, François Ewald, and Jacques Lagrange (1984; Paris: Gallimard, 2001), 1498–507.

—, 'Kant on Enlightenment and Revolution', trans. Colin Gordon, *Economy and Society* 15:1 (1986 [1984]), 88–96.

Fraenkel, Ernst, *Deutschland und die westlichen Demokratien* (1964; Frankfurt am Main: Suhrkamp, 1991).

Fraser, Nancy, and Linda Gordon, 'A Genealogy of *Dependency*: Tracing a Keyword of the U.S. Welfare State', *Signs: Journal of Women in Culture and Society* 19:2 (1994), 309–36.

Fundación de los Comunes, *Hacia nuevas instituciones democráticas* (Madrid: Traficantes de sueños, 2016).

Fustel de Coulanges, Numa Denis, *The Ancient City: A Study on the Religion, Laws, and Institutions of Greece and Rome* (1864; Baltimore: Johns Hopkins University Press, 1980).

Gago, Verónica, et al., 'How Would You Go to Strike? The Women's Strike and Beyond', special issue, *South Atlantic Quarterly* 117:3 (2018).

—, '#WeStrike: Notes toward a Political Theory of the Feminist Strike', *South Atlantic Quarterly* 117:3 (2018), 660–9.

— (ed.), 'How Would You Go to Strike? The Women's Strike and Beyond', trans. Liz Mason-Deese, *South Atlantic Quarterly* 117:3 (2018).

—, *Feminist International: How to Change Everything*, trans. Liz Mason-Deese (London: Verso, 2020).

—, and Marta Malo (eds.), 'Against the Day: The New Feminist International', trans. Liz Mason-Deese, special issue, *South Atlantic Quarterly* 119:3 (2020).

Galcerán Huguet, Montserrat, 'Demokratie, Gouvernementalität und das "Gemeinsame" in der spanischen 15M-Bewegung', in *Inventionen 2: Exodus. Immanenz. Territorium. Reale Demokratie. Biopolitik. Maßlose Differenz*, ed. Isabell Lorey, Roberto Nigro, and Gerald Raunig (Zurich: Diaphanes, 2012), 62–75.

—, 'The Struggle for Social Change Reaches the Institutions', trans. Kelly Mulvaney, *transversal: multilingual webjournal*: 'monster municipalisms' (September 2016), transversal.at.

—, Pablo Carmona Pascual, 'Los fututos del municipalismo: Feminización de la política y radicalización democrática', *transversal. multilingual webjournal*: 'monster municipalisms' (September 2016), transversal.at.

Gardner, Jane F., *Being a Roman Citizen* (New York: Routledge, 2010).

Geber, Eva, 'Zur Einführung', in *Louise Michel: Texte und Reden*, ed. Eva Geber (Vienna: bahoe 2019), 7–26.

Gilligan, Carol, *In a Different Voice: Psychological Theory and Women's Development* (Cambridge, MA: Harvard University Press, 1982).

Gould, Roger V., *Insurgent Identities: Class, Community, and Protest in Paris from 1848 to the Commune* (Chicago: Chicago University Press, 1995).

Graeber, David, *Debt: The First 5,000 Years* (New York: Melville House, 2011).

Graff, Agnieszka, Ratna Kapur, and Suzanna Danuta Walters, 'Introduction: Gender and the Rise of the Global Right', *Signs: Journal of Women in Culture and Society* 44:3 (2019), 541–60.

Guattari, Félix, 'Transversality', in *Psychoanalysis and Transversality: Texts and Interviews 1955–1971*, intro. Gilles Deleuze, trans. Ames Hodges and Rosemarie Sheed (1972; Los Angeles: Semiotext(e), 2015), 102–20.

Gutiérrez Rodríguez, Encarnación, *Migration, Domestic Work and Affect: A Decolonial Approach on Value and the Feminization of Labour* (New York: Routledge, 2010).

Hall, Stuart, 'Popular-Democratic vs Authoritarian Populism', in *Marxism and Democracy*, ed. Alan Hunt (London: Lawrence & Wishart, 1980), 157–80.

—, 'Authoritarian Populism: A Reply to Jessop et al.', *New Left Review* I:151 (May/June 1985), 115–124.

Hamilton, Alexander, James Madison, and John Jay, *The Federalist Papers* (1787–1788; New York: Bantam, 2003).

Haraway, Donna, *Staying with the Trouble: Making Kin in the Chthulucene*, Experimental Futures (Durham, NC: Duke University Press, 2016).

Hardt, Michael, and Antonio Negri, *Assembly* (Oxford: Oxford University Press, 2017).

—, *Multitude: War and Democracy in the Age of Empire* (New York: Penguin, 2004).

Hark, Sabine, and Mike Laufenberg, 'Sexualität in der Krise: Heteronormativität im Neoliberalismus', in *Gesellschaft: Feministische Krisendiagnosen*, ed. Erna Appelt, Brigitte Aulenbacher, and Angelika Wetterer (Münster: Westfälisches Dampfboot, 2013), 227–45.

—, Paula-Irene Villa, *The Future of Difference: Beyond the Toxic Entanglement of Racism, Sexism and Feminism*, trans. Sophie Lewis (2017; London: Verso, 2020).

Harney, Stefano, and Fred Moten, *The Undercommons: Fugitive Planning & Black Study* (London: minor compositions, 2013).

Hartman, Saidiya V., *Scenes of Subjection: Terror, Slavery, and Self-Making in Nineteenth-Century America* (Oxford: Oxford University Press, 1997).

Harvey, David, *The Enigma of Capital: And the Crises of Capitalism* (London: Profile, 2010).

—, 'The Urban Roots of Financial Crises: Reclaiming the City for Anticapitalist Struggle', *Socialist Register: The Crisis and the Left* 48 (2012).

Hegel, G.W.F., *Elements of the Philosophy of Right*, trans. Samuel W. Dyde (1821/1896; Mineola, NY: Dover, 2005).

—, *Hegel's* Philosophy of Nature: *Part Two of* The Encyclopedia of the Philosophical Sciences *(1830)*, trans. from Nicolin and Pöggeler's Edition (1959), and from the *Zusätze* in Michelet's Text (1847), trans. Arnold V. Miller (Oxford: Clarendon, 2004).

—, *The Phenomenology of Spirit*, trans. Arnold V. Miller (Oxford: Oxford University Press, 1977).

—, *Jenaer Systementwürfe III: Naturphilosophie und Philosophie des Geistes. Vorlesungsmanuskript zur Realphilosophie*, ed. Rolf P. Horstmann (1805–6; Hamburg: Meiner, 1987).

—, *Lectures on the History of Philosophy*, trans. Ruben Alvarado (1857; Aalton: WordBridge, 2011).

Heimeshoff, Lisa-Marie, et al. (eds.), *Grenzregime II: Migration – Kontrolle – Wissen. Transnationale Perspektiven* (Berlin: Assoziation A, 2014).

Heinz, Marion, 'Zur Konstitution geschlechtlicher Subjekte bei Rousseau', in *Geschlechterordnung und Staat: Legitimationsfiguren der politischen Philosophie (1600–1850)*, ed. Marion Heinz and Sabine Doyé (Berlin: De Gruyter, 2012), 163–80.

Heller, Hermann, 'Die Souveränität: Ein Beitrag zur Theorie des Staats- und Völkerrechts', in *Collected Works*, vol. 2, ed. Martin Draht et al. (1927; Leiden: Sijthoff, 1971), 31–202.

Hendicks, Wanda A., *Gender, Race, and Politics in the Midwest: Black Club Women in Illinois* (Bloomington, IN: Indiana University Press, 1998).

Hess, Sabine, and Bernd Kasparek (eds.), *Grenzregime: Diskurse, Praktiken, Institutionen in Europa* (Berlin: Assoziation A, 2010).

— et al. (eds.), *Der lange Sommer der Migration: Grenzregime III* (Berlin: Assoziation A, 2016).

Hobbes, Thomas, *De Cive–Philosophical Rudiments Concerning Government and Society* (1651), public-library.uk/ebooks/27/57.pdf

—, *Leviathan – or the Matter, Forme, and Power of a Common-Wealth, Ecclesiastical and Civill* (1651; London: Ely, 1909).

Hochschild, Arlie Russel, 'Global Care Chains and Emotional Surplus Value', in *On the Edge: Living with Global Capitalism*, ed. Anthony Giddens and Will Hutton (London: Jonathan Cape, 2000), 130–46.

Iglesias Turrión, Pablo, 'Understanding Podemos', *New Left Review* 93 (May/June 2015), 7–22.

—, 'Spain on Edge', *New Left Review* 93 (May/June 2015), 23–42.

InfoSex, 'If Women Are Becoming a Multitude All Around the World', *Dinamo Press*, 14 December 2016, dinamopress.it.

Jörke, Dirk, 'Demokratie in neuen Räumen: Ein theoriegeschichtlicher Vergleich', *Österreichische Zeitschrift für Politikwissenschaft* 40:1 (2011), 7–19.

Jullien, François, *The Philosophy of Living*, trans. Krzysztof Fijalkowski and Michael Richardson (2001; Kolkata: Seagull, 2016).

Kant, Immanuel, 'On the Common Saying: "This May Be True in Theory, but It Does Not Apply in Practice" ', in *Kant: Political Writings*, ed. H.S. Reiss (1793; Cambridge: Cambridge University Press, 1991).

—, *The Conflict of the Faculties*, intro. and trans. Mary J. Gregor (1798; Lincoln: University of Nebraska Press, 1992).

—, *Anthropology from a Pragmatic Point of View*, trans. and ed. Robert B. Louden and Manfred Kuehn (1798; Cambridge: Cambridge University Press, 2006).

Karakayali, Serhat, 'Volunteers: From Solidarity to Integration', *South Atlantic Quarterly* 117:2 (2018), 313–31.

Keeanga-Yamahtta Taylor (ed.), *How We Get Free: Black Feminism and the Combahee River Collective* (Chicago: Haymarket Books, 2017).

Kimmerle, Heinz, *Derrida zur Einführung* (Hamburg: Junius, 1988).

Klinger, Cornelia, ' "Für den Staat ist das Weib die Nacht": Die Ordnung der Geschlechter und ihr Verhältnis zur Politik', in *Geschlechterdifferenz: Texte, Theorien, Positionen*, ed. Doris Ruhe (Würzburg: Königshausen & Neumann, 2000), 61–100.

Knittler, Käthe, 'Wissensarbeit und militante Untersuchung: Zwischen Produktion und Rebellion. Über Möglichkeiten widerständiger Wissensproduktion', *Kurswechsel* 1 (2013), 74–83.

Knoll, Alex, Sarah Schilliger, and Bea Schwager, *Wisch und weg! Sans-Papier-Hausarbeiterinnen zwischen Prekarität und Selbstbestimmung* (Zurich: Seismo, 2012).

Korolczuk, Elzbieta, and Agnieszka Graff, 'Gender as "Ebola from Brussels": The Anticolonial Frame and the Rise of Illiberal Populism', *Signs: Journal of Women in Culture and Society* 43:4 (2018), 797–821.

Kreisky, Eva, and Birgit Sauer, *Feministische Standpunkte in der Politikwissenschaft: Eine Einführung* (Frankfurt am Main: Campus, 1995).

Kubaczek, Niki, and Gerald Raunig, 'The Political Reinvention of the City', trans. Kelly Mulvaney, *transversal* (November 2017), transversal.at/blog.

Kuster, Brigitta, *Choix d'un passé: Transnationale Vergegenwärtigungen kolonialer Hinterlassenschaften* (Vienna: transversal texts, 2016).

Kuster, Friederike, *Rousseau – Die Konstitution des Privaten: Zur Genealogie der bürgerlichen Familie* (Berlin: De Gruyter, 2005).

Laclau, Ernesto, *On Populist Reason* (London: Verso, 2005).

Lang, Sabine, and Birgit Sauer, 'Hat die europäische Krise ein Geschlecht? Feministische und staatstheoretische Überlegungen', in *Europäische Staatlichkeit: Zwischen Krise und Integration*, ed. Hans-Jürgen Bieling and Martin Große Hüttmann (Wiesbaden: Springer, 2016), 241–58.

Lange, Lynda (ed.), *Feminist Interpretations of Jean-Jacques Rousseau* (University Park: Pennsylvania State University Press, 2002).

Lazzarato, Maurizio, *The Making of the Indebted Man: Essay on the Neoliberal Condition*, trans. Joshua David Jordan (Los Angeles: Semiotext(e), 2012).

—, *Governing by Debt* (2014), trans. Joshua David Jordan (Los Angeles: Semiotext(e), 2015).

Leighton, Marian, 'Der Anarchofeminismus und Louise Michel', in *Louise Michel: Ihr Leben – Ihr Kampf – Ihre Ideen*, Frauen in der Revolution, ed. Renate Sami (Berlin: Kramer, 1976), 17–56.

Lefebvre, Henri, *La Proclamation de la Commune: 26 Mars 1871* (Paris: Gallimard, 1965).

Lenze, Anne, and Antje Funcke, *Alleinerziehende unter Druck: Rechtliche Rahmenbedingungen, finanzielle Lage und Reformbedarf* (Gütersloh: Bertelsmann-Stiftung, 2016).

Lissagaray, Prosper Olivier, *History of the Paris Commune of 1871*, trans. Eleonar Marx (1876; St Petersburg, FL: Red and Black, 2007).

Locke, John, *Two Treatises of Government* (1689; Cambridge: Cambridge University Press, 1994).

—, *Second Treatise of Government*, in *The Founders' Constitution* (1689; Chicago: University of Chicago Press/Liberty Fund, 1986).

Lorey, Isabell, 'Governmentality and Self-Precarization: On the Normalization of Cultural Producers', trans. Lisa Rosenblatt and Dagmar Fink, *transversal: multilingual webjournal*: 'machines and subjectivation' (November 2006), transversal.at.

—, *Figuren des Immunen: Elemente einer politischen Theorie* (Zurich: Diaphanes, 2011).

—, 'Maßlose Differenz', in *Inventionen 2: Exodus. Reale Demokratie. Territorium. Immanenz. Maßlose Differenz. Biopolitik*, ed. Isabell Lorey, Roberto Nigro, and Gerald Raunig (Zurich: Diaphanes, 2012), 154–7.

—, 'The 2011 Occupy Movements: Rancière and the Crisis of Democracy', *Theory, Culture & Society* 31:7–8 (2014), 43–65.

—, 'Das Gefüge der Macht', in *Gouvernementalität und Geschlecht: Politische Theorie im Anschluss an Michel Foucault*, ed. Brigitte Bargetz, Gundula Ludwig, and Birgit Sauer (Frankfurt am Main: Campus, 2015), 31–61.

—, *State of Insecurity: Government of the Precarious*, trans. Aileen Derieg (London: Verso, 2015).

—, 'Ekstatische Sozialität', *engagée: philosophisch-politische einmischungen* 2 (2015/16), 20–3.

—, 'Die Wiederkehr revolutionärer Praxen in der infinitiven Gegenwart', in Isabell Lorey, Gundula Ludwig, and Ruth Sonderegger, *Foucaults Gegenwart: Sexualität – Sorge – Revolution* (Vienna: transversal texts, 2016), 77–103.

—, 'Präsentische Demokratie. Radikale Inklusion – Jetztzeit – Konstituierender Prozess', in *Transformationen der Demokratie – Demokratische Transformationen*, ed. Alex Demirović (Münster: Westfälisches Dampfboot, 2016), 265–77.

—, 'Precarisation, Indebtedness, Giving Time', in *Maria Eichhorn: 5 weeks, 25 days, 175 hours*, ed. Chisenhale Gallery (London: Chisenhale, 2016), 38–49.

—, 'Sorge im Präsens: Verbundenheit, Sorge, _Mit_', in *Ökologien der Sorge*, ed. Tobias Bärtsch et al. (Vienna: transversal texts, 2017), 113–22.

—, 'Emancipation and Debt', presentation at the Emancipation Conference, Technical University, Berlin, 27 May 2018, philosophycommons.typepad.com/disability_and_disadvanta.

—, 'Lucha de clases', in 'Conceptos para comprender la sociedad contemporánea', *Cuadernos de Teoría Social* 4:8 (2018), 126–8.

—, '8M – The Great Feminist Strike', trans. Kelly Mulvaney, *transversal* (March 2019), transversal.at/blog.

—, Gerald Raunig, 'Das gespenstische Potenzial des potere costituente: Vorbemerkungen zu einem europäischen konstituierenden Prozess', in Antonio Negri and Raúl Sánchez Cedillo, *Für einen konstituierenden Prozess in Europa: Demokratische Radikalität und die Regierung der Multituden* (Vienna: transversal texts, 2015), 9–36.

—, Gundula Ludwig, and Ruth Sonderegger, *Foucaults Gegenwart: Sexualität – Sorge – Revolution* (Vienna: transversal texts, 2016).

Ludwig, Gundula, 'Desiring Neoliberalism', *Sexuality Research and Social Policy* 13 (2016), 417–27.

Lutz, Helma, "Life in the Twilight Zone: Migration, Transnationality and Gender in the Private Household," *Journal of Contemporary European Studies* 12:1 (2004), 47–55.

Luxemburg, Rosa, 'The Mass Strike, the Political Party and the Trade Unions', trans. Patrick Lavin (1906; Detroit, MI: Marxist Educational Society of Detroit, 1925).

mac1, 'The Municipalist Manifesto', *transversal: multilingual webjournal*: 'monster municipalisms' (September 2016), transversal.at.

Macherey, Pierre, *In a Materialist Way: Selected Essays*, trans. Ted Stolze (London: Verso, 1998).

Macpherson, C.B., *The Political Theory of Possessive Individualism: Hobbes to Locke* (1962; Oxford: Oxford University Press, 2011).

Maihofer, Andrea, 'Familiale Lebensformen zwischen Wandel und Persistenz: Eine zeitdiagnostische Zwischenbetrachtung', in *Wissen – Methode – Geschlecht: Erfassen des fraglos Gegebenen*, ed. Cornelia Behnke, Diana Lengersdorf, and Sylka Scholz (Wiesbaden: VS Verlag, 2014), 313–34.

—, 'Pluralisierung familialer Lebensformen: Zerfall der Gesellschaft oder neoliberal passgerecht?', in *Kapitalismuskritische Gesellschaftsanalyse: Queer-feministische Positionen*, ed. Katharina Pühl and Birgit Sauer (Münster: Westfälisches Dampfboot, 2018), 113–38.

Marso, Lori Jo, *(Un)manly Citizens: Jean Jacques Rousseau's and Germaine de Staël's Subversive Women* (Baltimore: Johns Hopkins University Press, 1999).

Malo de Molina, Marta, "Common Notions, Part 1: Workers-Inquiry, Co
-research, Consciousness-Raising", trans. Maribel Casas-Cortés and
Sebastian Cobarrubias (Notas Rojas Collective Chapel Hill), *transversal: multilingual webjournal*: 'militant research' (April 2006),
transversal.at.

Martin, Randy, *Knowledge Ltd: Toward a Social Logic of Derivative* (Philadelphia: Temple University Press, 2015).

Marx, Karl, *Critique of Hegel's Philosophy of Right*, trans. Anette Jolin
and Joseph O'Malley (1843; Cambridge: Cambridge University Press,
1970).

—, 'On the Jewish Question', in *The Marx-Engels Reader*, ed. Robert
Tucker (1843; New York: Norton & Company, 1978), 26–46.

—, *Comments on James Mill, Éléments D'économie Politique* (1844),
marxists.org.

—, 'The Eighteenth Brumaire of Louis Bonaparte', in *The Marx-Engels
Reader*, ed. Robert Tucker (1852; New York: Norton & Company,
1978), 594–617.

—, 'First and Second Drafts to *The Civil War in France*', in *The Civil War
in France* (1871; Peking: Foreign Languages Press, 1966).

—, 'The Civil War in France', intro. Friedrich Engels, in *The Marx-Engels
Reader*, ed. Robert Tucker (1871; New York: Norton & Company, 1978),
618–52.

Matthes, Melissa, *The Rape of Lucretia and the Founding of Republics:
Reading in Livy, Machiavelli and Rousseau* (University Park: Pennsylvania State University Press, 2000).

Mitropoulos, Angela, *Contact and Contagion. From Biopolitics to
Oikonomia* (London: minor compositions, 2012).

Maus, Ingeborg, *Über Volkssouveränität: Elemente einer Demokratietheorie*
(Frankfurt am Main: Suhrkamp, 2011).

Mauss, Marcel, *The Gift: The Form and Reason for Exchange in Archaic
Societies*, trans. W.D. Hall (1925; New York: Routledge, 2001).

Michel, Louise, *The Red Virgin: The Memoirs of Louise Michel*, ed. and
trans. Lowry Bullit and Elizabeth Ellington Gunter (1886; Tuscaloosa:
University of Alabama Press, 1981).

—, 'Die Frau in der Freimaurerloge', in *Louise Michel: Texte und Reden*,
ed. Eva Geber (1904; Vienna: bahoe, 2019), 27–31.

Mosès, Stéphane, *The Angel of History: Rosenzweig, Benjamin, Scholem*, trans. Barbara Harshav (Stanford: Stanford University Press, 2009).

Mouffe, Chantal, *The Democratic Paradox* (London: Verso, 2000).

—, *For a Left Populism* (London: Verso, 2018).

Movimiento por la Democracia, *Carta por la Democracia* (Madrid: self-published, 2014), http://blogs.traficantes.net/wp-content/blogs.dir/9/files/2014/03/Carta_por_la_Democracia_1pag.pdf

—, 'El Movimiento por la Democracia, en la nueva coyuntura', *Diagonal*, 25 June 2014, diagonalperiodico.net.

Müller, Jan-Werner, *What Is Populism?* (Philadelphia: University of Pennsylvania Press, 2016).

Nancy, Jean-Luc, *The Experience of Freedom*, trans. Bridget McDonald (1988; Stanford: Stanford University Press, 1993).

—, *Being Singular Plural*, trans. Robert D. Richardson and Anne E. O'Byrne (1996; Stanford: Stanford University Press, 2000).

Negri, Antonio, 'The Constitution of Strength', in *Insurgencies: Constituent Power and the Modern State*, trans. Maurizia Boscagli (1992; Minneapolis: Minnesota University Press, 1999), 303–36.

—, 'Constituent Republic', in *Revolutionary Writing: Common Sense Essays in Post-Political Politics*, ed. Werner Bonefeld (New York: Autonomedia, 2003), 243–53.

—, and Raúl Sánchez Cedillo, 'For a Constituent Initiative in Europe', *transversal* (January 2015), transversal.at

Neilsen, Brett, and Ned Rossiter, 'Precarity as a Political Concept, or, Fordism as Exception', *Theory, Culture & Society* 25:7–8 (2008), 51–72.

Nietzsche, Friedrich, 'On the Uses and Disadvantages of History for Life', in *Untimely Meditations*, ed. Daniel Breazale, trans. R.J. Hollingdale (1874; Cambridge: Cambridge University Press, 1997), 57–124.

—, *Thus Spoke Zarathustra*, trans. R.J. Hollingdale (1883–1885; London: Penguin, 1974).

—, *On the Genealogy of Morality*, trans. Carol Diethe, ed. Keith Ansell-Pearson (1887; Cambridge: Cambridge University Press, 2007).

Nigro, Roberto, and Gerald Raunig, 'Transversalität', in *Inventionen 1: gemeinsam, prekär, potentia, Kon-/Disjunktion, Ereignis, Transversalität, Queere Assemblagen*, ed. Isabell Lorey, Roberto Nigro, and Gerald Raunig (Zurich: Diaphanes, 2011), 194–6.

Non Una di Meno, *Abbiamo un Piano: Piano femminista contro la violenza maschile sulle donne e la violenza di genere* (2017), nonunadimeno.files.wordpress.com.

Notz, Gisela, 'Wir wollen Brot und Rosen', *Ada Magazin*, 23 September 2018, adamag.de.

Nowotny, Stefan, 'Swarm of Events: What Is New in History and the Politics of Enunciation', trans. Aileen Derig, *transversal: multilingual webjournal*: 'inventions' (January 2011), transversal.at.

—, and Gerald Raunig, 'Instituent Practices: New Introduction to the Revised Edition', *transversal* (May 2016), transversal.at/blog.

Nolte, Paul, *Was ist Demokratie? Geschichte und Gegenwart* (Munich: Beck, 2012).

Ober, Josiah, 'The Original Meaning of "Democracy": Capacity to Do Things, Not Majority Rules', *Constellations* 15:1 (2008), 3–9.

Observatorio Metropolitano, *La apuesta municipalista: La democracia empieza por lo cercano* (Madrid: Traficantes de sueños, 2014).

Pateman, Carole, *Participation and Democratic Theory* (Cambridge: Cambridge University Press, 1970).

—, *The Sexual Contract* (Stanford: Stanford University Press, 1988).

Piketty, Thomas, *Capital in the Twenty-First Century*, trans. Arthur Goldhammer (Cambridge, MA: Belknap, 2017).

Precarias a la Deriva, 'Adrift through the Circuits of Feminized Precarious Work', *transversal: multilingual webjournal*: 'Prekariat' (July 2004), transversal.at.

—, 'Cuidados globalizados', in *a la deriva: Por los circuitos de la precariedad feminista* (Madrid: Traficantes de Sueños, 2004), 217–48.

—, 'Of Questions, Illusions, Swarms and Eeserts: Notes on Research and Activism from Precarias a la Deriva', trans. Maggie Schmitt, December 2006 [2004], crashcourse666.wordpress.com.

—, *Was ist dein Streik? Militante Streifzüge durch die Kreisläufe der Prekarität*, trans. Birgit Mennel, introd. Birgit Mennel and Stefan Nowotny (2004/2006; Vienna: transversal texts, 2014).

—, 'Projekt und Methode einer "militanten Untersuchung": Das Reflektieren der Multitude in actu', in *Empire und die biopolitische Wende: Die internationale Debatte im Anschluss an Hardt und Negri*, ed. Marianne Pieper et al. (2005; Frankfurt am Main: Campus, 2007), 85–108.

—, 'A Very Careful Strike: Four Hypotheses', *The Commoner* 11 (2006), 33–45.

—, '¡La Bolsa contra la vida! De la precarización de la existencia a la huelga de cuidados', in *Estudios sobre génerro y economía*, ed. María Jesús Vara (Madrid: Akal, 2006), 104–34.

—, 'Die Prekarisierung der Existenz: Ein Gespräch', in Renate Lorenz and Brigitta Kuster, *sexuell arbeiten: eine queere perspektive auf arbeit und prekäres leben* (Berlin: b_books, 2007), 259–72.

Preciado, Paul B., 'Let Your South Walk, Dance, Listen and Decide', *documenta 14 Public Paper* 2 (2017), 2.

Pope Francis, *Encyclical Letter: Laudato Si of the Holy Father Francis – On Care of for Common Home*, 24 May 2015, para 155, vatican.va.

Rancière, Jacques, *Disagreement: Politics and Philosophy* (1995; Minneapolis: University of Minnesota Press, 1999).

Raunig, Gerald, *Art and Revolution: Transversal Activism in the Long Twentieth Century*, trans. Aileen Derig (2005; Los Angeles: Semiotext(e), 2007).

—, 'Instituent Practices: Fleeing, Instituting, Transforming', trans. Aileen Derieg, *transversal: multilingual webjournal*: 'do you remember institutional critique?' (January 2006), transversal.at.

—, 'Instituent Practices, No.2: Institutional Critique, Constituent Power, and the Persistence of Instituting', trans. Aileen Derieg, *transversal: multilingual webjournal*: 'extradisciplinaire' (January 2007), transversal.at.

—, *A Thousand Machines: A Concise Philosophy of the Machine as Social Movement*, trans. Aileen Derieg (2008; Los Angeles: Semiotext(e), 2010).

—, 'Confluences: The Molecular-Revolutionary Force of the New Municipalismos in Spain', trans. Kelly Mulvaney, *transversal: multilingual webjournal*: 'monster municipalisms' (September 2016), transversal.at.

Rebentisch, Juliane, *The Art of Freedom: On the Dialectics of Democratic Existence* (2012; Cambridge: Polity, 2016).

Rigney, Ann, 'Remembering Hope, Transnational Activism beyond the Traumatic', *Memory Studies* 11:3 (2018), 368–80.

Rodriguez López, Emmanuel, *La política en el ocaso de la clase media: El ciclo 15M-Podemos* (Madrid: Traficantes de sueños, 2016).

Rosanvallon, Pierre, *Le capitalisme utopique: Critique de l'idéologie économique* (1979; Paris: Points, 1999).

Ross, Kristin, *The Emergence of Social Space: Rimbaud and the Paris Commune* (London: Verso, 2008).

—, *Communal Luxury: The Political Imaginary of the Paris Commune* (London: Verso, 2015).

Rousseau, Jean-Jacques, 'Discourse on Political Economy', in *The Social Contract and Discourses by Jean-Jacques Rousseau*, trans. G.D.H. Cole (1755; London: Dent, 1923), 249–87.

—, 'Economy [abridged]', in *The Encyclopedia of Diderot & d'Alembert Collaborative Translation Project*, trans. Stephen J. Gendzier (1755; Ann Arbor: University of Michigan Library, 2009).

—, *Politics and the Arts: Letter to M. D'Alembert on the Theatre*, trans. Alan Bloom (1758; Ithaca, NY: Cornell University Press, 1968).

—, *The Social Contract: Or, the Principles of Political Rights*, trans. Rose M. Harrington (1762; New York: G. P. Putnam's Sons, 1893).

—, *Emile, or Education*, trans. Barbara Foxley (1762; London: Dent, 1921).

—, 'Plan for a Constitution for Corsica', trans. Christopher Kelly, in *The Plan for Perpetual Peace, On the Government of Poland, and Other Writings on History and Politics: The Collected Writings of Jean-Jacques Rousseau*, vol. 2 (1766; Hanover, NH: University Press of New England, 2005), 123–55.

Salazar Parreñas, Rhacel, *Servants of Globalization: Women, Migration, and Domestic Work* (Stanford: Stanford University Press, 2001).

Sánchez Cedillo, Raúl, '15M: Something Constituent This Way Comes', trans. Mara Goldwyn, *South Atlantic Quarterly* 113:3 (2012), 573–84.

—, 'Rajoynato, municipalismos, sistema de contrapoder', *transversal: multilingual webjournal: '*monster municipalisms' (September 2017), transversal.at.

Sarachild, Kathie, 'Consciousness-Raising: A Radical Weapon', in *Feminist Revolution* ed. Kathie Sarachild (New York: Redstockings, 1975), 144–50.

Sauer, Birgit, 'Krise des Wohlfahrtsstaates: Eine Männerinstitution unter Globalisierungsdruck?', in *Globale Gerechtigkeit? Feministische*

Debatte zur Krise des Sozialstaats, ed. Helga Braun and Dörthe Jung (Hamburg: Konkret Literatur Verlag, 1997), 113–47.

—, 'Authoritarian Right-Wing Populism as Masculinist Identity Politics: The Role of Affects', in *Right-Wing Populism and Gender: European Perspectives and Beyond*, ed. Gabriele Dietze and Julia Roth (Bielefeld: transcript, 2020), 25–44.

Scheele, Alexandra, 'Widersprüchliche Anerkennung des Privaten: Eine Kritik aktueller Entwicklungen wohlfahrtsstaatlicher Politik', in *Staat und Geschlecht: Grundlagen der aktuellen Herausforderungen feministischer Staatstheorie*, ed. Gundula Ludwig, Birgit Sauer, and Stefanie Wöhl (Baden-Baden: Nomos, 2009), 167–82.

Scherl, Magdalena, *Ersehnte Einheit, unheilbare Spaltung: Geschlechter-ordnung und Republik bei Rousseau* (Bielefeld: transcript, 2016).

Schmitt, Carl, *Political Theology: Four Chapters on the Concept of Sovereignty*, trans. George Schwab (1922; Chicago: Chicago University Press, 2005).

—, *The Crisis of Parliamentary Democracy*, trans. Ellen Kennedy (1926; Cambridge, MA: MIT Press, 1988).

—, *Constitutional Theory*, ed. and trans. Jeffrey Seitzer (1928; Durham, NC: Duke University Press, 2008).

Schrupp, Antje, *Nicht Marxistin und auch nicht Anarchistin: Frauen in der ersten Internationale* (Königstein: Helmer, 1999).

Scott, Anne Firor, 'Most Invisible of All: Black Women's Voluntary Associations', *Journal of Southern History* LVI:1 (1990), 3–22.

Scott, Joan W., 'The Uses and Abuses of Gender', *Tijdschrift voor Gender-studies* 16:1 (2013), 63–77.

Segato, Rita Laura, 'A Manifesto in Four Themes', *Critical Times* 1:1 (2018), 198–211.

Sieyès, Emmanuel-Joseph, 'What Is the Third Estate?', in *Political Writings*, trans. Michael Sonenscher (1789; Indianapolis: Hackett, 2003), 92–162.

Skinner, Quentin, *Hobbes and Republican Liberty* (Cambridge: Cambridge University Press, 2008).

Smith, Adam, *An Inquiry into the Nature and Causes of the Wealth of Nations*, ed. Edwin Cannan (1776; London: Methuen, 1904).

Snyder, Claire R., *Citizen-Soldiers and Mainly Warriors: Military Service and Gender in the Civic Republic Tradition* (Lanham: Rowman & Littlefield, 1999).

Social Anthropology, 'The Other Side of the Crisis: Solidarity Networks in Greece', special section, *Social Anthropology* 24:2 (2016).

Stoler, Ann Laura, *Race and the Education of Desire: Foucault's History of Sexuality and the Colonial Order of Things* (Durham, NC: Duke University Press, 1995).

Stuckler, David, and Sanjay Basu, *The Body Economic: Why Austerity Kills* (New York: Basic, 2013).

Terranova, Tiziana, 'Red Stack Attack! Algorithms, Capital and the Automation of the Commons', *EuroNomade: Inventare il comune sovvertire il presente*, 9 March 2014, euronomade.info.

The Invisible Committee, *Now*, trans. Robert Hurley (Los Angeles: Semiotext(e), 2017).

transversal: multilingual webjournal: 'monster municipalisms' (September 2016), transversal.at

Transmaricabollo, 'Manifesto del orgullo indignado 2011', madrid.tomalaplaza.net.

Trouillot, Michel-Rolph, 'Unthinkable History: The Haitian Revolution as a Non-Event', in *Silencing the Past: Power and the Production of History* (Boston: Beacon, 2015).

Trujillo Barbadillo, Gracia, 'La protesta dentro de la protesta: Activismos queer/cuir y feminista en el 15M', *Encrucijadas: Revista Crítica de Ciencias Sociales* 12 (2016), 1–18.

Tsing, Anna Lowenhaupt, *The Mushroom at the End of the World: On the Possibility of Life in Capitalist Ruins* (Princeton: Princeton University Press, 2015).

Virno, Paolo, *A Grammar of the Multitude: For an Analysis of Contemporary Forms of Life*, trans. Isabella Bertoletti, James Cascaito, Andrea Casson (2001; Los Angeles: Semiotext(e), 2004).

Wieling, Hans, *Die Begründung des Sklavenstatus nach ius gentium und ius civile: Teil I des Corpus der römischen Rechtsquellen zur antiken Sklaverei* (Stuttgart: Steiner, 1999).

Wingrove, Elizabeth Rose, *Rousseau's Republican Romance* (Princeton: Princeton University Press, 2000).

Young, Brigitte, 'Gendered Dimensions of Money, Finance, and the Subprime Crisis', in *Gender and Economics: Feministische Kritik der politischen Ökonomie*, ed. Christine Bauhardt and Gülay Çağlar (Wiesbaden: VS Verlag, 2010), 258–77.

Zechner, Manuela, 'Let's Play? Citizenship, Subjectivity and Becoming in Municipalism', *transversal: multilingual webjournal*: 'monster municipalisms' (September 2016), transversal.at.

Zelik, Raul, 'Podemos and the "Democratic Revolution" in Spain', *Global Research*, May 2015, globalresearch.ca.

Zerilli, Linda, *Signifying Woman: Culture and Chaos in Rousseau, Burke, and Mill* (Ithaca, NY: Cornell University Press, 1994).

Websites

Barcelona En Comú, barcelonaencomu.cat

Barcelona En Comú, *Ethical Code*, barcelonaencomu.cat/sites/default/files/pdf/codi-etic-eng.pdf

Carta por la Democracia, http://blogs.traficantes.net/wpcontent/blogs.dir/9/files/2014/03/Carta_por_la_Democracia_1pag.pdf

Dossier de la Comisión de Feminismos Sol, madrid.tomalaplaza.net

Fearless Cities, fearlesscities.com

Femicides in Europa, europeandatajournalism.eu/eng/News/Data-news

La PAH, afectadosporlahipoteca.com

mac1, mac1.uno

mac2, mac2.uno/en

mac3, mac3.uno

mac4, elsaltodiario.com/palabras-en-movimiento/mac4-de-municipalismo-y-contrapoder

Málaga Ahora, facebook.com/malagaahora

Marcha Popular Indignada, marchapopularindignada.wordpress.com

Mareas, 15mpedia.org/wiki/Lista_de_mareas

Movimiento por una vivienda digna en España, es.wikipedia.org

Partido X, partidox.org

Yo sí, sanidad universal, yosisanidaduniversal.net

Index